FROM VEILS TO THONGS

FROM VEILS TO THONGS

An Arab Chick's Survival Guide to Balancing One's Ethnic Identity in America

Dalel B. Khalil

iUniverse, Inc.
New York   Bloomington

FROM VEILS TO THONGS
An Arab Chick's Survival Guide to Balancing One's Ethnic Identity in America

Copyright © 2008 by Dalel B. Khalil

All rights reserved. No part of this book may be used or reproduced by any means, graphic, electronic, or mechanical, including photocopying, recording, taping or by any information storage retrieval system without the written permission of the publisher except in the case of brief quotations embodied in critical articles and reviews.

iUniverse books may be ordered through booksellers or by contacting:

iUniverse
1663 Liberty Drive
Bloomington, IN 47403
www.iuniverse.com
1-800-Authors (1-800-288-4677)

Because of the dynamic nature of the Internet, any Web addresses or links contained in this book may have changed since publication and may no longer be valid.

The views expressed in this work are solely those of the author and do not necessarily reflect the views of the publisher, and the publisher hereby disclaims any responsibility for them.

ISBN: 978-0-595-48168-2 (pbk)
ISBN: 978-0-595-60262-9 (ebk)

iUniverse rev. date: 12/12/2008

Printed in the United States of America

To thine own self be true.

—William Shakespeare

Three-day road trip to Syrian Embassy to obtain entry visas … $900.

Lunch in Syria with 20 of your relatives who don't speak a word of English … $150.

Buying clothes, makeup and having your hair done to meet a potential husband … $75.

Going to Syria with your father for the very first time …   *Priceless.*

This book is dedicated to my wonderful parents and to my best friend and sister, Leila.

Thank you, Mommy for teaching me to appreciate all the richness life has to offer, and to love life itself. You presented before me a rich, lavish tapestry full of exotic definition, color, and texture. You brought the world to us and made us love other cultures. Thank you, I love you so much.

Daddy, you came to this country and didn't speak a word of English. You had a third grade education, and yet you lived the American dream. You came here, worked hard and earned your own success. You love this country and genuinely appreciate all that it has done for you. You constantly give to the needy, the hungry, the hopeless and the forgotten. You are an honorable, humble man and I love you so much. I am proud to be your daughter.

And to Leila my sister. There are simply no words to describe how precious you are to me. Thank you for everything, for being my sister and best friend.

Contents

AUTHOR'S OFFICIAL DISCLAIMER xvi

Part I
The Basics (Everything You Need to Know About Becoming an Arabic Bride) 2

Chapter 1
How To Get Married Without Really Trying 3

Mishwarring: The Language of Love in the Middle East 13

What to Do If You're Being Questioned by the FBI (The Fadis, Bassams and Ibrahims) 15

Chapter 2
How to Become a Sit-el-Beit When You Don't Even Know What One Is 18

Chapter 3
Matching Your DNA With Your Behavior 28

What's Your Combination? 28

Identify Yourself: Are You a Village Chick, Vain Princess, or Urban Goddess? 33

Chapter 4
How to Catch a Syrian Doctor in Your Freshman Year 37

Chapter 5
The Wife-Material Olympics—Live from Dubai! 39

Chapter 6
Stereo, Tabal and the Wedding: A Fun-Filled, Three-Day Trip to the Altar 52

Chapter 7
I'm Married! Now What? On Your Mark ... Set ... Breed! 62

Chapter 8
Help! I Think I Just Married My Brother! 64
How to Avoid Marrying Someone You Think Might Be Your Brother 65
Why Do We Marry Our Cousins? 66
Why Do We Still Have Arranged Marriages In This Day and Age? . . 69
And What Exactly Do They Mean? 69

Chapter 9
Oh Crap! I Forgot to Get Married! Now What? 74
How To Create a Scandal 81
What To Do If You Find Yourself In One 84

Part II
The Extras (Everything Else You Need to Know About Simply Being Arabic) 88

Chapter 10
What They Don't Want You to Know: Hip-Hop Has Its Roots in the Streets of Damascus 89

Chapter 11
The Eleven Life Laws of Dupkeeing 106

Chapter 12
The Much-Envied Zalghouta Queen 119
Bonus Tips On How To Get A Zalghouta Queen For Your Village. . 122

Chapter 13
Um Kalthoum 126

Chapter 14
Why We Spend So Much Time Hanging Out 129
Bizzer: Sewing the Seeds of Gossip 137
Why We're Like Royalty 141
Why We're Always Late 144
"B'tehkay Arabay?" 148

Chapter 15
The Sperm in the Air Theory 150

Chapter 16
The Lebanese Hairdresser—Your New Best Friend! 161

Chapter 17
French Women Aren't The Only Ones Who Don't Get Fat 166

Chapter 18
Takin' the Jitney to Homs 173

Chapter 19
Why Kids in the Middle East Drink and Drive—and Why it's Okay 182

Chapter 20
 Restaurants, Real Estate and Retail: The Universal Language of
  Immigrants 192

 Businesses That Don't Have the Slightest Chance of Success in the
  Middle East *201*

 What You Won't Find in Abundance in the Middle East. *204*

 Before You Go *207*

Chapter 21
 Shunkleesh and the Bush Conspiracy. .212

Chapter 22
 The Art of Grapeleave Picking and Baking Bread: Your Key to
  Legitimacy. 218

Chapter 23
 In Conclusion 222

GLOSSARY 225
 Welcome to the First-Ever ***Zalghouta*** Challenge Sponsored by Dalel B.
  Khalil. 228

Do you come from a culture where women wear veils but your friends wear thongs?

Does at least one of your parents speak English with an incomprehensible accent?

Did your parents have an arranged marriage … are they cousins?

Well folks, you've come to the right place. You are literally holding in your hands the coveted answers to every question you ever had about your insane existence – herein lies all the information you need to understand about why you're crazy!

And trust me, you are crazy!

That's right. It's true. You can't deny it.

Put this book down and you condemn yourself to a life of insanity. Turn the page, and you're on the road to recovery.

Natives of non-Western countries, particularly females, will discover critical information in these pages. Information that you need to be able to function sanely (or at least fake it really well!)

It is particularly essential for those persons who are from India, Greece, Japan, Pakistan, Turkistan, Tajikistan, Afghanistan, Uzbekistan—what the hell—all the Stans! And finally, it is an absolute must-have for princesses of all nations.

Despite the misleading title, *From Veils To Thongs* is not limited to those who are profiled … *S**t!.* … *uh, I mean* classified as Arab-Americans. It is open to a much larger group of people, including every single ethnic minority whose parents emigrated from non-Western countries. And believe it or not, the Amish as well!

It is also a very helpful tool for our American friends; they will find our strategies quite useful in fighting the current War on Terror … *dammit!* … *I mean* ideology! Like us, many Americans are struggling to find their position in this escalating socio-political cultural war. They are torn between conservatism and liberalism, tradition and progression, fidelity and fun, flats and pumps!

It's hard to find balance. It really is.

Westerners, as well as those arriving FOB (Fresh Off the Boat) will be able to apply these principles to achieve their specific goals. In fact, this country would serve itself well if it issued free copies of this book at all ports of entry, customs offices, and designated border patrol areas.

This survival guide will not only save you thousands of dollars and years of therapy, but most importantly, will teach you how to come out the winner each and every time.

Happy Reading!

AUTHOR'S OFFICIAL DISCLAIMER

This book isn't for everyone. It's only for a certain group of very special people. It is not for those Arabic females who were raised to make independent choices for themselves and their futures, free of cultural or gender expectations. Nor is it for the girl who grew up in a liberal family, one where she was encouraged to boldly state her opinion, defiantly challenge convention or fearlessly pursue her daring ambitions. And it is most certainly not for the Arabic female who dated freely and openly—at least not the way Westerners are accustomed to.

It is, however, for the Arabic girl who grew up in America and didn't know which way to turn. Who sat in her room alone, crying in pain because she didn't understand the world around her, or where she fit in it. It is for the girl who didn't understand how to own, or articulate, her own feelings—let alone validate them. It is for the girl who survived a life full of contradictions—of being raised in one culture while, at the same time, living in the extreme other. And it is for every ethnic minority who, at this very moment, lives directly in the cross fire of the final "war of the worlds"—the Old World versus the New World.

It's for the girl who was raised with the mentality that her sole purpose was to get married and have babies, *then* figure out what she wants to do with her life; who understands that family always comes first, and who has a clear understanding of honor and dishonor. As well as blatant distortions of it. It's for the girl who is frustrated because she's studying to be a surgeon when all she really wants to do is throw down the books, rip off the façade, and shoot hoops for the WNBA, but she knows deep inside that ain't never gonna happen.

It's for the girl who had strict parents and an army of *ready-to-die-for-the-cause* uncles to make sure she never disgraced the family name even when *they* did. And who, no matter what she was doing or who she was with, it seemed that every time she turned around, she was either questioned, accused or just plain bombarded with *ibe!*[1]

---

1. *Ibe* means shame or dishonor.

It's for the girl who was raised in a "village" right smack in the middle of New York City, Miami or L.A. Or Paris, Amsterdam or Vienna; who steps into an upside down world full of contrasts, the moment she steps outside.

It's for the girl who knew what would happen to her if her hypocritical brother found out that she had a boyfriend—let alone lost her virginity to him. It's for the girl who understands that her brother's word counts more than hers, anyway, and knows that if she were to even *think* of behaving like his girlfriend does, she'd face a whole different set of consequences.

It's for the girl who told her parents that she was going to the library, stuffed her club gear in her backpack, changed in the car, and dashed to the concert along with her bestfriend/cousin. Oh yeah, and somehow made it home by 11 p.m. sharp, only to creep out the cellar door at 2 a.m. for the after party. It's for the girl who risked it all to have one last fling before heading over to the old country to marry a chosen suitor. It's for the girl who fundamentally understands the concept of arranged marriages more than she does a one-night stand. And for the girl who had to explain to her puzzled American girlfriends why she wasn't at all shocked when she saw those cute little wrapped-up Taliban chicks over in Afghanistan and then found herself painfully questioning why the Taliban's insane rationale makes any sense to her at all.

It's for the girl whose parents were slightly liberal enough to let her go on Spring Break but found herself in a precarious situation; standing paralyzed in front of an elevator door not knowing whether to push the "up" button and accept a cute guy's invitation to go back to his hotel room because, for the first time, no one's watching her.

Being a traditional Arab-American ain't easy. It's like a war raging inside of you. It's like waking up everyday in the combat zone, dodging Molotov cocktails. The assaults on your psyche are merciless. Yup, being a traditional Arab-American is your own little personal insurgency right inside your brain.

However, if you were born anytime after 1980 and part of the "new generation", or if you were raised more like *Shakira* rather than, let's say, your 45-year-old unmarried aunt, or if you are of Lebanese descent then, you can just go ahead and put this book down right now; it ain't gonna do you a damn bit of good.

You couldn't even *begin* to understand.

Believe me, I say that with the utmost respect. The truth is, the Lebanese have always been more open-minded in their ways than the rest of the Arab world. As a result, most didn't suffer the way the rest of us did. Despite having gone through so much historically and politically, the Lebanese have always picked up the broken pieces and pushed forward, *quite fashionably,* I might add.

But they aren't the only ones who won't understand. There are many people who claim to be both equally Arab and American, but the truth of the matter is that they are not because when it comes right down to it one side usually dominates the other and, therefore, eliminates a true culture clash.

You see, the traditional Arab-American has an entirely different set of pressures, stresses, and challenges that are unique to her specifically *and only* because she was raised as *a traditional Arabic female in a liberal, Western country.* That precise, lethal combination is exactly what makes her particular experience that much more difficult than everyone else's. That's it. Nothing else.

Since many others did not have the same "opportunities," they didn't experience the severe dissonance that comes with having to confront a "culturally dangerous" situation. Generally speaking, choices were already "made" for them based on cultural acceptance, family expectations, and social norms. So, in a sense, these people didn't *have* to decide. No pressure. No stress. No confusion. Some, Arab at heart; others, red-blooded Americans. As a result, their particular cultural rules shaped—and eventually defined—their respective behaviors and identities.

However, my friend, when you are *both traditionally Arab and uniquely American,* you're basically screwed. You are confronted with making decisions that are often at complete odds with each other. The question incessantly swirls around in your head: *"Who am I?"* It's almost as if you're constantly having to choose. Choose between *who you are,* and who you have been *told* you are. Between what you *want* to do and being told what you *must* do. Between your own boundless dreams, and the rigid ones outlined for you. You end up with two sets of friends: your *real* friends, and *the friends your parents actually know about;* two personalities: your *raw* personality and your personality *when family members are present.* Sometimes they're one in the same; sometimes they're not.

We are not victims though, because the bottom line is that we are responsible for all of our choices. However, ethnic people know that growing up with such strong familial and cultural ties makes the process of "becoming yourself" that much more difficult. For example, every Arabic female understands, in no uncertain terms, that her behavior can cause irreparable damage to her entire family. So keen is her understanding of this concept, that she has unconsciously mastered the art of image control. She's had to. It's a matter of self preservation. She innately knows that on some level, she is being watched. Not necessarily in a stalking, creepy, psycho kind of way, but in a way that she is aware that she is being observed. Sort of like the National Security Agency wire tapping way. That's a lot of pressure. Some Arab-American girls have been able to handle the strain better than others. And others? Well, they pretty much cracked.

Take it from me, having dual identities can make your head split, especially when you truly love both sides. It's not hard when you live in a homogeneous society where everyone is essentially thinking and behaving the same way. It's only hard when you're truly a product of both. It's only hard when you have a ticket to a Steelers playoff game in one hand and a ticket to a *never-to-be-repeated hafli*[2] in the other, and just about five minutes to decide which one to go to. That's when it's hard. That's when it's hell. I secretly envy those who are on either end of the spectrum. At least they have clarity. Being precisely in the middle of fire and ice, of heaven and hell, of veil and thong—*now that's hard!*

Thankfully, Arab life has changed radically over the past couple of decades, so things aren't as dreadful as they used to be. You see, back in the day, average, traditional Arabic girls weren't running around doing many adventurous things, like running track, rock climbing, or backpacking Europe—at least not in my neck of the woods they weren't. If you did, well then, you were the exception. I know that for sure because I was one of the exceptions. And sometimes it felt weird. But, then again, I was weird. Today, however, there are tons of open-minded, traditional Arabic girls who have assimilated very well into mainstream America. They have absorbed all the great things about Western culture so much that hearing about their mother's generation is a way to entertain themselves all night during sleepovers.

All twelve teenagers shake their heads and laugh. They say,

"Arranged marriages …! That's so funny (ha-ha)! So mom, tell us more. … Did they tell you who you were going to marry beforehand, or did they just pop it on you at the last minute (ha-ha)? Did you think daddy was cute, or were you just scared of his twelve brothers (ha-ha)? Hey mom, did they give you time to think about it, or was the two-day engagement long enough (ha-ha)?"

---

2. Arabic party.

And then, right in the middle of earsplitting, girly-girl giggles, they abruptly stop breathing! All twelve of them. Like lightening, it strikes them! It's at that precise moment that they realize they ain't that damn far removed from their mother's life, after all. The prissiest one of them all stands in the center and blurts out her terrifying epiphany:

"Oh no! Wait! Hey guys, you know Binda Maharta Vishnu that Indian girl in my biology 2 class who wears those real pretty sari thingies, and is always studying in the library? Well, Jennifer Lockbury told me that her mother is taking her to New Delhi this summer so that she can get engaged to her cousin, who she never met before!"

Brats.

Prissy, little, spoiled brats.

They're not suffering. They don't know how to. They *wouldn't* know how to.

Those girls are the ones who are playing all kinds of sports. They're going off to Hawaii for band camp, competing in soccer tournaments, and posing for prom photos with their parents *and* boyfriends. They are also the only ones in their schools who are bi-lingual, have international dual citizenship, and regularly enjoy summers on the Mediterranean.

They're not crazy.
They're balanced.

Change.

Change is good.
But, then again, so is tradition.
Progression balanced with tradition

Now that's sanity.

Unfortunately I, like so many others, had to earn my sanity the hard way. You see, I recently came back from my first-ever trip to Syria. It took me a very long time to open up to the idea of going there. It was a life-changing experience. Everything in my life changed. Everything in my body changed. Everything in my mind changed. I changed.

But, then again, I don't really think that's completely true at all.

You see, it was all there the whole time. It was just that I had buried it so deeply inside that when I finally did experience Syria, it was as if my body, mind and soul, all went into simultaneous uncontrollable convulsions. I had a great time in Syria, but it was also very painful and emotional for me. I can't tell you how much I regret not going every summer as a teenager. Had I known that I had been mistaken and actually had taken the trip earlier, my life would have been completely different.

But I didn't know.

I cried the whole way home. I had nine, mind you! Nine glasses of white wine on the plane in between all the tears. I cried when I got home. I cried every day for three weeks. Then I kept crying. I cried for one month. Then for two. I didn't want to be here. I wanted so desperately to go back. I never wanted to leave in the first place. I was severely depressed and unable to function—to think, talk, or see straight. It was terrible.

You see, before that, I was fine. I was an American girl at the top of her game. Physically, mentally, and emotionally, you couldn't touch me. I was on it, baby. Sharp. Right. Fierce. I had a plan. All I wanted to do was get this family trip over and done with so that I could get on with my fabulous and exciting career. Ten days, tops.

Boy, when life throws you a curve ball ...

I had no idea what was about to happen to me. I swear I wasn't ready for any of this. It was like someone picked up a 1,000 pound sledgehammer, and, with all the force in them, swung it right across the side of my head. *BAAM!* I spun around so hard, I got knocked out cold! I haven't been the same since.

Syria is a beautiful place, a little piece of heaven. It is the specific piece of heaven that I needed so badly growing up. Syria was the light my soul yearned for while it was frantically searching in the dark, cold abyss. It was the missing link, the one single piece I needed to bring me back home, to myself.

My soul was hurting. I had desperately needed to experience Syria. But I didn't know it.

The consequence was a lot of unnecessary pain, confusion and lost time. But everything happens for a reason, right? Perhaps I would have had a less positive experience had I gone when I was younger. Perhaps it could have been so negative that I may have never returned. Anything could've happened; we just don't know for sure what might've been.

But when I looked up at the mountain in the village of *Kaffram* at five o'clock in the morning, and the stars were shining so brightly and the moonlight was glowing softly and brilliantly. The vast, mighty universe was strangely calm and gentle. The night was quiet and stunning. And the church was right in the middle of the village, comforting everyone. It was so beautiful and peaceful. I knew right then and there that I had missed something so profound, so timeless. I was missing the very thing that my soul was aching for all of my life. It was as if my body finally found my soul, and I was able to breathe again. I wanted to live and die there. I wanted to die right then and there, in heaven, and spend eternity there. I didn't want to go to sleep, unless it was forever, in Syria.

I kept trying to figure it all out. I couldn't understand why the hell my people came off the mountain in the first place. To me, it's a mystery. I still can't understand. But perhaps my own reconciliation of my bi-cultural identities might help someone who is yearning for the same thing—peace within themselves.

Let me be clear, I always knew *who* I was but, by the same token, I was constantly struggling. At my very foundation, I am a village girl—always was, always will be—and I like it like that. I am a simple girl, just like my mother. Fancy cars, cash and glamorous titles never impressed me, but a white heart[3] always took my breath away. I was a Syrian village girl born and raised in a modern American city. A girl who was, and still is, bound to her heritage, but who tried to find just the slightest, most minuscule thread of logic in a universe whose eternal laws could never be logical. I was determined.

I was crazy.

As I've already mentioned, many girls have fallen through the cracks. Some have turned to self-destructive behaviors, some are in denial and others just got lost. No joke, baby. I'm talking about being a *traditional Arabic girl AND a modern young American*. Not either/or, but both. I'm a survivor. Yup, a straight-up vet, with all the hellish war stories to tell. To be honest, I'm really proud of my wounds. I kind of show them off once in a while. They make me feel ... *I don't know ... tough, maybe?* But despite all the distress, I wouldn't change a thing. I can bounce from one

---

3. Someone who has a pure heart.

culture to the next without skipping a beat. And I genuinely love both. Somebody once told me that I had an American mind, and a Syrian heart. I like that.

It is so important to keep the old country with you while appreciating the blessings of this new country. No matter how flawed things might be, what mistakes we've made, or what administration is currently in power, try to have faith in America's fundamental principles. Believe me, I am certainly not the only Arab-American who is upset with what is going on politically. I have very strong opinions about King George ... *S**t! Ah, I mean* ... about certain administrations and their imperialistic ... *dammit! Uh, I mean* ... its responsible and virtuous foreign policy. However, this is not a political book nor will I make it one.

And if, for some reason, you still can't see how blessed you are, just turn on CNN. A nice dose of Somalian street warfare will sober your ass up good 'n' plenty.

Speaking of street warfare ... I ain't tryin' to start any, either, so let me throw in a few more disclaimers. First of all, there are about 300 million Arabs worldwide and most are not Christian. However, I am. In fact, I am an Antiochian Orthodox Christian. I am Arab by culture—Christian by faith. So keep in mind that this is written from my perspective. But also keep in mind that the religious aspect doesn't really change the cultural influence to any real significant degree. Yes, there are obvious differences, (i. e. drinking alcohol) and yes, they do count, but we all basically share the same values (i. e. faith, family, honor, tradition, etc).

As a side note, not only is this the case for all descendants of Abrahamic tradition, but also includes the majority of all non-Western traditional cultures as well (i. e. India, China, etc.) As a matter of fact, these ideas are so universal that they even speak to the Amish. Because believe me, that little Amish girl clip-clopping 5 miles an hour in her little horse and buggy in the middle of a bitter, cold, minus 5 degree snowstorm is struggling. She's in this battle, too. Somewhere in her brain she is painfully questioning how the simple, beautiful, natural and innocent idea of progression and modernity got such a damn bad rap. I know in my heart that somewhere deep inside she secretly wishes that she could get into that warm, cozy, heated, lush Mercedes Benz that just drove by. She is struggling. She is struggling just like the rest of us.

And since I wrote a book about being in the middle of two contradictory worlds, it should be expected that I actually contradict myself. So, here it is: Even though the very first line in this book stated "This book isn't for everyone," it kinda really is. It really is for everyone, because these ideas are really so universal. As much as it is about being an Arab girl in this predicament, it's also for anyone and everyone who is caught in the middle of two extreme worlds—whatever those worlds may be. And it's not limited to age, race or gender, either. Struggling with his own cultural conflict and search for identity, Barack Obama wrote that he used drugs and alcohol to "… push questions of who I was out of my mind."[4] Talk about being a survivor! And if that's not enough to convince you, just look at both the political and social landscape in America. We're in a deep divide. We're all struggling. We're struggling right down to our core issues and beliefs.

So, back to the original point, regardless of religious—or any other affiliation for that matter—the overall picture is basically the same.

Secondly, specific traditions and details differ significantly throughout the region, but again, the overall picture is basically the same. Thirdly, assume my statements mean "generally speaking," and not "all." I am well aware that there are lots of loopholes in the system, but I can't deal with technicalities, they get on my nerves, so don't take everything I say so damn literally!

For example, when I say traditional Arabic girls don't really date, I don't really mean that. They do, it's just done *Middle Eastern style.* And I'm not talking about sneaking around, either. I mean, come on! Everyone sneaks around for goodness sakes! How the hell else are you gonna have any fun? But girls, don't get me wrong either. We do have our healthy share of loose women. Oh, yes, we do. Trust me. We sure do! However, what I am referring to is the unspoken, established cultural dating rules, which, *generally speaking,* are accepted by the collective majority. And when I talk about *ibe*, I'm not saying to get rid of it all together. *Ibe* is good—it keeps us in line. We just have to use it in the proper context, you know, without overdoing it and all.

And let me be crystal clear about one very, very critical point.

This book has absolutely nothing to do with religion whatsoever. So don't try and make something out of nothing, *because I know some of you are just dying to!* Dig a little deeper into what I am saying, and don't take everything so literally. This book has nothing to do with veils and thongs, as in the religious attire or lingerie, but rather symbolically represents the mentality behind the basis of each. It is a metaphor of the extremes.

---

4. From his book entitled, *Dreams from My Father.* (It should've been called *From Kenya to Kansas*).

It speaks to those who left a conservative society (the East) to emigrate to a liberal one (the West). Veils representing all things traditional; thongs representing all things liberal. My worlds are two—saturated and represented by both. And both cultures are equally my birthright. No woman has ever had to have physically worn either to understand life in this realm.

Got it?
Good.

And finally, it is important to understand that significant social changes have only occurred within the past 200 years or so, which means that the ideas and customs in this book are not exclusively Arabic at all. In fact, most of them were, more or less, the universal norm throughout history up right up until about the Industrial Revolution. For example, 10,000 B.C.—1920 A.D.—illegal for women to vote. See what I mean? It's only been 88 years since women's suffrage—not counting 12,000 years of leg work, of course.

Listen, I have to tell you that it took about three weeks to write this book and forever to revise it. I worked very hard to honestly try and describe each culture as fairly, accurately, and truthfully as I possibly could. However, after many late night rewrites, all-nighters, and way too many carbs, I finally realized that no matter how hard I try, or no matter what I do, somebody, somewhere, is gonna get pissed off about something. So I said, the hell with it. It's a free country. If you don't like it, go write your own damn book! Leave me alone!

Sorry ... now that I've gotten all that off my chest, I shall continue. And I'll try to be nicer.

All right. So, you bought this book because I promised that I could help you get sane by answering your questions, most specifically about your identity.

Well ... Here it is. Ready?

You're crazy!

Yup! That's what you are.

What are you kidding? Get real. Nobody grows up in such extreme worlds as you and remains sane. Come on! You might come out of it, life might go on, but there's still a little bit of craziness in you, and you know it.

There. That's it. We're finished. Thank you for buying my book. Go home now.

What?! I told you! You're crazy! What more do you want? Oh, I see. I see. You're in denial, aren't you? You don't think you're crazy. That's all right. It's fine, honestly. Look, honey, it's real simple.

Have a seat.

The reason that you are crazy, my dear, is that you know deep down in your heart that having *sito*[5] screaming from the top of the highest mountain about someone stealing her chickens is just as normal to you as attending a high-brow luncheon for the Republican National Party in which you are the guest speaker. And that's a scary thing. You know that's a scary thing. You are, by definition, at least partially crazy, whether you like it or not. And guess what else? There's no getting out of it.

You may be able to fool your friends, your co-workers, and even your fellow country club members, but those of us who are Arab-Americans know your dark little secret. We know what's in your soul because it's in ours as well, so don't try to cover it up—at least not with us, anyway. Besides, since we're all pretty much related to each other by marriage, that same woman is most likely our *sito*, too.

Now, first and foremost, if you don't know anything else about your identity, know this: as an Arab-American female, or for that matter, any other non-Western female, the sole purpose of your life is to get married and bear male offspring.

Got it? Good.

Keep your goals high. If you can produce, oh let's say, five to seven male children who grow up to become doctors—dare I say brain surgeons—you will have achieved the accomplishment of a lifetime. You *sooo* made it, baby! Your success will earn you the coveted *International Breeder Cup* until, of course, someone else comes along and smashes your winning record. But it will have been all yours, even if just for a brief, shining moment.

So basically, as an ethnic chick, that's the reason for your whole existence. That's it. But don't fret just yet; there is good news. Not only can the process be quite fun but even more than that, we are not alone. You see, this whole marriage/procreation speil is not just an ethnic thing at all. The truth of the matter is that

---

5. Your embarrassing, missing-tooth, bloomer-wearing grandmother.

pretty much all women, regardless of nationality, *were born to breed*. We ethnic people just intensify it a little more. All right, a lot more.

Plus, Western women just aren't into that whole "male heir" dynasty thing (except for British royalty, but that's totally understandable). Maybe that's why we do it; we want to be like royalty, you know, and have our own little kingdoms and such. Maybe we secretly envy them, so we just imitate their patterns. Just a thought. No doubt, though, if you're a member of the House of Windsor, you'd better be putting out little baby boys. That's a lot of pressure. Think about it. Imagine being the beloved crown queen and not producing a male heir for your subjects. Unspeakable! It's the same thing for us. Visualize being a wife of a traditional ethnic man and not producing male heirs for your mother-in-law? Treason!

Nevertheless, American women are born to breed, just like us. And just like us, our good friends also have a very loud-sounding biological clock. Not like Big Ben or anything, but it's still a clock. And it still ticks. You just can't hear it as much because the incessant corporate noise drowns it out. But trust me, it's there. See, they have glaring corporate noise; we have really loud relatives. Different sources; same excruciating, head-throbbing pain. Don't believe me? How many dating franchises can you count in your city? See what I mean?

Females between 20 and 30 rush to snag a husband like madwomen at a half-price clearance sale. Because when you're in your 20s, the big 3–0 is *scaarry!* Let me tell you. After 30, the blue light special kicks in, and it's a mad dash for the divorcees on the rebound. Let's face it, no matter where they come from, a girl is a girl is a girl. That's why we like to paint our nails, eat dainty little chocolates and stay up all night at parties, gabbing away until our sentences don't make sense anymore. We're girls! And it's fun to be a girl! And I don't care what anyone says: every girl dreams of throwing the biggest party of them all. The grande party! You know, the one where she gets to wear the gorgeous long white gown, eat a tiny sliver of the five-tiered cake and dance all night while daddy drinks away the thought of a $40,000 loan.

It's fun to be a girl *(Right, daddy?)*!

Now that that's all cleared up, let's get all this therapy out of the way quickly, so that we can get you married off and fulfill the purpose your family has specifically designated just for you. Quick! We don't have much time! Females aged 30 to 35 skip to the chapter that instructs you on how to find a husband—fast. Women in the 35 to 40 age group, stop reading this instant and immediately proceed to

Chapter 9 entitled *Oh Crap! I Forgot to Get Married! Now What?* Ladies 40 to 45 head to the church, mosque, synagogue or other house of worship as you are really going to need a miracle. Women 45 and older, please call my office for private consultations; the first five sessions are on the house.

Acceptance: The Final Stage
So soon?
Yes.

Now that you know who you are—and to think you've wasted all those years trying to figure it out—just accept it. Don't try to conceal any part of your ethnicity. And don't try to overcompensate for what is missing either. You'll end up being fake. Don't be fake. It's a big turnoff. Don't be like that woman who is so embarrassed of who she is. Outwardly she'll laugh during an awkward moment, but inside she is cringing. That corporate smile is her only protection. Be authentic. It's much better that way.

You know, we can learn a valuable lesson from our good friends, the *Aswaad*. [6] You see, the *Aswaad* had to deal with a lot of these issues long before us. So, after many years of facing racism, they decided to take matters into their own hands. They took it into their own realm and redesigned it to their own specifications. *And voila!* Just like magic, they came up with the concept of being *"Ghetto Fabulous!"* And they marketed the hell out of it.

So, here's my advice to you: examine your issues, reexamine them, do that at least three more times, have a martini, have a laugh, double the martini, think, break out the tequila, and the Bacardi Select, think a little more—but don't think *too much*—open a box of Kleenex, cry, listen to Peter Gabriel, cry some more, keep crying, and then embrace the good, the bad, and the not-so pretty. It's part of who you are.

Oh, and when your condescending *Miss Prissy 'I-just-got-promoted-to-Regional-Vice-President-of-Marketing'* co-worker asks you, "Hey, does your grandmother really scream on the top of the highest mountain, 'Who stole my chickens?'" take a deep, long breath. Stand tall, chest out, head back, look her straight in the eye and proudly and firmly say, "Yes. ... Yes, ma'am. ... She does" Then simply walk away.

---

6. African-Americans.

Go ahead. I dare you.
And make a loud chicken sound when you're halfway down the hall!

Look, if you really want to know how to deal with your crazy life then just read this book. It will tell you everything you need to know. Take it with a sense of humor, and call me if you're truly having an identity crisis. We can fix it up in a jiffy. In practically no time, you'll be as good as new.

I promise.

Part I

The Basics
(Everything You Need to Know About Becoming an Arabic Bride)

Chapter 1

▼

How To Get Married Without Really Trying

Believe it or not, you can completely avoid the dating scene and still get married, sometimes in just a matter of weeks. While others are spending their precious time reorganizing their portfolios or trying new fad diets that promise to lose pounds fast, in no time at all, you could go from being a single over-the-hill loser to a fashionable, much-envied bride! And all for about the same cost of most minor cosmetic surgeries. That's right. It's true. As with any marriage, no promise of happiness is 100% guaranteed, but it is safe and effective.

> *Note: The average turn around time for overseas marriage proposals is usually 24–48 hours from the time you initially step off the plane. But, if you are younger and have bona fide citizenship papers, you automatically jump the queue to the front of the line.*

Here are your (very limited) choices for finding a husband:

Plan #1
Plan #1 is basically your five star deal. It's the preferred choice for those with discriminating tastes. It's specifically designed for the busy executive who is in immediate need, enjoys the personal touch of having her own concierge, and who would rather meet face-to-face with a prospective client.

Plan #1—Break out the platinum American Express and kiss the single life goodbye.

Here's what to do:
Block out about a month on your calendar, preferably in August (that's when all the great parties take place). Hunt down one of your relatives who still speaks with an accent and tell them that you want to get married. Find out who else is going over to the old country, pack your bags, and take the first flight out with them. Waste no time my dear, remember, the early bird gets the worm. And it ain't like it used to be. There are lots more birds out there these days—*damn near vultures, some of them!*

As soon as the plane touches down, head straight over to your nearest associated village. Warning: you must have legitimate ties to this village. By this time, your original contact person will have already instant messaged your overseas relatives who then, of course, will have dispatched immediate press releases to all the single prospects in their particular village as well as to at least five others nearby.

Your job is to do your research and to do it well. Do not under any circumstances board the plane without being prepared that includes being briefed on what to do and what *not* to do. Every step has to be in the right order otherwise you'll sabotage it all. Bring your finest clothes, your best makeup and, whatever you do, don't forget to pack the travel adapter plug set because when them bachelors start lining the streets to come check out the sizzling American bombshell, that hairdryer better damn not fail!

Prior to your arrival, learn everything you can about your specific tribe. Who is the big shot? When did they come to America? Where did they settle? Most importantly, where do you fit in? Within hours you're guaranteed to have eligible suitors pack living rooms just to get a chance to meet wonderful you!

For those who just baulk at the whole concept behind Plan #1, I understand. Truly, I do. I could never wrap my mind around that whole idea. When everyone would tell me "Go to Syria and find a husband," I would lash out at them, "What are you freakin' crazy?! Just go over there and just pick one out? Like a car? Like a freakin' car? You insane people! Never!" It just ain't my thing—not by a long shot. But, hey it works for some people. And I have to inform you of all your options, so if you're in the market for a husband, and you're wanting to get married, I say, "Hey, go do your thing, girl"

Likewise, if you knock the idea of matchmaking—(uhhh…I can't do that one, either) just consider this: the only real difference between any dating service in this country and *Sito la'lias' kitchen*[1] is that *Busy Dating Professionals, Inc.* has DSL, sleek sales women, a brilliant marketing strategy—and a membership fee. And *Sito la'lias* has a rag in her hair, about twelve functional teeth, a phone, and the slickest network that even the CIA is dying to crack.

> *Insider's Secret Tip!* Buyer beware! In this day and age, you gotta be sharp. You gotta be a real savvy shopper. Remember, you are approaching and possibly doing business with the oldest, most experienced merchants in the world. You have to understand, us nomadic folk have been trading since the dawn of time. No one can match our skills. And, sad as it is to admit, obtaining a green card is often the number one priority for many potential mates. Not all, but enough. At least enough to make me warn you about it.

Also be aware of the tremendous power that Arabic men possess with regard to sweet talk, especially when it comes to an American who is not used to hearing such romantic and flattering rhetoric. For those of you who don't know, the Arabic language itself is akin to Shakespearean poetry. It's beautiful. Nothing is ever said simply as it is in English. So, when tall, dark, handsome *Mr. Syria* stares passionately into your eyes and tells you that you are as beautiful as the creation of life itself, or when he tells you that his soul awakened the moment he laid eyes on you, you're probably going to be swept right off your feet. *Shwoosh!* Just like that. And before you know it, you'll be embraced in his arms on your wedding night asking, "What the $@#! just happened?"

Mr. Syria may be saying those things because he really means it or he may be saying it with a hidden agenda. Only time will tell. The best situation is when you both know what the deal is up front. That way, you can go into the marriage with the benefit of full disclosure. Either way, the good news is that a green card marriage is not necessarily a bad thing. Many long lasting and successful marriages have been started this way, including my own parents and way too many relatives to list. But we'll get into all that later.

---

1. Elias' grandmother's kitchen.

Oh, and by the way, if you do get married to someone seeking a green card, you'd do yourself a big favor by enrolling in an immigration law class at your local college. Trust me, you'll be doing a lot of paperwork over the years.

One final note under Plan #1: if you chose to go with it, prepare yourself to almost immediately be bombarded by plenty of *Mr. Syrias* who might want to marry you. Within the first 24 hours of my stepping foot on land, I had a potential right there ready to go! The next day, I had another. The following day, I had two more. And so on and so forth. Before I knew it, I'd lost count there were so many bachelors coming around. Not necessarily for wonderful *me* but, you know, *for business*.

Plan #2
Plan #2 is your moderate selection. It's for the working woman who has slightly upscale taste, but unlike her Plan #1 counterpart, has not yet entered into desperate territory. She is not as high maintenance, therefore doesn't need a personal concierge. Her main disadvantage is that she doesn't have direct access to a contact person nor does she have the luxury of jet-setting overseas for a month. But, since her personality is more flexible, she will be open to a lot more realistic possibilities.

Plan #2—Take your time ... *but not that much.*

Here's what to do:
Since you don't have a connection overseas, make one here. Talk to your priest, community/religious/political leader or any one of those old, intrusive ladies that neb in everyone's business and just tell them that you want to get married.

Don't know any of us? No problem. Try this strategy: go on a lovely fact-finding tour to a small Middle Eastern grocery store, deli, or pizza shop. We own tons of them. Or, if you live in New York, Detroit, Los Angeles or Allentown, just open your front door and step outside. If, however, you live way out in the boondocks, you're going to have to trek a bit to get what you want. Take a Greyhound to the closest major metropolitan city, get off the bus, and you're bound to find at least one video rental/cell phone distributor/discount travel/satellite dish/knock-off designer watch distributor/small all-in-one discount dollar store. Once you've found one of our businesses, just walk right in and talk to the owner. They'll be glad to help you.

And, please, when you go to these places, do your research. Make sure that the people you are approaching are in fact Middle Eastern. Don't confuse us with Indians or Pakistanis. Don't lump us all together and stereotype us. It's not nice. We are different. Similar, but different. We're both "dark complected" and talk funny, and we're both really big on spices, but that's it. Otherwise, don't come crying to me if you accidentally find yourself on a 17-hour, direct flight to Bangladesh, sitting in the seat next to *Mister 'I-don't-need-a-shower-when-I-smell-so-good-like-curry' man!* Because it will be your own fault. And you'll have no one to blame but yourself.

<u>Plan #3</u>
Plan #3 is the Budget Plan.
With the budget plan, you don't get a fancy description.
Nor do you get free advice.

All right look, just go online and discretely profile yourself on all the websites that cater to Arab singles. Oh, and be sure to use a fake name.

There. That's Plan #3.

So, there you have it, your three basic plans for getting married without really trying. Chose the one that best fits your lifestyle, say a prayer and hope for the best. But whatever path you take to find Mr. Right, just make sure you obey the one Supreme Arabic Rule: Do Not Date! I mean that! At least not until your 40. By that time, who gives a s**t anyway? You know? I mean, you're freakin' 40 years old for goodness sakes! What have you got to lose? Go ahead, live a little! And while you're at it, break open that bottle of Jack Daniels. You deserve it! Jack never let you down. You've been putting up with all this double-standard crap long enough. Approval, acceptance, it never ends. Let your hair down. Have some fun!

(Psssst! Hey girls! Come here! Listen! If you do in fact date, do it discretely. Be smart and clean. Make sure your girl's got your back, and have a backup plan if you get caught. And, as every good, traditional Arabic girl with strict parents knows, if you do get caught, look them straight in the eye—and deny it!

Now that you've selected your optimal plan, let's take a few moments and go over some tangential, yet critical, finer points regarding the process.

We Do Business By Referral

Take it from me, in this game, it's all who you know. Referrals are about the only way you're gonna meet a potential husband. So, as an eligible female looking to get hitched, know that you won't be watched my dear, you'll be dissected. Everyone will be examining you under their own personal microscope. Your every move will be discussed and debated in excruciating detail. Mothers, sisters, aunts, nieces, neighbors, the damn dog even, they're all here to check you out. To see if the merchandise is, you know, worth the asking price.

Here's how it will work.[2] The man will never confront you directly, that's very disrespectful (and far too uncomplicated for us, anyway.) So during the initial pre-screening phase, their "agent" will represent them. Acting like a personal liaison, their job is to obtain basic vital information, get a feel for what kind of girl you are, and basically see what you're all about. When the "rep" comes over, they'll be analyzing you to see how you stack up. If you help with the dishes, be pleasant, smile a lot and are basically an all around sweetheart, you'll get high points. And conversely, unflattering behavior will cost you.

What's happening here is that the old adage, "the apple doesn't fall far from the tree," is being played out. You are being put to the test and rightfully so. As you've already learned, Arab-American females are automatically placed in a certain category based entirely on her family's reputation. If, for example, you come from a good family, then half the work is done. They just have to do a little investigating to make sure you're not the one "bad apple." And believe me, there's always one bad apple somewhere in the bunch. Plus, they want to see how you perform before they bring in the "v.p. or general sales manager," you know, to negotiate the final deal. It's not exactly a test drive, but I think you get my point.

You see, if you're behaving like the latest, brand new, fully-equipped BMW, they'll rush to get their unmarried brothers, uncles, and nephews over to meet you. They want the absolute best for their boys—and you're it! On the other hand, if you're running around like a high-maintenance, expensive, gas-guzzling SUV, the word will get around as well. Your lovely trip down the altar might make a u-turn, and

---

2. Generally speaking, of course.

wind up as an unexpected trip onto *Arabic eBay*—and it ain't no damn good being back on the auction block!

Another very important thing to know is that you really don't get private time, at least not like Westerners do, unless you're serious about at least entertaining the idea of perhaps getting married. For example, if you're in the village and a man's sister approaches you and tells you that her brother is interested in talking to you, unless you are interested in pursuing marriage, or at least getting to know him better for the purpose of possibly pursuing marriage—don't do it! Don't say, *"Sure, why not? He's hot, I'm bored. This could be fun! Let's get a beer!" Ahh,* it ain't happening quite like that, you know what I mean? People just don't date like that in the villages. Sometimes people don't date like that in America. Just don't try it over there. Because, one bad move, and the entire family's reputation is shot straight to hell. And besides, right or wrong, family honor is usually a whole lot bigger than you are or than you'll ever be. I know it's unfair but it's true—at least it is most of the time. You just always gotta be on your best behavior for everyone's sake, you know? It's kinda like that whole no "I" in "TEAM" thing.

I know … I know …

Ain't no damn "WE" in "TEAM" either!

<u>Get A Translator</u>
If you find yourself sitting with a single guy who is talking to you in Arabic and you don't understand what he is saying, get an interpreter. And keep your mouth shut until you do. Because if all of a sudden the room breaks out in a big *zalghouta,*[3] you might have just accidentally agreed to get married.

Let me tell you a little story.

My great-grandmother, *Sito Nejume,* was taken with her family to a real nice wedding in a nearby village. Oh, she had a great time! A ball! They danced. They feasted. It was just F-U-N! And the wine was good, too! *Sito Nejume* was just havin' the best darn time of her life. Well, when the wedding was over, she hopped into the carriage with everyone else to head back home. They picked her up and put her back out on the street. She hopped back in, again. They put her back on the street, again. She couldn't figure out why they wouldn't let her go home; it didn't make any sense, and she was so sleepy, too. Finally, they explained

---

3. Loud expression of joy and excitement (see Chapter 12).

to her that she wasn't going home because it was *her* wedding that she had just attended.

She was twelve.

Changing Your Mind About A Potential Mate

So soon?
No. Just a precaution.

In the very likely event that you completely got swept off your feet, accepted a marriage proposal and then realized what you just did, don't fret. You can still get out of the deal—most of the time. Just remember this golden rule:

Never *butlay*[4] more than three times.

Just three.
No more. No less.

Not five.
Not one.
But three.

Thou shalt not count to four.

Nor shall thou count to two, unless thou proceedeth to three.

Six is way out.
Three is the number.

Three is perfect because it means you're a spoiled little brat and a true princess. Fussy and all! It's everything an arrogant, small-minded man could ever want in a girl! However, after the third time you *butlay,* you inadvertently move from being an unattainable *"you're lucky you're even talking to me!"* princess to a bad ass *"ain't nobody wantcha spoiled little punk ass anyway!"* rejected ex-fiancé with a real need for an attitude adjustment. Essentially, you become a problem nobody wants. It's a real fine line. Be careful. Be strong. And don't let those donkeys wandering around fool you. We are in the 21st century and these guys know there are plenty

---

4. Break off an engagement.

of *Araabics*[5] in America looking to get married. They might just wait for the next plane load.

Disclaimer

Spoiled little princesses and narrow-minded men are not what the author (me) values by any stretch of the imagination. But she does recognize that in every culture there are gold diggers and arrogant men who prefer superficial relationships. However, this book is an equal opportunity educational tool and does not discriminate on the basis of vanity or financial status.

Your Competition

Single females looking for love have yet another obstacle to consider. Ever since 21st century technology found its way into the rural mountains, it has become much more difficult to compete for a husband. Thanks to the Internet and the satellite dish, those *foo-foos*[6] in the village can see what's going on outside and around the rest of the world. And those girls are getting real smart—real fast. They're beginning to throw those ruffled, 1970s shirts out the window faster than you can say *"Yeeeeh!"* They're reinventing their image, taming those out-of-control curls, and following the latest fashion trends. So, consider their new style transformation a direct threat to you.

Foo-Foo (n.)—A bubble-gum brained female with a very small I.Q. She smiles constantly, has fatal fashion sense and wants to get married in the worst way. Her signature style is ruffled, frilly, outdated '70s blouses, but her special trademark is long, curly, over-sprayed '80s hair. She is to Carson Kressley what kryptonite is to Superman. In fact, reports have recently surfaced of gay men suffering massive heart attacks upon random sightings. A code red alert has been issued by the global fashion police, and she is suspect number one on the *Extreme Makeover Most Wanted List*. Radical environmentalists want her dead or alive as she is the single most potent threat to the ozone layer.

---

5. Just a fun way to refer to Arabic people.

6. Dumb blond types.

Don't believe me? Here are just a few statistics to support my claim:

*According to a 1987 Congressional Report, the national average of hairspray used by a single, typical *foo-foo* was two to three aerosol cans per week.

—*Hairdoo Magazine, Special Edition, June 1987.*

**Foo-Foos* are solely responsible for 35.9% of the rapid deterioration of the ozone layer between the years of 1982–1986. They are also directly responsible for a staggering 40% increase in recent skin cancer cases.

—*U.S. Department of Environmental Services, Emergency Session, 1986.*

* "Oh it was just awful! He was just leaving the bar, and she popped out of nowhere! And then all of a sudden, I heard a real loud scream: 'Oh My God! No! ... No! ... Ahhh!' and the guy just collapsed right there!"

—*Eyewitness describing to reporters what he saw when a foo-foo startled a gay man to death.*

Sad, isn't it?
Not a friend in the world.

It wasn't always like that, though. Once upon a time (in the 1980's), if you were a *foo-foo*, you had men lining up for miles to marry you. If ever there were a feminine, wide-eyed, dumb-blonde type who could turn a man's head, you were it. Truly, these are wretched times. Men these days demand more from a woman. They're starting to require degrees, careers, portfolios and professions. Talk about outsourcing! It's a scary world out there. Real scary. Your modern, educated, well-established, bachelor would much prefer a working brain to go along with all that beauty. Even just a half a brain would do; but some is definitely better than none.

In all fairness, I should note that even though they are not so desirable, *foo-foos* are still a valuable commodity to an indiscriminate few. It's just that they're not as in demand as they once were. Granted, some old school *foo-foos* can still get by on pretty looks and a high-pitched cutesy voice but, at that point, they're pushing it.

Mishwarring: The Language of Love in the Middle East

If there is one single piece of vital information that you take away from this book, let it be this: if you ever go overseas, especially to Syria, you will fall in love.

Period. The end. No ifs ands or buts.

It's completely out of your control. It's so out of your control that it should be incorporated as a law of physics, right under that whole gravity thing. No matter how strong you are, no matter how independent you are, no matter how much you think it won't happen to you, guess what? It will. I guarantee it.

The region is beautiful. It's mysterious and comforting. Time is completely suspended in that enchanting land of romance and seduction. The nights are crystal clear. The moon is illustrious. The stars are brilliant. The mountains are breathtaking. And the music? The music is to die for. And every song is about love. All they do is sing about love, love, love. *My love this ... my love that ... the love I lost ... the love I found ... the love I need to find ... my lover's eyes ... the death of my own heart, killed by my lover's eyes.*

Allow me, if you will, to heighten your fears just a bit more. Thank you. When you do fall in love, *Ms. 'I-Don't-Need-A-Man-Thank-You-Very-Much,'* it will most likely come in the form of a sudden, intense, love-at-first-sight kind of way and knock you right off your feet!

But don't waste any time feeling guilty because it's not your fault. Not at all. You see, there is something in the air in Syria. And its name is *"Love." Love* is in the air. Love is so freakin' in the air that it is invisibly fused in with the oxygen that you breathe.

Let me explain.

If we were in science class in America, the chemical symbol for oxygen would look like this: O2. But test the *exact same sample of air* in Syria, and you've got an entirely different result. When you break down the molecules in Syrian air, it mysteriously appears as L2O—Love 2 Oxygen.

Researchers are baffled.

Many Middle Eastern countries are dangerously romantic. So when natives warn you that there is something in the air, please just believe it. If the bug catches you, that's it. You might as well just lay down and admit defeat right then and there. Love is all around you, it's what the whole freakin' culture is centered on. I'm telling you, we should bottle and export it. It should be part of our Gross National Product. We do it that well!

And when they *mishwarr,* just forget it. It's over. You are done.

Let me take a moment here to explain *mishwarring* so that you'll have a better understanding of just how powerful this stuff really is.

Mishwarr is what the whole village—make that the whole Middle East—does every summer night. It's crossing the threshold into enigmatic territory. Where innocent, yet spirited, flirtatious glances occur. It's where boy discretely meets girl. Tantalizing, isn't it? Enticing, isn't it? It's where secrets are sworn. Where whispers are exchanged in the dark. Thrilling, isn't it? Exciting isn't it? It's where passionate eyes first meet, stare and lock forever. It's where tender promises of giving one's heart are spoken. It's where people fall desperately and hopelessly in love. It's all the stuff that romance—since the dawn of time—is made of. It is sweet nectar.

You see, every evening, the masses go out for a leisurely summer stroll. Girls walk with girls, and boys walk with boys. No exceptions unless you're related or a family friend. [7] And they *shanglaay.* To *shanglaay* simply means to interlock your arms around your friend's arms as you promenade together. You know, like the Europeans do. Both men and women *shanglaay.* Some men, I think, *shanglaay* a bit too comfortably … ahh … but that's another book. At any rate, you'll have like five girls all holding on to each other and walking and, then maybe, seven boys a few yards behind them doing the same. It's kind of like a group date, where no one is actually dating, but everyone's making their final selections before they get to the check out line.

---

7. (Generally speaking, of course.)

Here is where the magic happens.

If a boy likes a girl, this is his chance. He's just gotta find the right moment to approach her. He's gotta play his cards just right. He's no dummy, either. He's gotta test the waters first. So, he'll work his magic by getting one of his boys to walk a little faster and say something quick and discretely to the girl. If she likes him, maybe she'll arrange to meet him under the apple tree near the mountain spring tomorrow evening. His boy will then report the information back to him. She'll flash back a quick, *"you're cute, and I like you"* million-dollar smile. Then, my dear, *it's been a really good mishwarr!*

That is Syria.

Doesn't it just want to make you fall in love right now? You're not even there and you're falling in love! See! That's why we affectionately refer to Syria as *"La-La Land."* It's pure fantasy. Ain't a bit of it even close to reality. No sir. Not for centuries. And that's just the way we like it.

What to Do If You're Being Questioned by the FBI (The Fadis, Bassams and Ibrahims)

If you find yourself suddenly surrounded by serious looking men who are interrogating you, don't panic; it's actually a good thing. You remain "a person of interest." Just be polite, sweet and answer all of their questions as briefly as you can.

If they ask you what your intentions are—tell them to get married and have babies.
If they ask you what your background is—tell them you're from a nearby village.
If they ask you where you've been—tell them you've been lost the whole time, waiting for you.
If they ask if you have been followed—tell them yes, but you lost "them" all.
If they ask you about your connections—tell them you are the daughter of "so and so."
If they ask for your papers—tell them they're at the altar ready to be signed.

Co-operate. But don't let them infiltrate. Personal details are classified top secret. Any leak of sensitive information will destroy the entire mission. Remember: *Loose Lips, Sink Chicks!* Do you understand? Your future security is at stake here. Operations must be clean and swift. Covert. Under no circumstances are you to affiliate with any outside, unauthorized person or organization not part of this exercise. You have all the information you need now. Just don't be too nervous. It will cause suspicion. Good luck.

Oh! And one more thing.

Sorry, I really did almost forget to tell you this but it is quite critical to the success of the assignment. Before you go any further and matters get any more serious, you need to know that the American style of getting married is quite different than the Arabic style. And in some cases, it's actually reversed.

In America, typically, you date, get to know each other, and who knows, maybe even live with the guy for a while. Sometimes you date for a year or two. Or three or four. Break up. Date other people. Get back together again. Date more. Sometimes have a kid together. Sometimes have *a couple of kids together.* Then you decide if this is the man that you ultimately want to spend the rest of your life with. If it all works out, then you get engaged and married. In America, of course, not all lovers go through each of these steps, but it is fair to say that those options are available to you, even if you don't take them.

In the old country ... *well ... it's kinda different, you know?* It's kind of like exactly the opposite way around. Over there, available suitors generally make their interest known. You, as a woman, check out the guy and review his qualifications. Evaluate what he as a man can do to provide for you and your future. Learn of his financial, educational and professional status. Is he a doctor? Lawyer? Cheap, lazy bum? Womanizer? Inspect it all. Verify his references and thoroughly investigate his family history. Do not underestimate this point. It's critical to do your research because you want to make sure that he is not the one "bad apple" of the family that I told you about earlier *(Hey, equal opportunity background checks, baby. No gender privileges here).*

After that, calculate the number of other potentially better offers. Weigh them out. Recalculate the number of other potentially better offers. Check daily bachelor reports to see if something better has come in since. Pow-wow all night with your girlfriends about it over *bizzer*[8] and *maté.*[9] Narrow your search down to the final four. Line up your negotiating terms. Have a high council meeting with your girlfriends, again. This time with chocolate. Get blood work done to make

---

8. Seeds we snack on (but very important in Arabic culture. (See Chapter 14).

9. A very special hot tea drink.

sure that if he *is* related to you, that it's not too close. Continue the process of elimination. Secretly choose the final lucky guy. Take one last, careful look to make sure he really is the one. Get engaged and married. *Then* get to know each other.

Yup! That's kinda how it happens—sometimes. Same research, different methods. But don't worry, whatever happens you'll find a way to make it work. I know you will. Love will come. Trust me. Even if you have to *make* it come.

Look, I don't mean to be facetious; I'm just trying to make a point. And the point I'm trying to make is that you can be with someone forever and never truly know that person. And conversely, in an instant, you can know if a certain man is the right one for you. The Arabic way of approaching marriage is much more practical. You find someone with the basic good qualities and build a foundation from there with the understanding that in time, love will grow. And trust me, *it will grow* because the culture, family, and society are all built around making sure the marriage works. In other words, it ain't real acceptable to get divorced ... *uhh* ... so you kinda stay married, even if you're not necessarily all that happy.

In America, we tend to look for love first, and then build from there. The downside here is that since we have this idea of what love "should" be like, we're often disappointed when reality comes barging in. Furthermore, because Americans have more individual freedom and less family pressure and interference, it's easier for us to throw in the towel when we feel trapped or unfulfilled. And then we wonder why we've got a staggering 50% divorce rate. *Hmmm...* Too much freedom? Not enough freedom? Makes you wonder which way is better, doesn't it?

The fact of the matter is that sometimes things work out, and sometimes they don't. It's just the luck of the draw. No matter how hard you plan or which method you use, unfortunately, life has no guarantees.

CHAPTER 2

▼

How to Become a Sit-el-Beit When You Don't Even Know What One Is

A *sit-el-beit* is arguably the best identity you can have (excluding princesshood, wife-of-renowned brain surgeon and/or mother-of-seven-male-doctors).

Sit-el-beit (n.)—The lady of the house. It is the common name used for the female (usually married, but not always) who takes care of the household. She does it all: cooks, cleans, serves coffee, and entertains with grace and ease. She might be described as the Arabic version of a slick-marketed, pre-prison Martha Stewart. She is the perfect hostess and ultimate homemaker.

Unfortunately, a *sit-el-beit* is never given her due credit. Very few can truly appreciate the amount of work and sacrifice she makes. The *sit-el-beit* is to the family what the secretary is to the billionaire CEO. She is, for the most part, exclusively in charge of preserving the family honor and stellar reputation. She is the superwoman behind the scenes. She is the damage-control expert, scrambling at the last minute to make the head of the household look like he's completely in charge, and actually knows what he's doing.

At times, the work can be downright exhausting. For instance, when the old, senile grandfather inadvertently puts his foot in his mouth in front of a room full of distinguished guests, *Ms. Sit-el-Beit* is always right there to clean up the big mess. Or when her absent-minded husband forgets that he promised to drive his niece, the bride, to the church on her wedding day, it is the *sit-el-beit* who rushes to get her there on time.

She's got wicked instincts and can spot a troublemaker a mile away. She instinctively understands her guests' needs; anticipates them, even. She is the multi-tasking queen of the universe. The girl gets up at 6 a.m. , throws in a load of laundry, then goes to the market to buy fresh fruits and vegetables. By 8 a.m dinner is completely prepared for that night, and two dozen shirts have been ironed to a crisp. All of her delicacies have been prepared in advance, and she always has a fresh *rakoui*[10] of delicious Arabic coffee on the fire, ready to offer visitors who drop by. She is always looking her best. Her hair and make up are done, but never overdone. Her work is absolutely impeccable, and she can do it all with a dazzling smile!

See, don't you want to be just like her?

I do.

Well, now that you've learned what a *sit-el-beit* is, let's get you started on becoming one. The following is a brief instructional guide to help you take the first steps toward becoming a great *sit-el-beit*.

The Unofficial *Sit-el-Beit's* Guide to Entertaining

1. Stock Up. As a *sit-el-beit*, you'll need to prepare a shopping list of necessary items and have them fully stocked in your cupboard. When guests drop by, all you really have to do is offer them coffee or tea, a sweet, and/or fruit. You're really not obligated to serve any food unless of course they drop by while you're in the middle of breakfast, lunch or dinner—then you gotta share. The following list contains only the minimal essential food stuffs you should have on hand:[11] Arabic coffee, tea, *maté*, sweets, sesame crunch candies, *arak, bizzer* (all three kinds),[12] assorted nuts (especially pistachios), wine, and the three main types of fruits which are guaranteed never to go stale—apples, oranges and pears.

---

10. Coffee pot.

11. A full list of definitions can be found in the upcoming *macdouse* section.

12. See Chapter 14.

Big Disclaimer

Not all Arabic households include alcohol among the beverages that are served. In fact, serving alcohol actually doesn't apply to the majority of Arabs (liquor is mostly consumed in Christian homes—not all—but enough).

During the holidays and other festive occasions, increase your menu to include more fruity wines, lots more *arak*, way lots more *bizzer*, lots of ashtrays, pretty colored Jordan almonds, and throw in a batch of expired sweets, such as the ever-popular Arabic gel nougat nut candy, preferably the ones with gold-laced wrapping. Unused ones from last year's wedding or *amadi*[13] is usually best. If you find yourself fresh out of those, call an old aunt. No doubt, she'll have plenty. But by all means, stay away from your aunt's stale *American* candy. You know, the plastic butterscotch ones where the wrapping is stuck to the candy or the unwrapped, fused together, after dinner mints. Somehow, it's just not right. And don't forget to include plenty of fruity tobaccos and charcoal for your *argeelee*. [14]

2. Purchasing Power. Own at least one membership to a Sam's Club, Restaurant Depot, or any other *members-only-buy-ridiculous-amounts-of-supersized-products-in-volume superstore*. This is not an option; it is mandatory. While you're at it, buy at least two large freezers and keep them in the garage. Fill them up with prepared meal time foods, such as grapeleaves, baked chicken, kibbee saynee, bread, hummos, and spinach pies because when company drops by unannounced, there's gotta be enough to go around.

Also, be sure to have the following ready-to-serve delicacies available for general emergencies: *macdouse, shunkleesh, bizzer*, olives, fruit (remember: *"the three with the guarantee"*), *lubnee*, feta cheese, *zait-oo-zatar*, pickled vegetables, bread, nuts, jellies, cheeses, dates, figs, small sweets, Arabic coffee, tea, *maté*, and, if you really want to go all out, an *argeelee*.

3. Visiting. When visiting, follow the proper protocol, and by all means, make the visits count! Look your best by visiting the most important families first, and let the word spread about your graciousness because

---

13. Baptism.

14. Shisha.

the points really do add up. Remember, the more points you get, the closer you are to achieving glory while, at the same time, embarrassing your competition. First visits are always reserved for the patriarchs and matriarchs of the family, as well as the elderly aunts and uncles. Persons arriving from or leaving to the old country come next, as it is a great cultural insult to *diss* them. New mothers follow, and, after that, it's on to newlyweds. Then it just trickles down after that. Sunday brunches are generally good ways to socialize with new acquaintances, but if it's just you and the girls—no kids and no husband—the Chinese buffet is definitely the spot.

Oh and by the way, if you want to send something overseas, this is your chance! Forget FedEx; they're nothing. Find out who's going back to the old country, drop by at the last possible minute when the traveler has almost completely finished stuffing the very last item into their already bursting suitcase, and ask if they wouldn't mind if you squeezed a little package in to give to someone who lives the next three villages over. Throw in a couple of *Alla ykhaleekees!*[15] and baby, you're in!

Sit-el-Beit Insider's Secret Bonus Tip! If you find yourself completely overwhelmed by all of the familial obligations and know there is no possible way you can visit everyone you're required to, try this handy dandy little trick. It always works for me. Visit only the head member of each family unit—and only for a half hour. Give them a little gift to pass along to the other family members. Come up with a good explanation as to why you have to leave and get out, fast!

Don't underestimate this, girls. Like I said, these points count big because it will get around that you did in fact pay a visit and that you were considerate enough to offer something in lieu of your absence. It doesn't have to be expensive. Something from the dollar store will work. Candle holders, rose soaps, lacy table coverings—anything. The gesture itself carries a lot of weight, and it will make you look really good. Trust me. You can easily earn at least three to five points for this one. And during holidays, it jumps to seven to eight points! No kidding!

Secret Sit-el-Beit Payoff! If you have ungracefully fallen from your throne, holiday visiting is your prime chance to redeem yourself—*if you play your*

---

15. Good old fashioned blessings.

cards right. By making the rounds, you will erase all the negative perceptions others have of you and be back on top in no time. They will completely absolve your misdeeds and forgive your bad behavior. And once again, you will reclaim your spot as champion *sit-el-beit*.

4. Entertaining. When entertaining, never let your guest sit without refreshments. Make sure to remove all used place settings quickly. Keep the *bizzer* dish full, and the shell dish empty. Absolutely keep your cool when they take only one tiny bite of each item, rendering you unable to salvage anything. It's just a cultural thing; don't take it personally, especially when you've spent all day in the sweltering heat to prepare the perfect *baklawa*.

And when it is *you* who are the guest, take only one bite of dessert and say with a demure smile, *"yislamoo."*[16] You don't want to appear ... *well* ... *you know* ... like you really *want* to eat the whole piece of cake.

5. Fake it. Smile—even when it hurts. And trust me, sometimes it will.

6. Fake it more. Don't lose your cool with your kids—until after the company is gone.

7. Be Feminine. Sing a little when you talk, but only a little, please. What I mean here is you should slightly fluctuate the intonation of your voice so as to sound very feminine and girly. Don't actually bust out and sing a song.

Big Secret Sit-el-Beit Payoff! A really good *sit-el-beit* will always pass up a serving of gossip, no matter how delicious, tempting, or juicy it is. However, if you do find yourself unable to resist the demons calling your name, do it diplomatically and quietly, and only with the most trusted of guests.

There really is so much more to cover, but I don't want you to get too overwhelmed, especially since the very idea behind being a good *sit-el-beit* is basically all about overwhelming yourself.

Now, here's a surprise pop quiz that just blew out of nowhere—just like company!

---

16. Just a fancy shmancy way to say thank you.

Scenario:

Three of your high-powered *jidus*[17] come over after church to discuss some very serious family business, such as a scandal, territorial threat, land dispute, etc. You, as the *sit-el-beit* or single "good daughter" …

  a. Completely ignore them all together, go in the sunroom with a bowl of low-carb cookie dough ice cream and a carton of chocolate milk and watch *E! News Live* so you can get the latest scoop on celebrity divorces.

  b. Pleasantly greet the *jidus,* serve them coffee, and then suddenly excuse yourself because you just remembered that you were supposed to go over to your cousin's house at 2 p.m. to call the boy that you met last night when you were out "shopping at the mall." *(He was so cute, too!)*

  c. Demurely serve coffee while you silently watch three grown adult men screaming at the top of their lungs about a "devastating" situation—a situation so utterly ridiculous that it leaves you dumbfounded, questioning how someone as bright and intelligent as you got mixed in with this bunch of clowns in the first place.

I'm not going to grade you on this one just yet. You figure it out. But let me just give you a little hint: If you didn't pick #3, you're wrong.

As a professional *sit-el-beit*, not only are you required to have your ready-to-serve items but *you, yourself,* my dear, must be ready-to-serve. Literally. Literally ready-to-serve when unexpected company drops by.

And unexpected company always drops by.

You can never let them catch you off guard. Ever.

There you are lounging on the couch, feet up all over the place, curlers in your hair, with a can of Diet Coke, and a bag of Hostess Ho-Hos. You're watching

---

17. Grandfathers (also refers to grand-uncles).

Seinfeld reruns and trying to get the last few crumbs out of the Pringles can. And then, out of nowhere, DING DONG! The doorbell rings! Your heart stops.

*Ohhh S**t!*

What's a girl to do?

Don't panic. It's all taken care of.

Quick! Pull out three essentials from your well-stocked Arabic items: the *bizzer*, the assorted nuts, and the *baklawa*! Grab the remote and flip on the *Al-Jazerra* channel! Rip out those curlers as fast as you can with your left hand and with your right hand, fill the *rakoui* with water and throw it on the fire. Make sure that coffee is on *before* you answer the door—it needs time. Remember, practice makes perfect. So, set up some practice drills, and you'll be a pro in no time.

The following are brief descriptions of those strange-sounding items:

Arabic coffee (n.)—Arabic coffee (makes espresso look totally wimpy).

Arak (n.)—100 proof alcohol. Unless it's homemade, then I think it jumps to 1,000 proof. The important thing to know is that it's a really strong drink. In fact, it's so strong that you have to cut it with water to drink it.

Argeelee (n.)—A shisha or hooka.

Bizzer (n.)—Seeds we snack on. That's all they are but, they're very important in Arabic culture. There are three basic types (see Chapter 14).

Lubnee (n.)—A much less offensive cheese than *shunkleesh*. It's like our own cute, little Arabic version of Philadelphia Cream Cheese.

Macdouse (n.)—A horrific-looking delicacy, often resembling a really gross ... um ... forget it. *Macdouse* is pickled baby eggplant stuffed with garlic, walnuts, and red peppers. It's robust and full of flavor. The garlic is so potent that it should only be eaten with the closest of friends. The longer this delicious delicacy is aged, the more fabulous the taste. Served with bread and hot tea, it is truly to die for. Just don't look at it while you're eating it.

Maté (n. or v. we really don't know)—But it's a very special hot drink that is served when people really like having you around (see *maté*, below).

Shunkleesh (n.)—So dangerous that you might be arrested for possession. A pungent, horrific-smelling, aged cheese that can also be used as a very powerful lethal weapon and is frequently swapped on the black market. It is slightly less deadly than ricin and more abundant than uranium. The latest figures point to some one million lost and forgotten *shunkleesh* balls in remote locations all over the world. A government-issued warning suggests they are likely giving off toxic levels of radiation at this moment. However, this ghastly smelling cheese is absolutely delicious to eat.

Zait-oo-zatar (n.)—A mixture of spiced thyme and olive oil that is eaten with bread.

A Sit-el-Beit's Well-Guarded Bonus Secret Tip! Whatever happens, do not get your *macdouse* from a jar; it is a sure sign of an amateur. It's equivalent to someone putting a note on your back that reads *"Help! I don't know what the #*!@ I'm doing!"* However, if you can speak Arabic fluently, you are automatically exempt from this rule. That is, you need not be ashamed to use *macdouse* from a jar. But if you do not speak the language and you can't make it yourself, you're gonna have to buy it from somebody in the community.

Another thing to know is that there is a certain way to make Arabic coffee and a certain way to serve it. If you don't already know how to make it, or how to serve it, just give it up. Don't even try. Coffee just isn't something you want to mess with, you know? At least not with Arabs.

Sit-el-Beit's Insider's Secret Bonus Tip! When company stops over, the usual custom is to give them coffee and a small sweet. Generally speaking, in most villages, two cups and about an hour-and-a-half later is widely considered a short visit. Once they're out, it's time to get ready for the next round of visitors. But if you've got some company that you really want to keep around, you know, like people you actually *like*—baby, then that's when you break out the *maté!*

<u>What the heck is *maté,* anyway?</u>
I'm so glad you asked.

Nobody really knows for sure, but what they do know is that *maté* is a very special hot drink. When someone offers you *maté,* they are offering you warmth, love and affection. They are essentially telling you that you are so cool to be around that they want to hang out with you for a really long time. Everyone gets coffee—but not everyone gets *maté.* You know what I mean?

Maté is a grainy something or other, wannabe-loose-tea-thingy, that your host mixes with hot water and sugar. [18] You can drink *maté* for hours, literally. Trust me, I have. I'm not sure what it was that I actually drank, but I do know that it was fun to drink! And *maté* is even more fun to drink because of the way it is served.

Your host will bring out these tiny tea glasses that can't hold more than two ounces at a time. You know, like those cute, little pre-measured cups you get when you buy cough syrup. Well, *maté* is served in really small, adorable glasses with the cutest little steel straws you ever saw in your whole life! It looks like you should be having tea with Barbie in her dollhouse or something!

I don't think anyone really enjoys the taste, but everyone agrees that drinking *maté* is just something to do—you know, while you're basically doing nothing. It tastes a little like the henna that you put on your hair, which tastes awful, but it's the reason *why* we drink it that matters. The important thing is that you are spending quality time together, sipping on some muddy, green stuff, you know, so that you're not just sitting there all "coffeed out." I mean there's only so much coffee you can drink in a day while visiting before you get totally wired!

That's why they invented *maté!*

And here's the thing. If you are really well liked—I mean *really* well liked,—then they'll break out the *argeelee.* But you gotta be extra special for that one because they'll be up smokin' all night. So, just remember this: When someone serves

---

18. All right, if you want the real definition, go ahead and look, it's in the glossary.

you *maté,* take it as a big compliment. When someone serves you *maté* and an *argeelee! Girl ... you are so "in" you just do not know!*

Chapter 3

▼

Matching Your DNA With Your Behavior

What's Your Combination?

SAP—Syrian-American Princess?
LAP—Lebanese-American Princess?
SLAP—Syrian-Lebanese American Princess?

> <u>Disclaimer</u>
>
> *There are 22 Arab countries in the world. Although we are proud to have so many sisters, space restrictions will simply not allow us to list them all. Please find your own acronym and adjust accordingly.*
>
> *Thank you,*
>
> *Management*

A princess is a princess is a princess. That's that. It's just the country from which you descend that makes the difference. Us Arabs are all a bunch of fun-loving people who know how to have a good time. We agree on that, right? However, just like anywhere else in the world, there are slight regional characteristics that distinguish one group of people from another. For example, we all know that

Floridians are totally different from Alaskans, and Texans are worlds apart from New Yorkers. We will examine those kinds of distinctions in further detail, but first let's take a closer look at SAPs.

SAP—Syrian-American Princess

Syrian people are fun. The psychology behind it is actually quite fascinating. Since we've got no over-inflated pride, no false superior attitude, no nothing, we seem to let go a lot more than others.

For the most part, we pretty much think of ourselves as regular, down-to-earth, unpretentious people. Except for the educated, sophisticated, fancy schmancy city dwellers, most Syrians are hardworking middle-class folk. We've got plenty of farmers who work the land up in the mountains and we're cool with that.

Even if some upper class Syrian snobs boast a long history of nobility, somebody at some point, started out as a farmer, okay? And we know that. So, no matter how high up the social ladder you get, you can never become too uppity because we'll always be able to trace your family roots back to the mountain where your *jidu* and my *jidu* stole their neighbor's chickens and, at that point, you've just lost all your cool points. And believe me, we have no problem putting you in your place if you act that arrogant with us. We don't play those games. We keep it real. We keep it "for real" real *(even when there are times when we probably should fake it a little)*

We are very proud of our "rough-n-tough" reputation. We have backbone and we know it. There is even a song in which the singer proudly boasts that he, his father, and his grandfather are all farmers. I have the CD in my car. I listen to it all the time. *Ana Fillah! Baya Fillah!*[19] I'm personally proud that we don't have too many sissy, gumball types running around bragging about how rich they are or guys who spend hours in the mirror styling their hair. *Blah! Yuk!* We got real men! Strong, Braveheart, manly-men! *RAAAAH!*

You see, many of us live in countless little villages where, at any given moment, the water or the electricity may suddenly be turned off. So, we take it as it comes. We kinda think, "Hey, it's been four hours and the electric is still on. I have a great idea. Let's have a party!" So, we break out the *arak* and dance a lot. We just kind of accept our circumstances and make the best of it. Plus, we're friendly and nice, too.

---

19. I'm a farmer! My dad's a farmer!

We like people. You could say that we're "people-people." Someone once told me that Syrians buy convertibles just so they can say "Hi" to everyone.

LAP—Lebanese-American Princess
Lebanese people …

Hmmm… How can I say this without … um … okay … forget that. Let's just say the Lebanese have a slightly different take on things, if you will. And that's primarily due to their history and their rare sense of fashion. Many Arabic countries had been colonized by Europeans, but, when they finally achieved national independence, most let go of the foreign influence. The Lebanese, I guess, apparently liked the French culture so much that they let it linger around until it became a permanent part of Lebanon itself. I see nothing wrong with that. In fact, in a moment we'll see how the merger actually benefited the Arab world.

But first, let's get our facts straight. Technically, and officially, Lebanese are Arabs. But they're kind of "French-Arab", in a weird way. You know what I mean? They're just a bit different from the rest of us. Not bad, not good—just different. Actually, from a Biblical perspective, they're really "Phoenicians" which historically, as a people, are really Syrians … *kind of … well … at least to some degree …* depending on whom you ask and what kind of mood they're in. But, regardless of their origination, much like Syrians are proud to be "real," the Lebanese are proud to be … *well …* "Lebanese".

The contributions resulting from this marriage to the French are simply immeasurable. For one thing since they've been heavily influenced by their ways, the Lebanese seem to be a bit more refined than the rest of us, which comes in pretty handy every once in a while. In all fairness, it should be said that they probably tried very hard to help us Syrians change, but they likely got fed up and just moved on. Being regular folk and all, we just couldn't adapt to their fancy schmancy etiquette. Too much fuss, you know?

Let me put it to you this way: the other day my niece asked me where the *bizzer* was. I said, "Oh, it's in my pocket," so I pulled out a handful and offered her some. She said, "You're so ghetto." I replied, "I know … and you're half Lebanese. If it were up to you, you'd have your *bizzer* organized in nice, neat Ziplock bags, color coordinated, with all the shells separated into individual compartments."

She didn't like that comment. At all.

You see, the Lebanese bring a certain air of sophistication and modernity to our region of the world. They are very progressive, open, and liberal in both their thinking and culture. Some would argue *a bit too progressive, open, and liberal in both their thinking and culture.* Surf, skiing, clubs and casinos—not for the tourists, honey, but for the natives. I mean, come on! The Lebanese drink Starbucks, prance around in their bikinis and listen to Frank Sinatra during poolside happy hours.

It's not the Middle East.
It's California.

Look, regardless of what you or I think, or how true, or untrue the stereotypes might be, the Lebanese have always challenged the status quo, pushed the envelope and strived to become more open and free. They are doing what they want, despite constant criticism from the Arab world. Many argue that they've lost their Arabian identity, flaunt too much, and overemphasize the importance of appearances. But hey, just think: If it weren't for the Lebanese, the Arab world would be hated for its horrendous fashion crimes—not terrorism.

And don't try to tell me that the other Arab nations have always been in vogue. They weren't. And you know they weren't. They only caught up-to-date after satellite dish technology provided 600 channels and all of a sudden they could watch style makeover programs 24/7.

Before that, it was a fashion nightmare. Ruffled shirts, bad hair, overdone makeup, mixed-matched patterns. *AAAAHH!* But, thankfully, the Lebanese have always remained a beacon of light in the dark storm. Their couture, high fashion, and overall French-influenced style have bled into the rest of our region somehow, and we are grateful. We owe it to our Lebanese friends to say "thank you." Thank you Lebanese people!

SLAP—Syrian-Lebanese-American Princess

SLAPs are really messed up. They are the worst case scenario, ever. These girls are completely torn apart inside. You see, their Syrian, grounded, playful side is constantly at war with their uppity Lebanese sophistication. And, as you know by now, to be Lebanese, is to be part French. So, as a SLAP, not only are you Syrian, but you are also Lebanese—and, by default, also French. And, if that's not enough to drive you crazy, you got the whole American thing to sort through on top of all that.

SLAPs are confused between identifying with the great and mighty cedars of Lebanon and the endless, freakin' apple orchards of Syria. They are caught between driving in their fully-equipped sports cars to spend the morning sunbathing half-naked at the beach and carrying buckets up to the mountain spring so that they can take a full shower without running out of water.

Even their spices confuse them. They don't know whether to use garlic in their foods or cinnamon. Or, even worse, *both*. It's just too much. It hurts their brains sometimes. Last I heard, the medical community classified the problem as some sort of rare syndrome and is now working on a fancy name for it.

My niece is a SLAP.
I mess with her head all the time.

PAP—Palestinian-American Princess *(now that's an acronym that doesn't sound good at all)*.
Palestinians are a fun bunch of people. I'm telling you; they really are. They know how to throw down, and they're just so cool. If Syrians are *real*, then Palestinians are *"for real, real,"* you know? They have heart and soul. They're as raw as it gets. And they are such genuine, good people.

JAP—Jordanian-American Princess *(not to be confused with Jewish, Japanese, or Jamaican-American princesses)*.
Jordanians are also very fun. Pretty much the same deal as the Palestinians—warm, likeable, good people. And King Abdullah is the man. I love him. He's like the coolest guy in the world, you know? Like if you hung out with him you'd feel like you were just shootin' the breeze with your boy, you know? Plus, their almonds are pretty good.

EAP—Egyptian-American Princess *(not to be confused by dyslexics with the Environmental Protection Agency)*.
Egyptians are the funnest bunch! And they're some *funny* people, too. I'm talkin' *fun-ny!* You'll be laughing so hard, you'll bust a gut. They are jolly, lighthearted people who are always smiling and enjoying life. I don't know why, but it's like in their blood or something. Maybe it's because their country is situated in Africa,

and we all know how fun the *Aswaad* are. They're probably the most laid back and easy-going of the whole crew.

<u>The Gulf Countries</u>.
Princesses?
Oh no.
No. No. No.

They're on a totally different level than the rest of us. Those countries are rich. *Really rich.* They are so wealthy that money just oozes out of their wallets. Seriously. It's not all that uncommon for Gulf girls to have servants and chauffeurs at their disposal. No kidding. So, our idea of a real live princess is probably their idea of the average high school teenager.

<u>Arab-Israelis</u>.
Ouch!
Talk about being at war with yourself.
Damn.
I can't even go there.

Identify Yourself: Are You a Village Chick, Vain Princess, or Urban Goddess?

(How to tell the difference and if necessary, change your unwanted status.)

You've matched your DNA with your behavior and figured out your combination. Now, it's time to take the next step. So, let's dig a little deeper, peel off a few more layers, and find out who you really are inside.

No marriage can ever truly be successful unless you understand who you fundamentally are. Take it from someone who's never been married. Knowing yourself will allow you to open your heart to both yourself and to another. Furthermore, living authentically as "you" will also provide the strong foundation necessary to withstand the uncertainties that come with a lifetime of love.

So, if you haven't done your "inner-self" work yet, you're going to have to break down and do a little soul searching because, let's face it, you can only fake it for so long. I mean come on, the real you is bound to come out at some point. And I say, do the dirty laundry when no one's looking, you know?

So, let's get started.

There are only three choices to pick from, so please select carefully:

Option #1—The Village Girl
She really doesn't have to come from a village at all; we're just saying that to market it better. She may actually be raised in the most cosmopolitan of cities, but it's her heart that we're concerned with here. It's the fact that her heart is bound to her village, her culture, and to her people.

The village girl is completely unimpressed with status or material things. She cannot be persuaded or bought, and she dislikes superficial people. Her soul is rich, and she knows that's the only thing that matters, anyway. She typically uses little or no makeup, is obedient, and cooks exceptionally well. She isn't threatened easily because her humble nature won't allow it. She always gives to others before herself and is very kind, sweet, and generous. She loves her parents and will do anything for them. What she wants most is to have a houseful of kids and to be a good mother.

> *Disadvantage:* Doesn't exactly understand that men are visually stimulated and that it's, at least in part, *her* job to keep him stimulated. The majority of her "inner self" work is complete, but her "outer self" needs some serious renovation. A style makeover and some time off for herself would do wonders.

> *Advantage:* Virtually has no attitude and would make a great wife. No matter how awful a situation, she will always be there with a smile and a cup of fresh Arabic coffee for her man. She's very low-maintenance and easy to please. She doesn't need to be whisked off to Paris to know that her man loves her. A small picnic in the field with her hard-working husband is what she cherishes most. She'll pack in fruit, sandwiches, and mountain-spring water. If a man can get her, he's got gold. But he's got to treat her well because all she asks for in return is to be loved.

Option #2—The Vain Princess
Strike a pose!

The vain princess has "it" but nothing else. The sleek outer package is basically all this shallow woman has to offer. There may be some potential for goodness, but she is too preoccupied with her own vanity to give it a second thought. She knows she's the s**t and makes sure that you know that you are not. *Thank you very much!* She's just better than you, you know?

There are actually two kinds of princesses. Underneath they are exactly the same except for one minor difference: one smiles and the other just gives off deadly venom. The former tends to smile and stare so far off into oblivion that she may appear to be lost. But she is working here. She is smiling and staring so that she can focus on being pretty, which requires a lot of energy. Please, don't break her concentration. In extreme cases, the smiling princesses can be so deeply absorbed into princesshood that they may appear robotic or clone-like. Go ahead, it's okay to touch them; they're real. Just do it gently so they don't get distracted. They aren't dangerous or anything—just gone. Even if her world is falling apart—*and I'll bet you, it damn sure is*—she keeps smiling. Nothing is ever wrong. Everything is perfect. All the time.

The ice princess actually believes that she *is* an international cinema star—a true diva—and, therefore, doesn't utter a word. She's also posing. *Shhhh …* don't break her concentration, either. If you do, she will slowly turn her head as smoke rises from her cigarette and stare you down with a cutting look that will make you wish you were never born. It's usually best to leave her alone.

Both princesses are equally threatened by others' beauty.

> *Disclaimer*
>
> *This information is loosely based on my own personal observations and is not intended to ignite anti-princessism. We wholeheartedly and firmly renounce all acts of anti-princessism in this country and abroad. It is our belief that we are all, in one way or another, guilty of being princess-like and, therefore, blameworthy of the same thing that we are outright accusing them of. Therefore, we refuse to take responsibility for any backlash that might occur as a result of these statements. So there!*

Thank You,

Management

Option #3—Urban Goddess *a.k.a.* The Perfect Woman
You can honestly be the sleek, sexy, ultra-modern woman of the 21st century while still having your heart planted firmly in the village of your choice. It just takes skill. You have to maintain the right balance with everything in your life. You can hold on to your old-fashioned values, but you have to be careful not to become homely. You can like drama, but you can't be a drama queen. You can have some attitude, but you're not interested in being a diva.

This is by far, the best option, and every man's dream. This woman is smart, strong, wise, and sexy. She knows herself and her inherent worth. She knows how to be a woman and how to please her man. She is carefree but not careless. And she takes care of herself—first. She is self-assured and unthreatened by others. She loves her life and is her own best friend. She is kind and gives generously from her heart.

When she walks in a room, it lights up. Everyone notices her. Her warm personality makes her beautiful. She has presence, and she is always present. There is something about her that is so special, so desirable, and so warm that everyone just wants to be around her. Her best kept secret is that she knows that everything she needs is already inside of her and, therefore, she seeks validation from no one. She has class, grace, and style, but she will put you in your place when necessary. Her face is full of mystery and she ferociously guards her privacy. She is a person of strong conviction and integrity. She has all these amazing qualities, but the one thing that makes her most attractive is her own self-possession.

You can aspire to be like her, but hard work will only get you so far. Whatever it is that you want to emulate must first come genuinely from within because, ultimately, people will see right through you. Besides, trying to be someone that you fundamentally are not is just a miserable way to live.

Chapter 4

How to Catch a Syrian Doctor in Your Freshman Year

It's the responsibility of your father to validate and to confer upon you your official "princesshood" status. That's his job in return for all your hard work as a respectable Arabic daughter. Give and take, babe! That way everyone wins. But for those of you who are seeking to build your resumé early, get a heads-up over all your girlfriends, and increase your available marriage options, here are a few suggestions:

Good girls get involved in the church, mosque, or any group that will better the religious or Arabic community as a whole. Political organizations are also a good place to start, although I'm not a real big fan of those. But any association that is working for—or makes you *look* like you're working for—the advancement of our culture is where to be.

For all others, the shorter the skirt, the bigger the attitude—the greater your options. There is overwhelming evidence that suggests that the amount of attitude is directly proportionate to the status of the doctor you are likely to catch. So, sign up for college, visit the Lebanese hairdresser[20] and head to the medical *muktabee*.[21]

---

20. See Chapter 16.

21. Library.

Girls, if you're looking to marry strictly for status, don't smile. It's a sure sign of weakness and desperation. That stone-cold, b**chy look usually gets the ones with the all money. Act like you're too good for your own self, you know? Take your attitude to the highest possible level. The sky's the limit here. You've gotta have an attitude bigger than anyone else's or it won't work. A half-hearted one, you know, showing that you actually care about another human being, and your cover is blown.

> *Disclaimer*
>
> *In extremely rare cases, it has been reported that females who pushed their attitude way over the top have had their heads abruptly blown off. Unfortunately, this was a direct result from the massive build-up of egotistical pressure compressing against the soft cranium tissue.*

Once you've got the attitude down, work the skirt. Wear the form-fitting cloth as high as you possibly can, right on the verge of—but without crossing over into—slut territory. Careful, it's a thin line. High micro-skirts, four inch heels and a low-cut shirt will definitely get you noticed at the library. The problem is that you just might feel a little uncomfortable being that overdressed to go study. But hey, it ain't like it used to be, there's some hot librarians around these days. And the wild ones hang out at after-hour libraries.

For those girls who just can't resist smiling, I say go ahead then, smile a lot. Actually, go straight for the fake smiles; they produce the best results. I know someone who has the very best fake smile in the whole wide world—and boy does she get results! She tilts her head slightly to one side and always acts surprised and interested in what you have to say, no matter what it is. She has great eye contact. However, she is careful not to allow *you* to penetrate those well-guarded windows to *her* soul. Even the casual observer will notice that she is so far off in *"La-la Land"* that you'd hardly even know she's there. In fact, I bet you that *she* doesn't even know you're there. As a matter of fact, I am not so sure *she knows that she is even there.*

Men have lined the streets for her.

Chapter 5

The Wife-Material Olympics— Live from Dubai!

Marriage is to Arabs what baseball is to Americans—their national pastime—except that it is much more fast-paced, even when the players are on steroids. It's actually more like basketball–Hell, it's March Madness! High speed, high energy, and rapid scoring!

Double teamed at center court—Whoa! A hook-shot! Airball!

Unbelievable! Rebound!

She shoots and scores!

Mariam is engaged to Samir!

For those who have been working hard all season to find a husband, getting married could be compared to the Super Bowl. But it carries much more prestige than American football. And like soccer's International World Cup, it almost always has global repercussions. Unfortunately, depending on how long a girl's been waiting, getting married might also be likened to the real Olympics, you know, like a single shot every four years.

And just like the Olympics, regardless of the particular match, there are essentially three standard prizes (plus one more because I just decided that I want to have four). You got your usual boring three: gold, silver and bronze, plus one more for the winner who demonstrates superwoman, supersonic, unrealistic ability. Mind you, this is not an easy task. Decades have passed without anyone being able to rightly claim this coveted prize. Don't be discouraged though. Have hope. It's there for the taking; you just gotta be hungry enough to go get it.

THE FOUR AWARDS

Outstanding Acheivement Award

You're already off the charts! There are no words. None. You've simply outdone yourself. We cannot express how proud we are of your rare and remarkable achievement. We are astonished. You have surpassed the most impossible expectations while under the most intense pressures. And in so doing, have earned your place in a supreme class all by yourself. Gold is an insult. Your triumph is worthy of receiving the Hope Diamond. All that hard, strenuous work taming those unruly curls combined with finding just the right amount of attitude, charm, and flair finally paid off. Even gracing us with your presence is much too kind; we are not worthy. We know you understand. Congratulations once again, and thank you so much for your autograph.

Gold Medal

Marry a surgeon and you take home the gold! Brain surgeon, heart surgeon, transplant surgeon—any kind of surgeon works. As a general rule, the more letters he has at the end of his name, the more zeros he has at the end of his paycheck—the more bags you can fit into your Benz. You understand? Good. Go for the whole damn alphabet if you can A to Z, babe. Throw in some damn numbers if it helps, you know? A surgeon will get you the brilliant, dazzling gold. Gold that is worthy of being sold at Tiffany's.

Then of course, there's the "beautiful, but relatively common" gold, which is any type of doctor as long as he's put at least four years into a legitimate medical school and has the abbreviation M. D. after his name. This particular kind of gold can be bought at fine jewelry stores everywhere.

And finally, you have your dentists. Dentists aren't really "dull" gold at all; they just don't glisten as brightly as "doctor gold." And you do want to glisten, don't you? I thought so. Look, if you're putting in all this effort to reach for gold, you might as well reach for the shiniest one of them all, right? 24kt. versus 14kt. ? What do you think? I'm thinking Home Shopping Network, QVC, you know? Credit card phone orders, catalogues, UPS shipping ... sounds a bit cheesy to me. I mean, come on, don't you think you should raise your standards a little?

All right, I'm sorry. That wasn't nice. Or fair. All right! Or true! There. I take it back. Sorry! Look, dentists are actually fine. They are. They have some letters at the end, like D. D. S, *(whatever that means)*. And you still have to use the word "doctor" when you refer to them, don't you? Plus, maybe they just offer something a little different. Not better, not worse—just different, you know? Like, maybe their specialty is not necessarily in gold, but, perhaps, say, in pearly whites, or porcelain, or metal. Those things are nice, too, in their own little way. So look, dentists count, all right? They're okay. Besides, you can tell all your friends that you're *flossin'* and it will be true. (All right, that was totally corny, but I couldn't resist). All I was trying to say is that medical doctors, specialists in particular, are just a better all around draft pick.

But surgeons, darling. Surgeons! That's the real reason we're here today. You got it?

Look, let's cut to the chase, here. I need to be straight with you. This competition only happens once every four years. And not everyone gets a chance to compete. On top of that babe, let's face it, you're way behind. I'm just trying to tell you that you got one shot at glory—and this is it, so don't blow it. Be smart and shoot for the brightest star in the galaxy. And remember girls, it ain't over till the last tick of the clock. Anything can happen.

<u>Silver Medal</u>
Coming in a close second is the ever popular engineer. Engineers are good. And since there are more of them than doctors, they are naturally more attainable. Just like a megaplex shopping mall, they offer a wide selection to chose from: civil, mechanical, chemical, electrical, computer, aeronautical, etc. The advantage is that they are regarded in very high esteem. The disadvantage is that their stubborn, rigid, analytical thinking can sometimes get in the way of emotional, feverish passion often associated with Arabic femme-fatale types, thereby causing unnecessary clashes in the relationship.

Bronze Medal

Bottom of the ninth. Four-Four tie. Bases loaded. Two outs. Three-two count. Payoff pitch is on the way. You gotta get a homer! You gotta win one for the team!

The bronze keeps you on the pedestal. It's the lowest and smallest pedestal—*but it ain't the ground*. The bronze medal goes to anyone with status and a long, well-established cash flow. It doesn't matter what the business is as long as it's legitimate. Gas stations, dry cleaners, car dealerships, they're all fine. Unfortunately, we don't breed too many lawyers, you just might have to cross over for that one, but that's on you, babe.

Now that you understand everything that is at stake and, more importantly, what you have to do to win, it's time to get ready.

The competition is about to start, ladies.

You know the rules. Shoot for the highest possible status. Stay focused. Competition is fierce this year, and you can't afford to slack off or get lazy. One false move and your girl's on your back, runnin' off with your trophy! Are you gonna let her do that? I don't think so! Keep your eye on the prize. Winning a competition like this takes strength, skill, stamina, and really good hairspray! Play nice—but play hard! May the best princess win! Good Luck!

Now, go get 'em, girls!

※ ※ ※ ※ ※

It's third down and three, with thirteen left to go in the final half. Samera in the lead with twenty, Muna trailing by eight, Selma barely on the board with four.

Number one seed Samera, just looking fantastic out there! Sharp and clean. Strong and confident. Her execution has consistently been flawless throughout this entire season. Watch how fast she's rolling those grapeleaves. ... Talk about speed! Her corners are perfectly tight ... her folds are nice and angular! Look at how crisp! That's the one thing these judges are going to be watching for closely this year. ... Regulations aren't as lenient as they were before the terrible *Mishtai* incident three years ago—they're cutting points for the smallest mistakes. They've just gotten real strict about everything. ...

There goes another one! ... And another one! ... The pot's almost full! ... Notice, Dan, how carefully she's stacking them in ... All those long hours of practice were definitely worth it. She's gotta be pleased with her performance tonight!

You know, Stan, that's the kind of skill and determination that Samera is known for. She's put in a lot of work and it's paying off for her tonight. She's the only person to win back-to-back Conference Championship Titles in both the grape-leave roll and the *mesbaha*[22] toss ... and that just demonstrates her grace, agility and overall domination in this sport.

Hashwee[23] is holding up nicely. It's looking good. Tight. Sticky. Firm.

Nine minutes to go ... Muna and Selma trailing by eight and four, respectively.

Samera, the 5-foot-7 senior from Aleppo who turned down a full scholarship to the prestigious University of Cairo to study engineering and philosophy, said she wanted to focus more on her career, and it seems like it's paying off, all right. Incidentally, the University of Damascus at Aleppo's rigorous grapeleave rolling program was recently ranked among the top five in the country.

Eight minutes left—Muna and Selma still trailing by eight and four.

Jump shot into the pot. ... Another one off to the side. ... She's looking for an opening. ... She finds it! She throws it! There goes another one! And another! Up off the back rim ... and it's in! Oh, she's really cookin' now ...!

Samera's putting her final points on the board!

This kind of amazing performance only comes with the level of persistence she's been consistently demonstrating since she made the decision to turn pro last summer. ... Her fans have come to expect only the best from her, and she just never seems to disappoint. ... Looks like they're already writing her name on the trophy, 'eh Dan? Someone's already bringing up the Gatorade bucket. ... Another victory for the favored for the two-time champi ... *WHOA! WHERE DID SHE COME FROM? ... WHAT! ... THIS IS UNBELIEVABLE!*

Underdog Reema racing around the bend! She's moving in fast! She's catching up! Look at her go! I can't believe what I'm seeing! Reema just blew in out of

---

22. Beads (it is discussed further in Chapter 11.)

23. Stuffing used in grapeleaves.

nowhere! ... She's storming up the 112 flights to the *Muktabee* with lightening speed! Makeup is still perfectly set! Her hair is handling the incredible stress of the wind, elements, and super-fast upward climb! Will you look at that? No flyaways what-so-ever! This is absolutely incredible! I can't believe what's happening right before my eyes! She wasn't even in the picture! If I didn't know any better, I'd think she's using some form of illegal performance-enhancing fortifying shampoo. She hasn't even broken a nail! What an execution out there!

The girl is totally oblivious to her four-inch high heels! Folks, this is mind-boggling! We haven't seen anything like this since Hala's breakthrough performance in the 2002 Amman Engagement Olympics! What a turnaround! Sensational! Look at Reema go! Her fans are going ballistic right now! She's got complete control over her skirt ... her books aren't even budging from her arms ... her briefcase is in tact! Talk about a triple threat! Folks this is really something! Battled out, and beating top seed, Samera! I've never seen anything like it! Samera had better get on it real quick if she wants to hold on to her title! Reema is about to blow her right out of the water!

Samera ... coming in from the curve ... taking a quick glance back at her new rival ... looking a little nervous right now ... looks like she's about to lose her edge. ...

Samera grabbing a handful of grapeleaves ... Looking for an opening. ... Can't find one ... She hesitates ... She's lookin' ... lookin' ... Clock's runnin' down ... She's under pressure ... Samera's about to get blitzed! ... She tosses a handful of grapeleaves into the pot ... OHH! OUT OF BOUNDS! And Reema takes the lead!

Boy, oh boy! What a spirited competition today! Talk about intensity! Reema took her opponent completely by surprise, breaking out and stealing the lead—killing her with the first turnover in the second half!

Stan, you know, you gotta give it to this group of girls, I mean, this is a really strenuous course! I honestly don't know how they're going to do it, and with over 1 billion fans watching worldwide, the pressure sure doesn't help.

Third place Selma ... coming in now ... strong and steady ... with a chance to lead ... I-formation inside the thirty-five ... Grips the *kibbee* ball ... Rolls out ... Play action fake ... fakes it to Nasema ... Throws long. Tosses it in to the end zone. Oh! Fumble! *Kibbee* deflected out of bounds!

Flag on the play.
They're resetting the clock …
Repeat first down …

She's out again … coming in steady … struggling to maintain control … easy … easy, now … She's under intense pressure out there … steady. Oh man! It looks like she's gonna break any second now … she's not holding up well at all … not good for Selma … kibbee balls are starting to look a little sloppy … they're not taking the right shape; they're actually beginning to look a bit deformed … and she's placing them in the pan too hard. Whoa! The oil is splashing up too much! The judges are definitely going to deduct points for that.

She's looking really tired out there. Her fatigue is surely affecting her ability to concentrate … and look at her hair! It's all coming apart! Selma had the best Lebanese hairdressers work on it all week, too …

Wait a minute! Hold on, here! Are they …? Are they …? It looks like they might be calling in the Medical Lebanese Hairdresser Team to take her off the field and do some emergency touch-ups …

Dan, are they going to penalize her? Can we get a confirmation on that? Hold on… (listening into ear piece). I think it's gonna be a coach's challenge.

Let's listen in…

After reviewing the play, Number Three Selma—Offense—charged with face mask(ara)—hair not holding—severely out of place. Illegal use of the kibbee ball. Drops kibbee ball out of bounds—visibly saturated with oil—intended to trip Number Two Reema on library steps—Unsportsmanlike conduct—15 yard penalty—automatic first down.

WHAT A DISASTER FOR SELMA! OH! HOW HORRIBLE! That's just gonna kill her! I don't know what's gotten into her that she would make such a big mistake! And then try to sabotage her competition? That's totally out of character for someone of her caliber. She's still pushing forward, but I'll tell you, Stan, it doesn't look good for her at all at this point. Her coach doesn't seem too happy, either. Certainly not a good day for *Sito La 'Essa*. She's looking very disappointed out there. She knows her protégé can do much better than this. That mistake is going to cost her big. Selma's gotta pull it together and just focus if any of this is gonna count at all.

You know, Dan, this match today has certainly had its share of rough spots...with two major players out of the picture, the competition is fierce. Samera's long time rival Iptesam out with a devastating eye injury from flying *bizzer* during the semi-finals in Cairo, and Najwa disqualified early on in the preliminary trials for using Vitamin D fortified cottage cheese during the *Shunkleesh* making phase.

Reema leading the pack by two ... Samera right behind her ... and Selma's trailing by a slim third.

It's down to the wire with only a minute left to go. Samera only needs seven more to win this competition and set a new world record, but she's gonna have to get past powerhouse Reema to do it.

In the meantime, we're gonna take a quick time out for station identification. Don't go away, we've got much more to come on the *Official Syria-WorldCom Aroos*[24] *Radio Network*. We'll be right back right after these messages. ....

❊ ❊ ❊ ❊ ❊

We're back. ... with less than a minute left to go.

Reema still leading the pack by two ... Samera right behind her ... and Selma trailing by a slim third.

Last snap of the half ... Ball carrier Reema rushing in ... She rushes up ... Coming in close to the end ... WHOA! INTERCEPTED BY SAMERA!

SHE'S DOWN TO THE TWENTY ... THE FIFTEEN ... SAMERA AT THE TEN ... THE FIVE ... TOUCHDOWN! IT'S A WIN FOR SAMERA!

SAMERA TAKING MATTERS INTO HER OWN HANDS JUMPS UP WITH A FLAWLESS INTERCEPTION AND WINS THE GAME WITH FORTY-ONE SECONDS REMAINING!

UNBELEIVEABLE!
WHAT A TURNAROUND!

SAMERA'S BEEN ABSOLUTELY UNSTOPPABLE IN THE FINAL SECONDS OF THE FINAL QUARTER! AND MAKING A COMEBACK

---

24. Bride.

LIKE THIS IS ALMOST INCONCEIVABLE! IT CAME RIGHT DOWN TO THE TICK OF THE CLOCK! AND SAMERA HOLDS ON TO DEFEND HER DIVISION ONE WMO TITLE!

ONCE AGAIN ... SAMERA ... CHAMPION OF THE THIRTY-THIRD SYRIA-WORLDCOM ALL-ARAB-AMERICAN AROOS WMO PLAYOFFS!

FINAL SCORE ... SAMERA TWENTY-TWO, REEMA TWENTY AND SELMA FOUR.

We're gonna take a quick break. We'll be back with some final thoughts right after this ...

※ ※ ※ ※ ※

Thanks for joining us on the Official Syria-WorldCom Aroos Radio Network, your home for in depth coverage of all major Middle East sports events.

SWC: Samera, how does it feel to be the Syria-WorldCom's All-Arab-American Aroos WMO Champion for the fourth consecutive time?

S: Well ... it's great (panting—breath—breath)!

SWC: The Super Husband Bowl isn't that far off from here ... What's it gonna take for you to get ready for the World Championship Trials in Damascus next month?

S: Well ... you just gotta try and stay focused ... work hard (panting—breath—breath) ... and just ... you know ... go out there and get the job done (pant—pant).

SWC: That was a lot of pressure out there for you. Reema was moving in so close, so fast. How did you manage to break her drive and finally regain the lead?

S: Well ... (panting—breath—breath) ... Just stayed focused ... did what I had to do ... just took care of business, you know? Stay focused ... get the job done ... (breath—breath).

SWC: How has it affected your performance with Iptesam and Najwa out of the picture? That certainly added a surprise element to the games.

S: Well ... you know, I just did what I had to do ... get the job done (pant—pant). You know, stay focused ... do what I had to do ... get the job done ... work really hard (pant—pant).

SWC: Well done, Samera! Congratulations on your fourth consecutive Syria-WorldCom All-Arab-American Aroos WMO Championship! Good luck and we wish you the best in the World Championship Trails in Damascus next month—and of course the best to you in the Super Husband Bowl!

S: Thank you (pant—pant)! Thanks (pant—pant)! Thank you (pant—pant)!

SWC: Once again ... Final score. Samera twenty-two, Reema, twenty and Selma at the bottom with four. Don't go away, folks. We've got more Syria-WorldCom post-game highlights and locker interviews coming up right after these messages. ...

> *The Syria-WorldCom post-game report has been brought to you by Salim's Overnight Shipping, "We work hard for you!" ... and by the friendly people from Basima's Baklawa, "Add a little sweetness to your life, with Basima's baklawa." ... And from the makers of Ahawee Arabeeyee, "We'll always have a fresh pot of Ahawee Arabeeyee on for you!"*

Our special thanks to Boomer Essa'sson, executive-in-charge of production: Statistics Research Director John "Johnny" Hanna; and, back in our Amman studios, Technical Director Joe "Deekey" Jinn and Senior Associate Producer Intay "Madge" Noon.

On behalf of Dan, Stan, and everyone here at the Syria-WorldCom Aroos Radio Network ... Good night.

※ ※ ※ ※ ※

Congratulations girls *(clap, clap)!* Good job! All of you *(clap, clap)!* Good job! You're all winners! All of you! You really put your heart out there, and nobody can take that away from you! God Bless You, all!

※ ※ ※ ※ ※

Now the rest of you, come with me! We've got a lot of work ahead of us. We're gonna pick up right where we left off.

Females…

Hey! Females! Get focused here! The game's over. It's done, okay? We don't have time to waste!

Helani! Noura! Eyes up here!

Girls, listen up … it is absolutely critical that you establish your boundaries from the get-go. Firmly state your position and make it crystal clear so that there is no room for any confusion. Make sure that every potential husband knows upfront—and in no uncertain terms—that you are a princess and intend to remain so after marriage. He's got to understand that he is lucky to even be talking with you in the first place. Got it? Good!

And when you do eventually get married, it's your responsibility to make certain that you remain princessy at all times. Because if you don't, it will be your own damn fault. And I'm telling you right now if you don't, do not come cryin' to me talking about how your life is such a mess. Take your worries to your old traveling buddy, *Mr. 'Curry-man'*, 'cause I'm not trying to hear it.

Now listen very carefully because I'm only going to explain this once. Many women are drawn to men who have their own, long-established and lucrative businesses. And yes, it's true, being self-employed does have a glamorous side to it, but it also has a very ugly dark side that most sheltered princesses don't even know exists. Like hustlers in Brooklyn or gangs in Compton, this stuff is hard-core, addicting and it destroys lives.

Mark my words lady, if you end up marrying into a small family business and you don't put your foot down, you will inevitably get sucked in like a vacuum and end up doing a lot of dirty grunt work. You'll start out just like everyone else does, innocently trying to win points by being sweet and helpful. You know, minding the store here and there, doing the payroll, going to the bank, that kind of thing. Before you know it, *BAMM!* You'll be in the basement fixing frozen pipes with just you, a cup of cold coffee, and a dim flashlight.

I'm telling you, it's like once they find out that they can get you to work for free—you know, because it's for you anyway—they'll start cutting the staff by 50%. It's like, why pay someone else, when you can do the job for free. That's dumb. (Didn't I tell you we're the savviest business people in the world?)

Now, let me scare you just a little more. Add to that scenario three or four kids running around in diapers with snot dripping from their noses and each one has an ear infection—because kids, for some reason, always get ear infections. Why? I don't know, but they do. Then you've got angry customers who are pissed off about their back orders, an anal retentive tax accountant who prudently declares *all* of your cash earnings to the IRS, and a wretched mother-in-law who constantly reminds you that if you were a strong woman to begin with, you would have had *all boys* instead of *all girls*, so that they could help out with the family business and run it right in the first place!

Within the first few years, you will be totally worn out and good for nothing. Hair frazzled, sitting by the dumpster in the back alley, smoking a cigarette and wondering how you ended up here to begin with. It all happened so fast. You don't remember anything. A vague image of a diamond tiara comes to mind, but just as you begin to remember more you suddenly black out again. The last thing you recall were disjointed fragments of your wedding day. You were sipping champagne in your stunning white gown, looking gorgeous, laughing, and dancing with your new prince. Then the next thing you know, you're trying to figure out how to lose the extra 25 stress pounds that *you really don't remember packing on.*

Nothing makes sense anymore. You're in bad shape. Keep going at this pace, and some customers might start mistaking you for your part-time, minimum-wage employee. You can't have that. It'll kill you! Listen, I've been around a long time, do you have any idea how many princesses I have seen fall from grace? It's horrifying. I wouldn't wish it on my worst enemy.

Grunt work is completely out of the question for real princesses and your husband has to know that upfront. Besides, if you were a *real* princess, you wouldn't have needed *me* to tell you all that, you would have already known it for yourself.

Now, in the very likely event that it becomes impossible to avoid marrying into a family business, at least steer clear of the food industry, particularly restaurants and pizza shops. Yes, they make a lot of money, but they are the hardest and most demanding (read Chapter 20, you'll see).

Try your best to stick to glamorous industries. Here's a business tip for you: sewing manufacturers seem to be making a strong comeback these days. Thanks to an abundance of FBI raids, and the ... *shhhh!* ... *the Patriot Act!* ... the sweatshop problems have been cleared up (we think). And so the government is using its spy capabilities much more efficiently and can now reserve its most powerful resources for fighting terror. *Go Homeland Security!*

As a result of this major crackdown, the textile industry has changed drastically over the past several years and, for the most part, so has the stigma. You don't have to run a sweatshop and you don't have to be thought of as a slave driver ... *necessarily*. Of course, you won't have the benefit of paying $2.50 an hour under the table to desperate illegal immigrants who put in 16-hour shifts, either. But you know, you win some, you lose some. Right? I'd just stay away from setting up shop near the southern border states. Just a suggestion. Them rednecks scare me a little.

Now before you turn your pretty, little princess nose up in the air, try to change the way you envision your business to be. With the right attitude, it can be established as an upscale, creative, and lucrative enterprise that may even evolve into a fancy schmancy boutique, catering exclusively to the rich and famous. *Hmmm...* Sounds interesting now, doesn't it? Think about it. Your executive in-house tailor can design eccentric clothes just for you, and you can market it as some obscure, rare, never-seen-before, French creation. And if you, yourself are trained as a seamstress, you'll be sitting real pretty. You can design and sell your own clothes, at your own obscene, designer prices.

Prêt-à-Porte, baby.
Prêt-à-Porte!

Look, I'm sorry sweetie, but not everyone can walk away a winner in the Wife-Material Olympics; it just doesn't work that way. You know that. But on the bright side, you can still be a wife, who has lots of material, so that you can create gorgeous gowns, so that you can always feel like a princess.

Chapter 6

Stereo, Tabal and the Wedding: A Fun-Filled, Three-Day Trip to the Altar

Arabic weddings in America are fun.
But Arabic weddings in the Middle East are off the hook!

They don't just have a wedding. They have a *wed-ding!* They are completely different than anything you've ever experienced. And I'm about to tell you why.

But first, I'm really mystified about something and, for the life of me, I can't seem to figure it out. As long as it takes to get some things done in the Arab world, you'd think you would have to prepare years in advance for that special day. But, for some reason, when it comes to putting on weddings, strangely enough, that's not the case at all.

Arabs overseas are suspiciously proficient when it comes to planning a wedding. What's more is that they seem to do particularly well with short notice type weddings. It's like this weird surreal experience where everything that is normally chaotic and disorderly suddenly gets systematic and super organized. Everything just seems to come together perfectly. And fast, too! Anything else in the Middle East—you know, like getting paperwork done, or negotiating the final price of a hotel room, or pleading with a taxi driver to take the shortest route—feels like running in a pool of molasses.

But weddings? They're a breeze.

They can put together the most extravagant weddings in a matter of weeks. I'm talking a 15-piece orchestra, 300 guests, and a wedding cake that takes center stage. In fact, they're so good that it could probably be done in a couple of days. Like, if you said on Tuesday that you wanted to get married, you could be at the church Saturday walking down the aisle. All the "village elves" would be working around the clock, like little busy bodies, to make sure it gets done. *Not that that actually happens—but it could.*

The best thing about the whole ordeal though is that compared to American standards, it's practically stress free. No calling banquet halls all over town to see if they might have an opening in two and a half years from next Saturday. You don't have all these RSVPs, formal head counts, or stupid fish or chicken cards to worry about. Nope, everybody's invited. And they're all getting chicken.

The brides rent their dresses for something like 75 bucks. Their bridal party is tiny since they usually only have a maid of honor and a best man. No army of fussy bridesmaids running around being all fussy and annoying. No stressed out, frazzled brides worried about if the wedding planner included the stupid formal utensils for the wedding cake. The photographer and videographer, which on occasion just might be the same person, shows up and does his job. The hairdresser comes to your house and does everyone's hair. The band is booked. You don't have to relinquish the hall at midnight—unless, of course, it's midnight two days later. You're happy because you just saved a thousand dollars by using your uncle's car and didn't blow away your future child's college fund on some silly, short, overpriced limo ride to the church. Everyone who loves you is there. And everyone is happy for you.

Well, most are, anyway.

Because you don't have to take out a second mortgage, put your father $40,000 in debt, or sell your nephew to pay for the big day, you're naturally more relaxed and, therefore, able to actually enjoy yourself. The entire process is just a whole lot easier to digest. And since there's no ridiculous checklist from *Cosmo* or *Glamour* pressuring you to make sure everything is absolutely perfect, you don't feel so nervous and overwhelmed. Everything is already perfect. It's perfect, sweetheart, because you're getting married.

That's probably why it's such a breeze.

Weddings in the Middle East are typically held in the summer, particularly in the month of August. Again, it's strategic. Kids are out of school, relatives are visiting from abroad and, by that time, everyone's already well established in party mode. There are a series of events that lead up to the actual wedding day, and those events are celebrations in and of themselves. What makes it so much fun is that all the preliminary festivities generate this great momentum that builds up and transforms what would otherwise be normal wedding excitement, into a whirlwind of exhilaration.

> ### Big Disclaimer
>
> *The following information is solely intended to further the public's general knowledge and should only be used as a general guideline to prenuptial festivities in the Middle East. As stated in the introduction, there are roughly 300 million Arabs worldwide, therefore it is inevitable that individual family practices will vary. The examples below are based on traditional "village" parties and do not reflect typical "city" parties ... necessarily.*
>
> *Not all celebrations are required to occur, nor is any family subject to adhere to the titles or creative descriptions of certain said parties—or party. The author (me) is not responsible for its content, inaccuracies, or just plain, flat out wrong information. For accurate information, please contact your local authorized licensed professional Arabic wedding planner, or any mother of the bride.*

In addition to the actual wedding, there are essentially three other major parties: the *khutbee*,[25] the *tabal*,[26] and what some refer to as the *stereo*. [27] All of the celebrations, except for the *khutbee*, take place right before the wedding. Plus, if you're

---

25. Khutbee refers to the overall formal engagement process. And it is also the name of the engagement party.

26. Also called *Hinnt al-aroos*.

27. Also called *Hinnt al-arees*. The stereo is relatively new, surfacing only within the past several years. (Prior to that the *tabal* was traditionally the party for both the bride and groom.)

an Arab-American, you gotta throw in a *layleeyee*,[28] which brings the grand total of prenuptial parties to a whopping four!

So, all in all, since the time you accepted the marriage proposal until some point after your honeymoon—which could very well be the span of only a couple of weeks[29]—you're basically the guest of honor to at least three or four major celebratory bashes, which were most likely all-nighters. Doesn't that just make you wanna kick your heels off right now? Damn, that's exhausting! I'm tired just thinking about it. No wonder people get married in their 20s. You'll never make it through in your 40s.

But you know what? None of that matters, anyway. You know why? Because not one single bride in the whole entire universe has ever said that she actually remembers her wedding day. Not one. No matter how wonderful or how spectacular the event, she always says—without fail—"You know what? I honestly don't know. I'm sorry. I really don't remember anything about that day. It was all such a big blur to me! I remember *(blah, blah, blah)* and then *(blah, blah, blah)*. Oh yeah, and *(blah, blah, blah)*, but other than that, it's all one big foggy cloud."

They totally zone out and go into "auto-pilot-bridal-mode." *"Thank you for coming." "How nice to see you, again." "So glad you could make it." "My new husband? … I don't know, but he's around here somewhere."*

Brides … they're totally wasted.

※ ※ ※ ※ ※

All right, you've gone through the formal dating rituals. He's asked you to marry him—*and cleared it with your parents*. You accepted. Now, you have an engagement party known as the *khutbee*.

The Khutbee

I'm not exactly sure what is being said during the *khutbee* ritual because I really don't understand it all that well *(see above disclaimer)*, but I do know that the

---

28. Wedding rehearsal dinner party.

29. Not all engagement periods are so short…*but they ain't all that damn uncommon, either!*

priest[30] shows up and performs a short ceremony. He says a few prayers, the wedding couple signs some legal documents and the party begins.

Don't quote me on this, but I think the priest performs an actual part of the wedding service, you know, just to kinda cement the deal a bit. So, in the event that ... *oh, I don't know* ... you have second thoughts, you get cold feet, or your future husband suddenly takes a strong, unexpected liking to your cousin ... *then* ... *let's just say* ... it acts as a modest safeguard, insurance for your investment, if you will. And that investment is further protected by presenting the bride with a generous dowry of gold.

All the *khutbees* I've attended took place on rooftops somewhere and let me tell you, they were sweet! Summer night, outdoor party, and the city as a backdrop—it's just way cool. Even if you're not rich, you *feel* rich. They dance, sing, eat, drink, and smoke *argeelee* until the early morning. They're happy. They're happy because there's going to be a wedding soon.

The Layleeyee[31]
It's getting close.

You've lined up your entire wedding party, and now all four of you practice walking down the aisle at the appropriate times. You listen for the cue. Now, there are only two cues. You, as the bride, wait for the second one. The priest does a quick, dry run of the ceremony. He tells you when to say, *"I do."* Probably advises you not to say, *"I don't."* He half-jokingly asks you to keep the kiss short and sweet—*and rated PG-13*—then the four of you walk back down the aisle, and that's it.

Congratulations. You've just rehearsed your wedding.

The *layleeyee* is the party that usually takes place afterwards. But, instead of the traditional, quiet wedding rehearsal dinner that Americans are used to, we have a ho-down.

Our more reserved American friends might have thoughts that sound something like this: "Wow, that sure was tiring, Aunt Mary. Gosh darn, what a big day we have ahead of us on Saturday. We'd better turn in early tonight and rest up."

---

30. In Christian *khutbees*.

31. The *layleeyee* is the wedding rehearsal dinner/party. In the Middle East, they don't really have a *layleeyee* because there's really nothing to rehearse. But they are relatively common in America.

Our thinking, on the other hand, might sound a bit more like this: "Yeah! Another reason to have a party! Great! What is it that we're celebrating, again? Oh, yeah, that we walked down the aisle with no trouble. Right, right. I gotcha. Because we got the cues down with no mistakes, right? I knew it! YES! Well hey, that's reason enough for me to stay up till dawn! Hey Iskandar, break out the *arak!* Mikhail throw down that pack of Marlboro Reds!"

Essentially, the *layleeyee* is your practice dry run of the *reception*. It acts as a precursor and provides critical information that will determine whether your wedding goes down in history as an incredible blow out event, or a lackluster, forgetful one. Suffice it to say that the *layleeyee* is to the wedding what the Golden Globes are to the Oscars.

The Stereo

When they told me I was going to the *stereo*, I thought, "Oh how cute. They're gonna bring out a stereo and play some music. That'll be fun! It will be just like when I was a teenager and danced in my living room."

Right.

They played music, all right. 'Til dawn.

And it wasn't in a living room. It was out in the streets.

Little did I know that the *stereo* is basically the groom's bachelor party. And everyone is invited, and everyone goes. Whoa! Hold on a minute! I know what you're thinking, and you're wrong! It's not like that. It's a completely different scene, okay? The only thing you'll find dancing on a man's lap is a two-year-old kid whose diaper needs changed!

The *stereo* is just a big block party in the groom's honor. Around 11 p.m. everyone comes out and has a *hafli*. Tons of people are dancing in the streets, kids are hanging out on roof tops, and adults are celebrating from their verandas. This goes on all night until, of course, it eventually ends and then everyone goes to each other's houses and drinks coffee until the sun comes up.

(Oooops! I forgot to tell you something really important, but I think you might have guessed by now. Nobody sleeps in Syria. Sorry. I meant to tell you that earlier. Yeah, they don't. So, just don't plan on getting a wink of sleep while you're there.)

The Tabal

The *tabal* is basically the bachelorette party. Again, it's not anything like what you're thinking. Trust me, Las Vegas, this is not. Besides, us Syrian girls know from experience that *"What happens in the village—Doesn't ever stay in the village!"* You know what I mean?

The *tabal* starts out real girlish and then gets real rough 'n' tough. At the *tabal*, all the women gather at the bride's father's house. They put on music and dance in the living room. During that time, there are a variety of traditional customs that make the occasion very special. One such custom is that the maid of honor paints henna on the bride's hands. The bride is also showered with rose petals as she dances the beautiful Arabic dance.

And her *sito*—her *sito*—stands in the middle of the room and, for lack of a better term, basically raps. I'm talkin' hooks and all. I ain't saying she's Kanye West or nuthin', but it's some tight a** s**t, especially for a 90 year old. *Sito rap,*[32] for real. She'll start bustin' out these rhythmic fertility blessings—even without a beat.

Inshalla bit jeebee sabay! ... Ou Inshalla bit shoofee ouladek! ... Ou oulad-ouladek ... Ou oulad-oulad-ouladek ... Inshalla kil sineh bit-dulee quaisee ... Aweeeeha ...!

(If God wills, you will get a boy. ... And if God wills you'll get to see your kids. ... And your kids' kids. ... And your kids', kids' kids. ... If God wills, every year you will stay prosperous. ... Aweeeeha ...!)

Sometimes, they get a little confused and get the blessings all mixed up, but they mean well.

So, *MC Lil' Sit2*'s rappin' for about ten minutes or until she can't holler anymore and her head starts to hurt. Then she starts b**chin' for someone to go get her a couple of aspirins. After a little while, they leave the father's house and take the party out to the streets where the rest of the village joins in.

The women escort the bride-to-be to the center where her fiancé has been waiting. They are then carried on the shoulders of their strong male, cigarette-smoking cousins. That statement is a literal one. They physically lift both the bride and the groom up into the air as a celebratory gesture. It's funny to watch their uneasiness. You can almost see the terror in the couple's eyes as they try to grasp each other for safety. One bad move and they know they're faced down on the

---

32. *Sit2 Dawg!* Das' wus up, yo!

ground. Especially if the guys have been celebrating all day with their good buddies, Johnny Walker, Jim Beam and, you know, the real rowdy one—José Cuervo. Fortunately, the human airlift only lasts about five minutes. Then they let them down—usually intact—and the party begins.

Now, unlike the *stereo*, which I'm guessing is probably named after the idea of playing music on a stereo, the *tabal* is named as such because they play music on a *tabal*. I think. I really have no clue. I'm just making this up as I go along. But it sounds right, doesn't it?

What they do is they get these gypsy guys, and yes, they are bona fide, registered gypsies[33] to play their *tabals*[34] at the *tabal*.[35] These guys are phenomenal. Their music is raw and their performance is incredible. They live in tents on the roadside in their own little tribal communities, and they'll travel anywhere for the party.

Tabal music is absolutely amazing. For example, when you are walking in the village on an ordinary day, suddenly, out of nowhere, you see hundreds of people coming down a hill and pouring into the streets responding to the mind-blowing drum beats. You are now right in the middle of a celebration. The tribal guys are in the back of a truck beating the hell out of the *tabal* with the entire village surrounding them, singing, clapping and dancing. Traffic is shut down. You got mules and donkeys trying to cut in line—but they know they ain't getting anywhere, they been through this before. Then the *tabal* guys jump out of the pick up truck, intersperse, and make the crowd go crazy with their rhythms.

These guys really do make the party.

And they deliver the same high quality entertainment during nighttime gigs, too.

The cool thing about the late night parties is that there is usually a table situated in the center and it is set up with fruit and water. Little kids come around to everyone in the dance line and offer a drink along with a small bite to eat.

---

33. All right, that's not true—back in the day they actually were gypsies, but now they all have cell phones, and even satellite dishes, so I don't know what they are. I guess, they're just plain old traditional tribal guys, but "gypsy" sounds more exotic.

34. Big, loud, goat-skinned drums.

35. The name of the party.

Strategy, baby. Keep the troops hydrated and well fed.

By now, you've probably guessed that the *tabal* is like a *kazillion* times better than the stereo could ever be. But, like everything else, it's all fun and games until someone gets hurt. And I don't mean hurt in a physical way. I mean it in an emotional way. You see, despite everyone's generous hospitality in welcoming you to the party, there are a few very strict rules with regard to dancing[36] at the *tabal* that you don't want to violate because if you do, you'll feel a sudden, sharp change in the wind. And it won't be a refreshing one, either.

As a guest, there are only two rules you need to concern yourself with:

The first rule is that there is one line—and one line only. And that line is tight. Despite all the wasted, excess, breathable room that is clearly available, you are to remain completely squished between your partners on either side, no matter how bad they might smell or how many times they might crush your feet. You are not the bride—and this is not your day. So, suck it up or leave the line all together, but don't you dare break off and formulate your own line.

The second rule is that the beginning of the line is reserved for the bride's family—only. She may choose to include her very close friends, but that's her option. And, if I were you, I'd make sure I found out ahead of time how close your relationship is with her. Don't break in unless she gives you a clear visual signal that it's okay to do so. Got it? Good.

<u>The Wedding Day</u>
Oh yeah, right. The wedding.
Sorry. I forgot about that.
Nothing special.
Just the same old usual thing, you know.

So, there you have it. You've been partying it up for at least three days straight, now. It's like you've gone on a weekend binge but without all the alcohol. Everyone is sleep deprived. No one is making sense anymore. Thoughts are just slurring all over the place. People are dozing off in mid-sentence, and everyone's

---

36. The *dupkee* (Arabic line dance—see Chapter 11).

got a headache. It's time to get some sleep, for real. You're tired. Go ahead, shut your eyes and sleep.

Because you got just about two days to recover before another wedding hits. And then the whole cycle starts all over again.

Hey, honey, it's the Middle East. It's March Madness in the Middle East! People are getting married all the time

Chapter 7

▼

I'm Married! Now What? On Your Mark ... Set ... Breed!

Pregnant yet?
What are you waiting for?

Follow princess rules, get engaged, get married, have a kid, and you're done. That's it. You're legitimized. Congratulations! That's all you had to do! Your official validation card will arrive in the mail between three to five business days. Once you receive it, you will be invited to parties everywhere and you'll gain an unprecedented amount of new respect.

Have a male child, and you are one up on the rest. Have a number of male children, and you are counted among the elite. Have *all* male children, and you are in a supreme class of your own. Produce five to seven male brain surgeons, and we're on our knees, touching your robe, and kissing your matriarchal ring.

Yes my darling, with that last conquest, your fate of becoming a powerful matriarch has been sealed. When you are 70-years-old, you can say anything you want, to anyone you want, whenever you want, however you want, about anything you want—and they will still worship, fear and revere you. Bar none.

After a few years of that though, you're pretty much done. In fact, I'm not so sure there's much more reason to keep on living, you know? I mean, after all, you've achieved the impossible. What's left? Oh wait, I know. I just remembered. You can yell at people. That's right. Yell at everyone—all the time. Go ahead and cause trouble. Gossip. Criticize everybody for everything and tell them how wrong they're doing it. That's your new job. There. See? You do have purpose.

Old people, especially Syrian matriarchs, are entitled to b**ch. And especially if those matriarchs managed to pull off what you have. So, go ahead, b**ch all you want. It's your prerogative. And be really cruel to the younger generation. Make them work, lazy bums! Make them go and get you all kinds of things, like a glass of water or a cup of tea. Scare the hell out of the bad ones, too. Send them to go get your teeth from the glass jar, right near the phone, by the overgrown *Chia Pet* in the next room. And when they walk into that dark empty room all alone, clap real loud so that your *"clap on"* lamp turns on without anyone being around.

Then laugh real spooky-like.

Go ahead. For all you've been through, you deserve to have a little fun!

Chapter 8

Help! I Think I Just Married My Brother!

Arabs.

We bring a whole new twist to the phrase "kissing cousins."

You come from a long line of close-knit family members. You're now of marriageable age and are looking into prospects for yourself. But, unlike your American girlfriends, you have a particularly unique challenge that they don't have or, for that matter, that they've ever even heard of. So, you must exercise even greater caution when choosing a potential mate.

Not only do you have to do all the normal things that other women must do in order to select a good husband like making sure he's honest, that he'll be a good provider, and ensuring that he's in it for the long haul, but because you are from a region of the world that likes to complicate things, you also have the extra added, nerve wracking stress of making sure that he's not *already* related to you. And, if he is, that it's not too close. Since we intermarry so much, the particular challenge facing you is that you have to be able to tell your would-be husband apart from your other male relatives.

How to Avoid Marrying Someone You Think Might Be Your Brother

It's very simple. Do your research. And, do it well. Find out who's who for at least three generations back. You know what? Make it four, just to be safe. On both sides—your mother's and your father's. Get a hold of as many family photos that you can and look at each one very closely. Study them. Look at the photos, and then look at the people who come over to your house during the holidays. Analyze their faces. Look at the photos. Then the Faces. Photos. Faces. Photos. Faces. Observe their mannerisms. Watch how they walk. Listen to how they talk. Notice how they hold their bread when they eat, which hand they use to drink. Are they a lefty or a righty? Notice what foods they seem to enjoy and what foods they dislike. Do this a lot. Your future depends on it.

If you find yourself sitting across the dinner table flirting with this really hot, sexy guy who has come over to check you out, and you're beginning to really like him, especially his intense, mysterious energy, but then strangely enough you begin to notice striking, almost bizarre similarities between this man, and … *oh … let's say … your father, maybe?* If all of the sudden seconds later you realize that the pattern is completely identical, whatever you do—don't panic! Stay calm. Keep your composure. And don't let anyone see that you just caught on. Breathe. Drink a sip of water, and politely excuse yourself. As soon as you get to the bathroom, take care of your stomach, and then politely excuse yourself for the rest of the evening. Go take a walk. Get some fresh air. And remember: keep breathing!

It's okay. Calm down. Nothing was promised. Nothing was exchanged. And, most importantly, *nothing happened!*

Your sexy, little hottie boy just might have been the son, from a previous marriage, that your father inadvertently left behind in the village some 30 years ago so that he could come to America and work hard to make a better life for you so that you could grow up and get married—TO YOUR BROTHER! … AAAGGGHHHH!!!

It happens, sweetheart. *It ha-ppens!* Don't worry. You're not the first, my dear, and you most certainly won't be the last. Just be grateful that you found out during the preliminary dinner rather than on the last night of your amazingly wild and unforgettable honeymoon!

Seriously, you should study your family members very closely and, if for some reason that approach isn't working, then the next best thing to do is go talk to an old relative. They know how everyone is related. Unfortunately, however, that's not a guaranteed safe bet either. The problem is that sometimes they're too old to explain it right. Or sometimes they're too old to *remember* it right. And that could be dangerous because one small slip of the DNA and you're right back to square one.

Just try to do your best not to marry too closely. And, if you do, well then, it just so happens that you did. I mean, if you actually end up marrying your brother, don't make such a big freakin'deal out of it. Relax, jeez! I mean, come on, he's only your brother for goodness sakes!

Why Do We Marry Our Cousins?

Because we like each other.
A lot.

And we like to hang out with each other and be really close—all the time. So, for example, if you're my first cousin and we've been playing together since the day we were born, then let's just continue the party!

You see, not only do we like each other, but we kind of like ourselves, too—in a good way. All of our family members are pretty similar to each other and we basically have the same genetic makeup. So, in a way, if we intermarry and have lots of kids, then essentially, we're just making a lot more of us. We're just multiplying the same DNA.

Human cloning is unethical, so we just do it the natural way and marry each other. That way our kids will be just like us. Our nieces and nephews will be just like us. Our grandchildren will be just like us. And sooner or later there will be lots of people who are just like us. Eventually, we can have our very own little village. In fact, some of us already do have our own little villages.

We're making "*mini-me's*"—legally.
It's the perfect formula.

We need a laboratory.
With lots of microscopes.
And lots of Petri dishes, clipboards, and men in long white coats.

Plus, we tend to generate really big families; it's just more cost effective that way. For instance, I personally have 58 first cousins. That's right, honey, 58. As in almost 60. *(Now do you understand why I'm writing a book about having an identity crisis?)*

But if you think about it, it makes a lot of sense. I mean, you already know the person you're gonna marry. And probably everything about them, as well. You're already related to the person and likely have the same last names, so you don't have to go through the hassle of changing them. You're already related to all of your in-laws. You're grandmother is probably already *his* grandmother. It's just so much easier that way. No fighting over whose house to visit during the holidays. No more arguing whether you're going to have dinner at *his* parents' house or *your* parents' house. Wherever you go, *everyone* will be there.

There's just one big downfall in all of this, though … Taxes. Tax forms can get kinda sticky, and I hate to admit it, but can trip you up if you're not super careful.

As a general rule, you never want to attract unwanted attention from the IRS, but this is especially true if you're an Arab living in post-9/11 America. Great example—Al Capone. No matter what he did or how brutal his offenses, he managed to escape the law completely unscathed. But, damn if they didn't get him on tax evasion! It's like, you could totally wipe out an entire neighborhood and come out perfectly clean, but God help you if you forgot to pay your annual $50 city occupational tax. You know? Just be careful with the paperwork, okay?

Other than that tiny potentially devastating problem, there are great advantages to intermarriage. Not only is it more convenient, but it's also a lot safer. Let me tell you, there are a lot of shady people out there. Straight up, wackos! It's scary. You don't know who these people are. You don't know their past or where they came from. You don't know their family history. You don't know *their* history. You don't know if they're wanted in four other states. You don't know if they're living a double life. You don't know if they're already married. You don't know where they've been or who they've been with. You don't know what they've got, what they want to get, or what they want to give.

Your family, at least you know.

And you know what the best part of intermarriage is? You can have a blast with it! Oh, man! You could have so much fun, you just don't know! Like, you and 20 of your cousins could go out to a bar, meet a bunch of guys and totally mess with their heads. Just freak them out all together. Like, you could stand around and point out each of your relatives and explain how they're all related to you—*and to each other.*

You could say, "Oh yeah, her? She's my niece, but she's 17 years older than me. And do you see the girl in the blue? That's my aunt, but I had to give her my passport to get in because she's only 16 years old. And that pretty girl over there with the dark black hair? She's my sister ... *and my sister-in-law. Awww and look ...!* There's my sweet husband. Isn't he handsome? He's also my first cousin's son.

Walk in just before closing time and get the really drunk ones.

※ ※ ※ ※ ※

The truth is my mother actually did marry her first cousin's son.
And she wasn't the only one who kept it in the family, either.

As a result, I am related to both of my parents, on either side. My mother is actually my first cousin twice removed and my dad is actually my second cousin—as well as the child of my first cousin once removed. [37] Which makes me, my own aunt—*and* my own niece.

Go ahead, do the math. I'll wait.

You see, if my father married a different woman than my mother, then my mother would still be my first cousin twice removed. And, if my mother married a different man than my father, then my father would still be my second cousin. So, either way, we're related. Which I should have figured out years ago, so that I could tell my dad to go straight to hell when he pissed me off!

---

37. On my mother's side, of course.

After all, he's just my cousin!

Why Do We Still Have Arranged Marriages In This Day and Age?

All right, you really wanna know the truth? Here it is …

We have arranged marriages because we're scared. That's right. We're scared. And we don't trust you. We have arranged marriages so that parents can choose for their grown adult children whom they will spend the rest of their lives with and with whom they will have children. They're afraid you might make a bad mistake—a devastating mistake. And, sometimes, people do.

Think about it. Your parents know what's best for you better than you know for yourself. They know who is best suited to become your lifelong partner. You might have a say in the matter but, if it's gotten to that point, you're probably too obedient of a daughter to resist anyway.

But in all seriousness, arranged marriages really aren't such a bad idea.

I'm not joking here. Your parents practically knew you all your life, at least ever since your first birthday. You guys hung out over the last 18 years or so, you know, sharing a house, meals, etc. Who else is going to know you better than them? Your parents want nothing but the best for you. They want to secure your future and make sure you have the best possible match. The only problem is *well…* when you're in love with someone else. *Then … uh …* in that case you're pretty much screwed. Sorry, can't help you with that one.

And What Exactly Do They Mean?

Arranged marriages only mean one thing: they mean that your marriage was arranged.

And not by you, either.

Probably not even by your fiancé, unless he's a really old guy with lots of money.

Technically, it should be said that it was *pre-arranged*. In fact, they should lobby for the name to be officially changed to *"pre-arranged marriages"* because, in a way, it's almost like false advertising.

And that's not right.

Plus, when you say *"pre-arranged marriage,"* ... *I don't know* ... it kind of adds a certain flair to it, don't you think? Like, it sounds sophisticated, somehow. Elitist. Exclusive. *Chic.* It just makes the whole thing sound modern and in vogue. Come to think of it, it's kind of like a status symbol, you know, like a pre-owned Jaguar or something. Hey, wait a minute, that sounds cool. Hold on, I think I'm on to something here. Listen to this idea ...

Take something that is ridiculed by others and seen as unfortunate and lowly, for example, arranged marriages. Then, like an old Mustang, revamp it to look hip, turn it around, and flaunt it right back in their faces. How's that for remarketing? Revenge is sweet, isn't it?

It can be done. Sure it can! It just takes work. Look, everything in history makes a comeback, right? Why not arranged marriages? Come on, *it's totally retro, babe!* All you have to do is redesign the concept and market it to fit into a young, 21st century modern, urban lifestyle. I'm telling you, it could be the next best thing!

Listen, you know how they took the old Cadillac car commercials and remixed it with the Led Zeppelin song to trick you into believing it's cool to drive an old person's car? Well, same thing. It's just a matter of how you present it because it's gotta be totally hot. And you gotta hit it really hard from the get go. So, play around with it, have a little fun, and see what works. Throw in over-the-top attitude, and then promote *pre-arranged marriages* as the most enviable status symbol ever to reach these shores. Rich, high-society types will definitely jump on the band wagon. Come on, they love being the first to have the newest, most trendy thing, regardless of what it is.

You can say something like, "Oh yes darling, well, I had a *pre-arranged* marriage. Yes, and let me tell you, it was fabulous, just fabulous! Well, I *personally* didn't have to do anything myself. No, no, no, it was all done for me. I was terribly busy, so I had it all *pre-arranged*. You see, I was vacationing in Fiji at the time with friends, so I just let my _____ handle it. *(Insert: accountant, manager, publicist, agent, personal assistant, stockbroker, staff, portfolio manager, butler—anything but parents!)*

Everyone will be so jealous of you. The Hilton sisters will be calling *you* up to party in Vegas.

Anyway, as I was saying, your arranged marriage was most likely organized by some people who are not you. Probably, lots of other people who are not you. In fact, they probably had a whole tribal high council consisting of aunts, uncles, grandparents, cousins, priests, neighbors, family doctors, kids, the mayor, former *zalghouta queens*[38] jitney drivers,[39] Pharisees, and Scribes all looking at the deal and putting their two cents in. That's not a bad thing, though. Come on, think about it, you're lucky to have that many people care about you.

On a serious note, back in the day, arranged marriages were necessary for survival. And to secure a family's future. And in some cases, it was also to retain property rights. It was also often used to expand financial wealth. And to attain permanent residency, reconcile family feuds, prevent wars, create wars, keep a blood-line pure, keep a girl pure—*you know from messing around and stuff.* In those days, a girl couldn't just go frivolously picking out who she wanted to marry. That would be insane. I mean, how about if she ends up with a bum who is allergic to work? Then where will she be? Huh? What will her future look like? Not very bright, now will it? And what if she finds someone whom she loves genuinely, from her heart? He could turn out to be a real playa' *and be lovin' the whole damn neighborhood genuinely, from his heart.*

It's best to leave the decision of marriage to others, lest you be blamed for your own actions.

Honestly though, arranged marriages are not such a bad idea.

My parents had an arranged marriage, sort of. But it wasn't like anything I explained above. My mother was a lively, independent, 28-year-old working woman when she got married and she knew the deal full well and upfront. She made a deliberate, informed decision. Nobody forced either one into the marriage, but it did have certain elements of, you know, a *pre-arranged kind of arrangement.* My dad's father talked with her about it and she agreed. But, for some reason though, I have a feeling that the whole village held a couple of high council meetings by themselves, anyway. Just something to do, you know, because you can get cabin fever up in those mountains sometimes.

---

38. See Chapter 12.

39. See Chapter 18.

She was his cousin. And it was for the green card. Consider it a really important multi-billion dollar international business deal, like the merger of DiamlerChrysler. It was so that she could bring my father to America, so that he could work, establish himself, and eventually bring the rest of his family here. By the way, that's a very common thing that immigrants do. One key person finds a way to get to America, builds his foundation, and then sends the boat back for everyone else. One by one, each family arrives, gets situated, and then reaches their hand out to help the next load cross the pond—or cross the border—depending on ... *well, you know.* At any rate, the process started from the time the Mayflower came ashore, and we've been at it ever since.

Fifty years after my father stepped foot on this land, well over 150 people are in this country because of my parents. That's no exaggeration. I am not only including the families that my parent's initially sponsored; I am counting all their descendants including their children, grandchildren, great-grandchildren, their old-country spouses, their old country spouses' respective families, all their descendants, their own American-born children, their own American-born children's children, and the countless other non-relatives who they helped to achieve permanent legal status.

Boy, if my mom only got a commission!
Great immigration lawyer, lousy saleswoman.

It's truly a beautiful thing to see how big our clan has grown over the years. Each one getting married, having children, and sprouting up new families and new businesses. God bless them. They have all worked very hard, prospered, and now enjoy great success of their own.

All because of my mom and my dad.

When my mother went to Syria back in 1956 and eventually married my father, she had no idea what the future would hold for her. But her very open, vocal, and non-secretive plan was to divorce her Syrian-farmer husband as soon as he got his green card.

They stayed married for 47 years.

The last day she spent with us in full consciousness, we were celebrating their 47th wedding anniversary.

He was holding her hand 10 days later when she died.

And he had anointed her body with holy oil only an hour before.

Arranged marriages—they're not such a bad idea.

CHAPTER 9

OH CRAP! I FORGOT TO GET MARRIED! NOW WHAT?

You forgot didn't you?

You never forget anything, but it just so happened that you forgot this.

Come on, just admit it.

You forgot!

Excuse me, *Ms. 'My life-is-so-well-structured-and-organized-that-everything-is-right-where-I-positioned-it-to-be,'* may I please have a word with you?

You're feeling a bit queasy now, aren't you? Aren't you? I know. It's that exact same hard punch-in-the-stomach sick feeling you get when you're late for work, rushing 90 miles an hour on the freeway, putting on your mascara and checking your cell phone messages, when suddenly you slam on the brakes and scream, "Oh S**t! Did I leave the iron on?"

See? You forgot something, didn't you?
And it's something way bigger than the iron!

You went ahead and got so busy with your high-powered career that you forgot the most important thing in the world to do before you die: get married. And have kids, but I'm not even gonna go there!

Hey! Don't play dumb with me, this is a big deal, here! No joke. And you mean to tell me that your company actually trusts you to handle multi-million dollar accounts? Please! You freakin' sit on a medical board that makes decisions for other people's lives? Members of the community view you as a role model and actually look up to you?

Unbelievable.

Look, you knew from the day you were born that being 30 was just around the corner. And don't give me that innocent *"but-I-didn't-think-it-was-gonna-come-so-soon"* garbage! Please! You knew that you would hit 30 years old in ... *oh ... I don't know? Let's just say, maybe ...* exactly 30 years! Jeez! You blew it!

Remember that list you made when you were 15 years old? You know, that critical list of things to do before you die.

1. Lose 10 pounds.
2. Attend Fashion Week in Paris.
3. Backpack South America.
4. Use Harvard International Law degree to work as economic advisor in developing countries.
5. Get married.

Dah! What happened?
Because sweetheart—*tick*—*tick*—*tick!*

All right. Calm down. Quit crying, already! Just listen. Look, I actually do have some good news for you, okay? Regardless of how I personally feel about your unbelievably stupid mistake, this is, technically, a survival guide. And, as your advisor, it is my responsibility to help you survive; therefore, I'm obligated to you—commercially, that is. Plus, even though I've been yelling at you for your amnesia for about a half-hour now, I really do have a heart. I'm a very kind, compassionate, and generous person. Consider this a one-time charitable gift.

In the event that you are not married by 30, there is a loophole. Yes, that's right, a loophole. Not many people know about it, so don't go rushing off to tell all your 30-something girlfriends; we certainly don't need a stampede around this place! You see, there's sort of a little "marketing mistake," if you will, that only a few of us know about. And yes, it's perfectly legal, so don't ask.

What it is, is an extended grace period. Yes, a grace period. *By the grace of God*, you are granted a five-year extension. Hold on, sweetheart! Not so fast! You're not off scott-free. Those years are considered probation. So, if by chance, you don't get married by 30, there is still a very small window of opportunity left. You can legitimately squeeze marriage in until the age of 35, but that's it! 30 to 35 is your last chance. You can fool people by being 32 and "still looking," by being 33 and "still searching," by being 34 and "still hoping"—up until the very last day of being 35, you can even grab someone, *anyone*, as a last ditch effort and marry him. Under the new laws, you are still well within your rights to blindfold, kidnap, and force a man to the altar—you even have the privilege to drop his jaw to mimic an emphatic, *"I Do!"* But, 35 is it.

Once the scale tips to 36, you're in the red zone. And the red zone ain't no good! You are basically beginning to be all washed up. And, it only gets worse after that. 37 is a very critical age. It's a conniving little number. It's very tricky, cruel and deceitful because it's so damn subtle and innocent looking that you just pass it off and think, "Oh, no problem. It's only 37. I'm still in my 30s, *technically*. It's not like I'm 40 or anything."

Yeah, right.

Remember how fast 30 came, and you were crying your eyes out because you didn't realize it was gonna come so soon? Well, I hate to break it to you, but 40 is not just around the corner, baby. It's on your front porch, and it's got one foot inside the house.

"Hello! Hello! Anyone home? It's me, 40. I'm a little early, I hope you don't mind!"

You know what else? As you get older, your hearing tends to go. Sounds become more and more faint. Except for one. The sound of your biological clock. That one seems to get significantly louder as you age.

BONG! BONG! BONG!

And more annoying.

And please don't give me that psycho-babble, "inner-self love," new age crap. There's a part of being single and alone that sucks, and you know it. Let's face it: deep down inside we all want someone around to fight about the remote with.

Now, if you'll be so kind as to allow me to rub just a little salt on that freshly sliced wound of yours. Thank you.

So, my dear, not only are you *not* married, but now you have everybody in the world wondering about you. They're all asking, "What's wrong with her? Why isn't she married? Such a pretty girl. There's gotta be something wrong with her. Can she have children? Maybe she can't have kids. She looks like she could have kids. I don't know. Poor thing. What a waste of beauty. Isn't that a shame? Hey, I know a fellow who might be interested in her; he's 67, good retirement income though; she won't have to work, you know? But I think his eldest daughter is older than her. Oh, poor dear, she'll never get married; she's just too old!"

And believe me, girl, they won't necessarily wait till you leave the room to say it, either.

It seems as though everybody in the community is talking about you. And you know what? They are. You're not being paranoid. They really are talking about you. Remember that spotlight you were craving when you were in your 20s? Well, when you get older, it's much too bright and harsh to withstand. The brilliance directly burns onto your blushing, humiliated, *"I-just-wanna-die-already"* red face.

So, what do you do?

Look busy!
Look *really* busy!
And when you're done doing that …

Look busy some more.
Just keep looking busy!

Look like you're running AT&T Worldwide—all by yourself.

In fact, tell them that you're running AT&T by yourself. … *you know … layoffs and all.*

There really aren't a whole lot of options, and I'm pushing it to help you out. So, you gotta work with me here, okay? Now, just like every other solution in this book, I've come up with only three. Take your pick.

1. Quit Your Job And Become Self-Employed
Opening your own business is by far the best solution.

You know that career that you worked so hard to get all of your life? The one that gave you all those big sore bumps from banging your head up against the glass ceiling? Yup, that one. That career. Give it up. Submit your resignation today.

I know, you're probably wondering why I, (the author), *a.k.a. Ms. 'Independent-Women-of-the-World-Unite!'* would suggest such a ridiculous idea? Well, here's why. A business—*any business*—will suck the very life out of you, especially if you're in it alone.

After hearing this advice, your natural response might be to consider getting a partner in order to alleviate some of the responsibility. I'll say this once and only once: Don't You Dare! It will defeat the entire purpose. We're shooting for torture here, not success. In fact, get success out of your head right now. You've had enough anyway, so just get over it, or I can't help you.

See, what you have to do, is torture yourself by working 27 hour days, without a break, so that you can justify why you don't have a husband and children.

Do you understand? You need an excuse. And this is the perfect excuse.

You see, my darling, businesses are very needy things. They are just as needy, if not more needy, than a husband and five kids. They will drain you—and that's what we're shooting for here. You're going to have to retrain your mind to think like a victim. The trick is to position yourself in such a way that lends itself to blame your surrounding circumstances and not *you*.

Now, if you have any sanity left, you're probably still confused by my suggestion. You might be questioning whether inflicting such torment onto yourself is really worth it. But I challenge you to look at the alternative. Surely, you can see that this particular agony is paradise compared to the thunderous, shrilling noise coming from everyone's big mouth. Imagine the ringing in your ears, from hearing, day after day, "Why aren't you married?" "What are you waiting for?" "You know, you're not getting any younger." "If you wait any longer, nobody is going to want you, you know."

Now, isn't my idea better?
I thought so.

Shall I continue? Thank you.

Your ultimate goal is to get your thinking process to automatically jump into defense-mechanism mode when someone chastises you for not being married.

Your response should sound something like this: "Can't you see that I'm stuck in this lousy business! What the hell do you crazy people want me to do? You think this is easy? I've got bills to pay! Open your eyes, can't you see I'm dying here! I'm here eight days a week, 27 hours a day! I have to run this business or I'm going to go bankrupt and lose everything!" If they see you in such throes of distress, they'll leave you alone—mostly though because they'll be scared of you.

Perfect example: Condoleezza Rice. Does anyone even dare question her? No. She's gotta run the freakin' country *and* stabilize the world! How dare you even think to bother asking her why she's not married? What's wrong with you? Listen, I don't care how prim and proper she is on the outside, she's still a *sista* and she'll go off on you in a minute! For real! Her head will start swerving side to side like a cobra, finger all up in your face, and all that pent-up street attitude will bust on out; *"Excuse me? What did you say, M**^&*f$**&#?! I know I heard you say something! Aww, hell no! I know you didn't! Come 'ere b**ch! That's right! That's right! You better run!*

Conde don't play! For real!

Now *Ms. 'Queen-Bee-of-the-corporate-world,'* since you're not nearly as important as Ms. Rice, you gotta come up with another plan. And this one is yours. If they see that you are working so hard—for yourself—they will have pity and compassion. In time, they will forgive you for being such an irresponsible failure to society and to your family, for making such a stupid mistake.

Now, *Ms. 'Queen-Bee'* you don't mind if I call you *Ms. 'Queen-Bee,'* do you? Oh, or shall I say *Ms. 'I-somehow-forgot-to-get-married!'* The important thing to remember is to make it *your own business* because the whole, long, drawn-out plan doesn't work if you're employed in a regular job working for someone else. [40] It just doesn't. And here's why: the logic behind this thinking is that "you kill yourself—<u>for yourself</u>" the good old-fashioned way. Us immigrants just don't understand it the other way around. We naturally think, "Why would you kill yourself to make someone else rich?" Other than a few obvious exceptions, it's gotta be … well … *like your own baby!* (Ouch! Didn't mean to put it like that! Sorry!)

Listen, if you want to challenge me and try to use my methods while you're still employed in a regular job, then go ahead. Girl, you will fall flat on your face! If your goal is to get people off your back, you'll just make matters worse by tamper-

---

40. Condoleezza Rice, Oprah, and Wonder Woman are exempt from this rule due to their overwhelming job duties and respective superhero status.

ing with my master plan. Everybody will be on you as to why you are working like a jackass for someone else. And believe me, the last problem will be bigger than the first. They will badger you to quit your job, go overseas, and get married. Do you see where I'm going with this?

So, open up your own business, and remember the key to success for you—is failure. Or at least to constantly struggle. Just don't do well. Keep struggling. Because, if business does go well and you actually do succeed, then you will be viewed as having plenty of spare time. And then, what's a girl to do with all that time? Which brings us right back to square one.

Got it? Good.

2. <u>Become A Caretaker</u>
Another good idea is to take care of an elderly relative. That's always a great excuse. Plus, people will not only be forgiving, but they will actually love you even more for your great acts of courage, sacrifice, and martyrdom. And sympathy? Whoa! You'll be swimming in it! The best part of this plan is that you'll automatically be excused for any erratic behavior you may exhibit because your relatives will blame it on the overwhelming stress that you're under. This is actually a great time to break a couple of those hard and fast restrictive rules that have suffocated you for so long. Keep it light, though, you don't want to go overboard, you know?

3. <u>Go Back To School</u>
Education is always a great way to get out of stuff! Any kind of stuff, whether it be work, marriage, or just plain reality. Just go back to school. Be a student. Take up any major, but make sure it's complicated, or at least sounds really complicated like engineering, medicine, or law. People will usually leave you alone if they know that you're studying.

Oh, and make sure you stretch out your program long enough until you find out what your next step is. Go for a masters degree. Hell, get a Ph. D. You can buy at least a decade with that one! And don't forget to throw in another couple of years to write that dissertation! Plus, if you do that, then everyone will be really impressed with you, and they'll invite you to all kinds of cool, international graduate school parties.

And you never know, you just might meet a doctor at one of those parties. Or at the library. Or in the hallway—*and voilà!* Your problem is solved after all!

How To Create a Scandal

HUGE Disclaimer

The author does not endorse any Arabic daughter to rebel against her parents, family, or culture, in any way shape or form. She wholeheartedly denounces all noncompliant behavior and strongly urges all Arabic daughters to remain honorable, obedient, and well mannered for as long as they are alive.

(Pssst!

Down here!

Shhh! … Listen! … Forget that crap … It's just for liability purposes. Look, you want your own spot in history, right? Then keep reading. I've learned a thing or two along the way and if you're smart, you'll follow my lead. I gotta be straight, though. Depending on how hot tempered your particular family is, you just might get killed. But, hey, you could also walk outside and get hit by a bus, right?)

So, here's the deal.

- Do anything that breaks the rules. Anything at all.

You know how I've been talking about strategy throughout this book? Well, you're an Arab; it's in your blood, so strategize. Make your plan methodical. First, define your goals. In the very first chapter, Chapter 1, your goal was to get married, right? But clearly that didn't happen. We've already progressed to Chapter 9, and you're still single. So, now, your goal is what? That's right. But it can't merely be to get attention. Come on, girls, reach higher. You need to get attention because …? Come on! Because? … Because? … Because, why? Look, I don't have time for this; let me just tell you!

Your goal is to become the star of the hottest, most controversial, sizzling gossip in town so that you can get the spotlight to shine back onto you so that men will once again notice that you exist so that, by some far-fetched miracle, you can possibly get one last shot at getting married!

Do you even *understand* that?

What? Did you guys, like, skip the entire first eight chapters of this book? Please do not tell me that I got stuck with the remedial class. I can't believe this. *Un-freakin-believable!* No wonder you're not married. You freakin' ...

Ugggh!

Look, here's the golden fool-proof formula, okay? Get a pen and write this down:

The stricter the tradition, the more forbidden the fruit ...
The more forbidden the fruit, the greater the temptation ...
The greater the temptation, the harder the fall ...
The harder the fall, the more severe the repercussions ...
The more severe the repercussions, the louder the gossip ...
The louder the gossip, the shorter the distance to your goal.

Make sense?

Whew! Thank goodness! There's hope after all!

Now, I'd like to share a little story with you.

Once upon a time, I knew a girl who, just like you, wasn't even a real princess, but she had one of the most juiciest, most sneakiest scandals in the whole history of scandals, ever. This girl was creative, smart, and beautiful. She also happened to have a little knack for dancing. Well, as the story goes, one day while she was enjoying an extended stay in Syria, her mother received a frantic phone call from her relatives overseas. They were begging this woman to come and rescue her daughter right away. You see, the girl had innocently ventured into dangerous territory. She had "run away" to dance professionally on stage with the internationally famous Syrian superstar *Sabbah*.

Word got around back to this country faster than the speed of light.

Within 10 days, the tickets were purchased, the bags were packed, the passports were expedited. And the plane was en route to Syria.

Urgency.
Now, that's the way it's done.

I told you she was good.
Damn!
She did it *well!*

The only problem was that when her mother finally arrived, things got a bit confusing for everyone around. You see, this lady didn't rush half way across the world to "rescue" her daughter from the dark influences of an eccentric theatrical group. She raced half way across the world to see her daughter shine on stage. This woman was beaming with pride and overwhelmed with joy. There, on stage, was her beautiful daughter, gracefully dancing the magnificent Arabic dance as if she were born in the ancient land itself. She was so thrilled that she went to see her daughter perform every single night for two weeks straight.

Now, a girl running off to dance with a troupe doesn't seem like much of a big deal at all, right? But at the time, it was. At the time, and in that particular, small community, it was the biggest scandal of the day, complete with all the spicy elements that made it so salacious. It had all the elements of an international sensational headliner. *Ahhh…* good old fashioned scandals, they just don't make them like they used to.

It's a lot tougher these days. You have to work so much harder just to get the same effect, you know? Since we've gotten so desensitized, things don't shock us like they used to. It's like now you have to totally put yourself on the line if you want to get any attention at all. It can still be done, but it takes a lot of work. A lot of *smart work*. The key is to find the one forbidden thing that your family unequivocally refuses to accept—and go do it! Again, they might kill you, or you could ruin your own life for the next 30 years but hey, no pain, no gain, right?

Now, if you've always been the "good girl" who has never made any waves, now's your chance to throw your own little personal tsunami! Oh, yes it is! *Ahh-hem …Excuse me, Poseidon … Thank you.* In one fell swoop, you could diminish everything your cliquish, petty little girlfriends ever worked for their whole lives and rise straight to the top. You're gonna be so good that they're gonna have to invent a whole new word just for you because "bad girl" wouldn't come close to describing your streak of wickedness.

That is, of course, *if you play your cards right.*

That means you gotta strike them hard and fast, before they even know what hit them. *Slam! Spin! Thump!* Knock 'em out! See what I'm saying? You got one shot, babe. That's it. No second chances. You can't screw up. Nothing can go wrong because, once you're out, *you're out!*

I'm warning you right now; if you come out with anything less than sheer annihilation, you better forget everything. You might as well crawl back into your dark, little hole for the next 40 years and hope everyone gets temporary amnesia. You really have to think long and hard about the whole thing, you know? Meditate on it. Evaluate the pros and cons. Consider what's at stake, not only for you, but for everyone involved as well. Calculate all risks. This is no small feat, my dear. Carefully map out the details. Run through every worst-case scenario you can think of. Assess all possible outcomes. Pray. Pray, some more. Shut your eyes. Hope for the best. And take the plunge.

What To Do If You Find Yourself In One

Shine baby, shine!
It's yours to relish in!

Well, you've certainly outdone yourself, haven't you?

Oh look …

CNN is breaking in with Christiane Amanpour. FOX News just dispatched a crew to the scene. The BBC is interrupting its regular programming to broadcast the events live to its affiliates around the world. Producers are scrambling to pick up the story live. Oh, and this just in, Anderson Cooper will host a live special edition of CNN—Special Investigations Unit, tonight at 8.

This is incredible!

I am so proud of you, my little protégé. Honestly. You have created a very rich scandal. How did you do it so flawlessly? Darling, I'm not sure if you realize this, but you are now the brightest star in the galaxy—make that the universe. You sit amongst the distinguished perpetrators of the most infamous and greatest scandals of all time—Romeo and Juliet, King Edward and Wallis Simpson, Elizabeth Taylor and Richard Burton.

And now *you!* I'm impressed.

But enough self-glorification, look at what you've done to benefit others. You've helped so many ordinary, everyday nobodies simply by implementing your risqué behavior. You might not fully grasp this concept yet, but you, my dear, single handedly jump-started the failing economy. What can I say? Darling, it's true.

AT&T Wireless stock jumped a whopping 55 points just moments after news of your story broke. Verizon cell phone usage increased 45% within the first three hours. Busy circuits and jammed phone lines caused a sudden, unprecedented surge in Internet usage, says AOL's chief financial officer. And as expected, coffee sales blew through the roof.

Starbucks posted the largest gain with a 125% increase in sales during the first day. Chief rival Seattle's Best came in just behind at 110%, and the world's largest retailer, Wal-Mart, reported a global sell out of all major coffee brands. Gas prices jumped from $4.12 to $5.50 per gallon in one hour as gossip-hungry women rushed over each other's houses to discuss the shocking news.

In overseas markets, *bizzer* sales increased by 60% (white pumpkin seeds, only), Marlboro Reds went up 75%, and Winston's up 65%. A surprisingly disappointing day for *maté*, though, posting less-than-expected sales during the first quarter with only a moderate increase just after the opening bell. Industry analysts speculate the light trading will pick up later in the week when more details of the scandal surface.

In medical news, emergency room visits soared within the first four days with the most complaints coming directly from *sitos*. Severe chest pains caused by excessive *"waaay-laaays"* [41] caused several elderly patients to be medevaced to local area hospitals.

Spiritually speaking, morale is up 90%. Your unmentionable actions have brought purpose to hundreds of women in your local community who have nothing better to do with their lives than to look around and point fingers at those who do.

And, finally, on the intellectual front, your controversy has stimulated spirited debates all over the country. A nation of women now have something challenging to talk about instead of the usual, not-so-thought provoking questions of which farmers market has the best price for baby eggplant.

And best of all …

---

41. Overdramatic wailing sounds that women make during a crisis. Or during a situation that they would like to *manipulate* into being a crisis (the real "pros" beat their breasts in angst).

TIME magazine just made you their "Person of the Year."

❈ ❈ ❈ ❈ ❈

All right, that's enough. Show's over.
Keep it movin'. There's nothing here to see.

Now, princess, here comes your dose of harsh reality. Sorry, I know, cloud nine was nice and comfy. But come on, clouds are just pockets full of condensation. They're bound to burst and pour down at some point.

Look, fame is a funny thing. As fast as it comes is as fast as it goes, *unless you know how to work it.* No single group of people have mastered this concept more than Hollywood celebrities. One day you're the hottest thing ever to hit the gossip circle, the next you're doing infomercials for teeth whitener.

People have short attention spans. Once the initial shock from the scandal has dissipated and time has passed, everyone just goes back to their ordinary, mundane lives. That's just what happens. The thrill is gone. The excitement is over. And then you're left all alone not knowing what the hell to do with yourself.

I know, sweetheart, it's confusing.

This is by far the most common mistake that princesses and drama queens make all the time. You think, "All that work, for what? It's not fair!" You ask yourself, "was all that suffering even worth it?" But the solution is simple, like everything else, just reinvent yourself.

But hold on, Cinderella, not so fast! There is a catch.

You can't do it right away. You have to wait. Give it some time, like 10 to 12 months because overexposure kills everything. But, you also want to be careful not to wait *too* long, otherwise the public may forget about you all together. And if that happens, you'll have to go *all the way back* to square one and start all over again with an *even more sensational* scandal than the original. Of course, then you gotta factor in the law of diminishing returns and the fact that some people won't be able to keep up with all the drama, so eventually they'll just give up. Plus, you have to consider the toll it will take on *you*. My gosh, you'll be totally exhausted! You can't keep torturing yourself every time you need attention! Crisis after crisis will wrinkle your skin, wear you down, and give you migraines. You don't want that.

Trust me, just disappear for a while, and everything will work out fine. I'm sorry, honey, but you have to. It's for dramatic effect. Think of it like being in the Witness Protection Program, but only for a short run. Besides, when you finally do reemerge, you will feel more invigorated and ready to take on greater challenges. Plus, bigger and better opportunities will be on the horizon waiting just for you.

Imagine: Your very own *E! True Hollywood Story.*

Hmmm… Sounds delicious, doesn't it?

Part II

The Extras
(Everything Else You
Need to Know About
Simply Being Arabic)

Chapter 10

What They Don't Want You to Know: Hip-Hop Has Its Roots in the Streets of Damascus

One word: Jay-Z.

Everybody talks about it now, you know, how the *Aswaad* are just like the Arabs, and the Arabs are just like the *Aswaad* but, I gotta tell you, I'm walking, talking living proof. I got credentials behind me. Strong credentials. I crossed over and found out first hand, and let me tell you, the *Aswaad* are more like us than you think. Truly, they are. I've always innately known that but, having experienced it first hand, not only solidified the whole theory lock, stock and barrel, but it also, inadvertently, revealed to me *just how much* we're alike.

You see, for almost four years, I was the morning show co-host for the number one urban radio station in Pittsburgh. I lived, ate, and breathed with the *Aswaad*. They loved me. I loved them. They were my family. They still are my family. Every single day, we laughed: we laughed at ourselves, we laughed at each other, and we laughed at all the craziness in the world and around us.

When I worked there, I had found my home away from home. When they joked about being so *ghetto* because they had two television sets (one for the picture and one for the sound), it was like I finally found my people! I said, *"No way! That's us! Hey! We do that! You guys do that, too? For real?"* I was ecstatic because that really did happen with my dad and uncle but, in retrospect, I think my co-workers were just joking about it.

At any rate, I didn't fit in with my white Caucasian counterparts so much and there weren't too many Hispanics running around the city at the time. So, based on our similarities, it was inevitable that we would click together so well. It was a perfect match. And the more I worked and hung out with them, the more I realized how strikingly similar we really are. Not just in the way that all God's people are the same, but rather in a specific, unique, genetic kind of way. Like, if you traced each of our roots back far enough you might find that we could be from the same damn tribe—*that kind of similarity*. And get this. Ready? Egyptian, Libyan, Algerian, Tunisian, and Moroccan-Americans are *technically,* African-Americans because those Arabic countries are situated on the continent of Africa.

Interesting ... isn't it?

But, as I was saying: Jay-Z.

Let me ask you, what was your reaction the first time you heard *Big Pimpin'* on the radio? Be honest, now. When I heard it, I was in the studio and damn near dropped my headphones. I totally flipped out. I was like, damn! Where the hell did that come from? That's our music! I couldn't believe it. Jay-Z and his entourage flew straight into the Arabian Desert, stormed some Bedouin tribe, snatched *sito* while she was baking bread, rounded up her clan, mixed it up in the studio, and made millions!

Bling! Bling!

Then there's Timbaland, Magoo and *ere'body else in the 'hood!* Only a brother could have the foresight to take our music, mix it up, and make a s**tload of money off of it! And if that weren't enough, not only do they have the business part down, but they've also got the science to back it up.

You see, the musical mélange works so well because our beats are damn near identical. Unlike rock music, which has no beat and does serious damage to the neurological system, our respective beats are tribal in nature, which, in turn, allows the body to instinctively respond to sudden, unexpected changes in rhythm. Tell me, how many times did you automatically switch into *dupkee* mode straight out of a hip-hop song without even realizing what you just did? Right in the middle of the club, and without missing a single beat! Come on, man. *Please!* You know you did! We all did. Hell, we all *do!* We can't help it.

See how hip-hop has its roots in Damascus?

And remember the late '80s song *Pump Up The Volume* with that one really cool Arabic part in the end? I swear every single Arab blasted it out of their cars; they were so proud. Boy, isn't that a shame though? If you only knew, you could have taken a cassette player into the kitchen, recorded your own *sito*, and had your own damn Grammy by now.

And how about the song *The Hotstepper?* It had a freakin' *zalghouta*[42] in it! A *zalghouta* for goodness sakes! It was a hard one too, like it came straight outta the desert. Plus, at that time, most people never heard that sound before. *Yaharam.*[43] Poor stiffees[44], they must've gotten really scared. Now, they're not only afraid of Black people, but they're scared of us, too.

Maybe even more so.

My *Aswaad* friend put it all in perspective when he hugged me and said, "*Thanks man! Whew! Used to be that we was at the bottom. Everybody hated us—they was always on our backs about somethin'! Wouldn't let a brother be! Now your people came around—and BAAM! Now ya'll at the bottom. Ahhh-haaa! They don't stop us no more, but they up all over you're a**es now! Ya'll some profiled M*'&^ **#*s, for real! Thanks, man, we needed the break. Good lookin' out, babe!*"

See? We even help each other out.

You gotta give it to the *Aswaad* though, they make everything cool. They just do. No matter what it is—fashion, athletics, music, dance, science—they make it cool. And if it was already cool, they make it even cooler. Venus and Serena Williams blew away the uptight tennis world and literally turned it upside down. Not just in their game, but in their style, fashion, and overall fierce presence. They hit it hard with fresh, strong attitude and made tennis exciting to watch. Talk about a grand-slam! Now, everybody watches tennis. And what about Tiger Woods? Can you even think of anything more boring than golf? Hell, they're so good they could make calculus and engineering chic!

---

42. Loud expression of joy and excitement (see Chapter 12).

43. What a shame.

44. From here on in, Stiffees, Mr. Stiff-Ass and/or Mr. Uptight refers to all the stiff, out of touch, ultra-conservative, narrow-minded people who don't have a sense of humor—regardless of race, color, creed or national origin.

Little kids all over the world want to be the next NBA superstar. The young and ambitious dream of being the next P. Diddy. Young girls wish they could become the next Beyoncé. And need I even mention Barack Obama? He, himself, practically single-handedly made politics exciting for the first time ever![45] It's like the *Aswaad* have this special, magic touch so that practically everything they put their hands on turns into gold. They take a boring—whatever it is—put in a little charisma, whip it up with their own blend of creativity and *voilà!* The ordinary instantaneously becomes the extraordinary! Just like that! I have no idea what it is, but that certain twist makes all the difference.

Let's take a closer look at this, shall we?

You see before the 1990s, Caucasian and African-American pop culture trends were, for the most part, relatively separate. There was certainly a sizeable degree of crossover, but nowhere near where it's today. At some point in the mid '90s, there was a huge cultural explosion, and everything just got infused. You'll notice as well that it was the urban side that ended up dominating the pop culture scene and not the other way around. As you can see for yourself, there are a lot more Eminem types around now than Vanilla Ices back then.

Another one of my *Aswaad* friends put it rather astutely when, during one of our plentiful discussions about life, he said, "Look around, man, it's all blowin' up! Everybody wants to be on this side now! And that's only happened, to this extent, within the past couple of years. Why? Because now it's cool to be Black. Black is in."

My friend was right. It's "in."

And it's not just "in" in America either, it's "in" all over the world. The whole urban cultural phenomenon just exploded and spread like wildfire around the globe. I'm not talking about in the big cities like Tokyo, Madrid or Paris; that's been going on forever. I'm talking about in the farthest, most remote corners of the earth—in ancient lands where their way of life has remained virtually untouched by Western influence. Where donkeys can be found roaming the streets. Where guys make a living by selling fresh baked bread from the backs of their beat up, 1960's diesel-fueled Chevys.

Let me explain.

---

45. All right, that's not all together true. Hillary did too, but that's only because she was Bill's wife—and we all know that Bill was the first black president, so she only made it cool, by default.

I was in Damascus, Syria, the oldest continuously inhabited city in the world. There I was in the heart of this magnificent metropolis waiting for an old vendor to finish making my falafel sandwich. His tiny shop was no bigger than two-feet wide and the storefront had to have been at least a thousand years old. I was surrounded by these archeological treasures containing remarkable pieces of history—secret underground churches, tiny jails cells where people were imprisoned, and beautiful ornate mosques. I was taking in every bit of the old world atmosphere, absorbing all of the incredible sights and sounds of a world undefiled, and forever lost in time.

I found myself trying to comprehend the fact that I was standing in the very same general area where almighty God spoke to Saint Paul nearly 2,000 years ago, where the beginnings of what took place would mark the spread of Christianity throughout Europe, then to the rest of the known world, and would change it forever. I was simply awestruck. It was truly a sacred moment. Then, all of a sudden, coming around the corner of a tiny, quiet intersection, I hear, *"It's getting hot in here ... so take off all your clothes ... I am getting so hot I wanna take my clothes off!"*

Boom! Boom! Boom!

I was like, *"What? What the hell was that? Naaw! That did not just happen!"*

It was Nelly bustin' out somebody's car! Loud as hell, too. I couldn't believe it. I damn near fell straight to the ground. Listen, you gotta understand, I know they play the music over there; that's not the point. But when you are in the streets of old world Damascus for the very first time like I was—in this ancient land halfway across the world, among holy places, and engrossed in a sacred moment—your head spins around when someone busts out some Nelly! Come on, man! It totally blew me away! Not here. Not now. You know what I mean? Don't mess with my head like that; I can't handle it. All the other cars were playing traditional Arabic music, but then from behind the corner—*BAAM! Nelly!*

Hip-Hop has its roots in Damascus.

I don't care what you say.

And they're in the gritty backstreets of Damascus, too.

As I've said before, the *Aswaad* are just like us. But here are a few examples that show just how much they're like us. Of course, there are plenty more, but this should at least get you started.

<u>We both have innate rhythm</u>
It must be something in our genetic makeup, but we both dance really well. You can count the Latinos on this one, too. We feel the rhythm and our body just naturally responds to the beat.

I have to say though that the Latinos must have some kind of extra, secret gene that makes them shake like 1,000 times faster than the rest of us. And the *Aswaad*, let's just say, really appreciate the freedom of movement with regard to dance and some aren't real shy when it comes to expressing themselves, you know what I mean? Especially during a nice, slow Jamaican beat.

And Arabs? Like I said, you could be in the middle of the club and the DJ can switch from Amr Diab[46] to 50 Cent, and you won't miss a beat. Some of you are funny to watch, though. Without knowing it, you'll go from a hip-hop groove straight into an Arabic dance step, then suddenly catch yourself just after doing it. You take a second to realize what just happened and another for your body to reorient itself back to what it was originally doing. And then you'll look up and smile real big at your dance partner, *like it was intentional the whole time. Please!*

<u>We're creative with our music</u>
Who, but a brother, could take a lame Broadway tune and turn it into a chart-topping hit, i. e., Hard Knock Life? Or even children's rhymes, i. e., "Shimmy shimmy cocoa pop, shimmy shimmy pop!" When I heard Country Grammar for the first time, I said, "Damn! They took a kid's rhyme and made it sound hot!

Unbelievable!

And, now Arabs are remixing all kinds of music. They even have the audacity to mess with *Um Kalthoum*.[47] That's sacrilegious, if you ask me. You don't

---

46. Famous Egyptian pop singer.

47. Legendary Egyptian classical singer (see Chapter 13).

remix *Um*. Not her. *Fairouz*?[48] Okay. *Sabbah*?[49] Okay. But *Um*? No. That's just wrong.

<u>Neither of us use taxis</u>
We use the *"serveece."*
They call a *"jitney."*

Same thing though. Both emit black smoke.

You do know by now, that *Mr. Stiff-A*** uses the taxi, right? He likes to know *exactly* what the meter says and wants to calculate the price to the nearest 10th of a mile.

<u>We all cram in together, holding on to our plastic grocery bags, and head to the big cities</u>
Mexicans are right up there with us on this one, too. We hop in, even when there are people *already* in the vehicle. That way, we pay less. It just makes more sense.

And we carry tons of plastic bags.

They are filled with all sorts of things: groceries, worn tennis shoes, candy wrappers, toothbrushes, pants that need hemmed, deodorant, letters from immigration officers, letters from probation officers, medical assistance applications, citizenship applications, baby formula, Holiday Inn housekeeping applications, Holiday Inn complimentary size guest soap, shampoo, and conditioner, coupons, loose change, a hair brush, your child's birth records, your child's immunization records, wrinkled up Kleenex, old fruit, nuts, and *bizzer*.

Plastic grocery bags ... the convenient, affordable carry-on luggage of choice.

<u>We're not exactly the first to be invited to the annual holiday office party—and neither are they</u>
We're both dark-complected and, some would contend, very suspicious looking. (Scoot over guys, we gotta make room for the Mexicans on this one, too.) Ultra

---

48. Famous Lebanese singer.

49. Famous Syrian singer.

conservative, narrow-minded, Archie Bunker types don't particularly like us, or trust us, very much. There are those who think that all Black men are criminals, all Mexicans are illegals and all Arabs are terrorists. Somehow though, they're very astute at being able to differentiate between 10,000 blond, blue-eyed, pale-skinned, surfer-dude looking guys. But, for some reason, we all still look alike to them.

<u>We do look alike, actually</u>
In all fairness to *Mr. Stiff-A*** and his friends, I must admit that there's a part of me that understands his dilemma. I mean, it's true, we actually *do* look alike. At least some of us do. Call the Hispanics in again *(actually—keep them close by, we keep needing to use them)*.

It's true. I know that you have at least one *Aswaad* friend who looks exactly like your Arabic cousin. Right? You even catch yourself doing a double take every so often. You're like, "Jamouli? Hey, Jamouli? Ahh damn! Jerome, sorry man, I thought you was Jamouli for a second, ya'll two look exactly alike!"

Plus, we get even more confused now that the *Aswaad* are using common Arabic names more often these days. As a matter of fact, that's really messing us up. "Yo', Khalil, meet my cousin, Khalil." … "Ahmed, Yo'! This is my friend Ahmed."

<u>We're just the ones who are … well … profiled a lot</u>
It kinda seems that people are interested in what we're up to these days. They just want to know, you know, what we're doing.

All the time.

And *why* we're doing it. And with *whom* we're doing it.

Around the clock.

It's not a big deal, really.

The local and state authority's focused on us. That's true.

And the national authority's, too. Yeah, you're right, so what?

Okay, yeah, especially all the big government department agency heads. That's fine. So, big deal.

Okay, I admit, most of the general population is and the border control guards as well. So what's your point?

Okay! Okay! Wall Street, the Red Cross, the UN, the EU, the entire telecommunications industry, the entire transportation industry, etc.

ALL RIGHT! WE HAVE THE WHOLE DAMN INTERNATIONAL COMMUNITY AUTHORITY'S ATTENTION!

There, I said it! Are you happy? Now leave me alone!

And let's not forget the friendly skies.

The airlines arbitrarily call passengers up to check boarding passes—and rightfully so. It's not a big deal. They call everyone up, randomly, you know, to verify confirmed seats and all.

"Will the following passengers please proceed to gate 17 ...

Jones ... Smith ... Collins ... Roberts ... Abdullah ... Mohammad ... Mustafa ... Yassir-Ibn-Abdul-Aziz ... Sheik Ahmed-Hussein-Abdul (the third) ... Hamdallah-al-Hyatt-Ahmed ... Ali-Rafik-Moushtawai ... Abdallah-Abdallah-Abdallah (the fourth) ... Zaid Al-Ibn-Il-Halawee ... Nasser-Ibn-Abdul-Halim-Hafez. ...

Thank you. If you would kindly step right this way; this will just take a moment of your time."

I'm not complaining. Oh no, I'm not. Not at all. Trust me. If there were nineteen highjackers from Asia, I'd be listening for names like Kim Hung Ho ... Chan Li Sen ... Hi Li Ho ... Ho Chi Mihn ... Kung Pow ... General Tso ... Beef Broccoli ... Shrimp Fry Rice ... Combination Special Number 1 and Number 2!!!

<u>We both know how to represent</u>
We're always having fun ... *you know* ... when we're not fighting or anything. Or when we're not at war, or anything. Even our demonstrations are fun. Hell! They're parties in and of themselves. I mean, I go to demonstrations just for the heck of it. I don't always necessarily know what I'm protesting or anything. Sometimes, I don't think they do, either. But, you know, sometimes you just gotta go to the town square, wave a flag, and stomp your feet a little. You just feel better afterwards.

Caucasian demonstrations are the worst! *Ugh! Bor-ing!* I'd rather watch paint dry. Sorry, to put it like that, but hey. No spunk, you know? Maybe a little jingle here and there but that's it. *Bor-ing!* Orderly, too. *BLAH!* At least we have fervor. We go all out in our demonstrations. We represent! *Yeah, baby!* Thousands of people come out into the streets and chant. And our chants have a solid beat to them, too. It's a slammin' rhythm (that's usually where the foot stomping comes in.) We gather in little circles, and we shoot off guns. Yup! Up in the air. Repeatedly. *TAAT! TAAT! TAAT! TAAT!*

I'm not condoning it ... *I'm just saying that we do it.* Sometimes. Like when we're really mad. Or sometimes when we're really happy. Or sometimes during a funeral. And even sometimes during a wedding. It all just depends. And we make lots of *zalghoutas.* I'm telling you; it's a big party!

The *Aswaad?* Well, they have interesting demonstrations, too, but; for some reason, they tend to be referred to as "riots." Come to think of it, our demonstrations have a different name too; they tend to be referred to as "uprisings." *Hmmm... Interesting.* But, the *Aswaad* represent! They sure do! And sometimes they shoot off guns too, but mostly when they get mad. Like when an entire city police department's officers are acquitted after a video tape shows them beating the s**t out of an unarmed Black man. Those kinds of things, I don't know, just sort of gets to them, I guess.

Disclaimer

The above example is used to demonstrate a point, not to incite any tension or violence. The author recognizes that a**holes come in all shapes, sizes and colors. And that there are good cops and bad cops and good citizens and bad citizens.

But in the spirit of discrimination (just kidding!) In the spirit of good relations, let's continue.

<u>*We're hustlers,*[50] *you know, businesspeople*</u>
It doesn't matter what the commodity, we're selling.

Whatever it is: T-shirts, incense, tablecloths, knock-off designer watches, purses, belts, fake cologne, packs of gum, picture frames, pirated videos—if we got it, we'll sell it to you. And most of the time we got it for damn near free.

We will, with no shame whatsoever, take sprigs of fresh mint from our backyard, boil a pot of water, throw in a tea bag, fancy it all up, decorate it with a lemon wedge that we got for free from our uncle's lemon tree, serve it in a little demitasse two-ounce glass, and sell it for $5. 75. And we'll be proud. Boast even!

"Ma'am, I make this special tea just for you. I get the fresh mint from my own back yard. I pick it myself. Only the best leaves ma'am. I grow it in the old country and bring it here for you! You like? And the lemon? It come from my uncle's lemon tree. It's a special lemon tree. Nobody else has this kind of special lemon tree. It's a special one ... special lemon ... from the old country ... but now it's in the new country ... I'ma so glad you like it. Thank you, ma'am very much. Here is your 25 cents change. Have a nice day, ma'am."

We know how to make money.

<u>*We're always late*</u>
They have C. P. Time.
We go on Arab Time.
Neither one is anywhere even remotely close to EST. [51]

---

50. All references to hustlers in this book are to be taken only in the positive sense, as in an entrepreneur/businessperson.

51. Eastern Standard Time.

Their scheduled one o'clock is actually around three o'clock. And that's the same with us. In other words, if you told both *Mr. Aswaad* and *Mr. Abdullah* to meet at the coffee shop at 1 p.m., they'd both show up, on time, at 3 p.m.

And *Mr. Stiff-A***? Well, let's just say, he'd be really mad.

For some unknown reason, neither of us care to acknowledge any of the scientifically-based, long-standing 24-hour time zones, that the rest of the international global community collectively agrees to operate on for the unified purpose of maintaining world order and punctuality. Most of us, admittedly, have never even heard of Greenwich mean time.

And sadly, most of us have never heard these words, either:

"Give a little. ... Help a lot. ... Support the Dollar Energy Fund. ... From the US Naval Observatory's Master Clock ... Current Eastern Standard Time ... 12:14 p. m ... Temperature 59 degrees."

It's really only a phone call away—time and temperature information—and it's free.

And let me just say that *Mr. Stiff-A*** has every right to be mad! Oh yes, he does! As soon as he gets that large stick out of his a**, he will probably march on over to Washington, D. C. and submit a bill to congress demanding that rich Black men, like P. Diddy, who wear $500,000 diamond-studded designer watches be punished by surrendering, upon demand, their timepieces—until they learn how to be on time!

I don't blame him.

We tend to take ownership of the cities that we live in

Dearborn, Michigan, has the highest concentration of Arabs in the United States.

Detroit, Michigan has the second highest concentration of African-Americans in the United States. [52]

---

52. I knew you'd check. Source: U.S. Census Data Report 2000.

Strange, isn't it? Detroit and Dearborn are situated right next to each other. Funny, how we just happen to be *jironies*?[53]

Even our cities look alike: Gaza/Compton. Fallujah/Flint. Baghdad/Bedford Stuy.

Hmmm...

<u>The media finds our worst 10% and uses them to represent our entire community</u>
Of all the available bystanders in any given run-of-the-mill tragedy, the media always seems to find the most messed up ethnic individuals to give their personal account of what happened. It's like they bypass every freakin' normal person and find the most illiterate, hostile, disheveled, missing-toothed witnesses to describe a scene in the most sensational way.

<u>We're both naturally funny people</u>
Funny how we seem to have the same *kind* of humor.

Take the movie *Friday* with Ice Cube and Chris Tucker. Insert *Tarek* and *Ahmed*, change the setting from a front porch in South Central to a front porch in the village, and replace a few taboo activities.

Not much would change.

<u>We both have the best music</u>
They got the drum.
We got the *tabal*.

But, we both got the beat.

<u>Everyone's a cousin, even if they're really not</u>
Everyone's a cousin, even if they're really not.

---

53. Neighbors.

They refer to each other as "sista" and "brotha"
We refer to each other as *"khaytaay"*[54]
And *"khayyaa"*[55]

(Kinda weird, huh?)

They're always looking for the hook-up
We're always looking for the hook-up.

God and religion reign
Do I even have to go there?

We both bling!
They prefer both gold and diamonds to decorate their bodies.

We just go for the obnoxiously long, arm-full of gold bracelets to adorn our bodies.

They are Ghettofabulous!
And so are we.

And finally—sorry, I hate to say it, but—we both cringe in front of the TV set during a national tragedy. We're hoping and praying. Praying, "Dear God, *please, please* don't let it be one of us!"

And How Cool Are We?
Say what you will about Arabs, but we have the best culture. We offer so many phenomenal things that I can't even begin to list them all. I say this with the utmost pride and with the utmost humility. I mean who can touch our music?

---

54. Sister.

55. Brother.

Our dance? Our hospitality? Our warmth? Our richness? Our tradition? Our values? Our customs? Our passion? Our mystique? Nobody. We have such a rich plate that we bring to the beautiful world banquet.

Our Arabic dance is like no other—sensual, mysterious, and womanly. Studios are overflowing with women who want to learn the captivating dance of our ancestors.

Then there's the whole diet thing. No matter what fad is in at the moment—low carb, low fat, low whatever—it always comes back to the simple Mediterranean diet. Time and again, it is proven that ours is one of, if not the most, healthiest. Fresh vegetables, extra virgin olive oil, and garlic are not only what make it so healthy, but they are also what make it so delicious. Even our desserts are served in teeny-tiny portions. They're so cute, petite, and innocent that they couldn't possibly make you fat! And most are filled with wholesome nuts or dates. Our coffee is always served in little, itsy-bitsy demitasse cups—small caffeine spurts to get you going instead of a whole 16 ounce cup to get you hyper and over the edge.

And didn't we offer the best to science?

Who do you think invented Algebra?
We did!
See ... And where would we all be without Algebra?

Everything in the world—all science, technology, and advancement—depends on the perfect logic of numbers. That which determines the future rests on the very foundation of the simple, yet absolute, mathematical laws of Algebra. Without it, there can be no progression. No forward movement. No evolution. No nothing (even though *I*, personally never had any use for Algebra after high school. And none of my friends ever had any use for it after high school. Nor did any of their friends. Or anyone else I could think of. Nevertheless, it is a very important contribution that Arabs so generously made to civilization! So there!)

And what about the alphabet? *Hmmm?* Who do you think came up with that? We invented that, too! And we certainly use that a lot, now don't we? Plus, we probably invented that cute little *A-B-C* song that goes with it to help children memorize it. We're so damn musically talented!

So there you have at least two major contributions Arabs have made to advance civilization. We basically invented the Three R's: Reading, Writing and Arithmetic. Wow! I just realized that. That's so cool! Go ahead, try to advance a civilization without reading and writing or solving, really big math problems! I swear we are so cool!

※ ※ ※ ※ ※

By the way, in case you didn't know, the Irish are a lot like us, too. They pretty much have the same values: hospitality, generosity, family, honor. And they too have a very funny sense of humor. Even our musical instruments are almost identical. They use big drums; we use the *tabal*. They use bagpipes; we play the *mijwez*. [56]

They drink beer in the afternoon. We drink *arak* in the afternoon. It's normal. Their kids go to the pub for a pint. Our kids break out the *arak*. [57] They've got that radical, liberation front IRA thing going on ... *ahh* ... and we're ... *let's just say* ... "politically energized."

The Irish truly value the time they spend together. They love to sit around with family and friends, singing, laughing, and telling great stories. They're passionate people, full of warmth and heart and they're humble, hard-working folk, too.

Their little villages are so romantic and picturesque. They kinda look like "the shire": blue skies, rolling hills, farmlands, and cute little cottages, except their front doors are not as round and the people don't look *anything* like Frodo and his gang of hobbits!

The guys are sweet, especially when they turn on that old Irish charm. And they're a blast to hang out with—fun and free-spirited. Have a pint in the pub and you'll be dancing with the lads all night; they're that friendly. And being mostly Catholic, they too have their own little *ibe* system. Everyone knows each other—who's in their family, what clan they belong to, where they came from, who fought who in the last feud, which family isn't speaking to which and just how many centuries it's been since they haven't spoken, that kind of thing.

---

56. Similar instrument as the bagpipe.

57. See Chapter 19—Why Kids in the Middle East Drink and Drive.

And you know what else? The Irish have long been known as the *Aswaad* of Europe.

Now, isn't that something?

CHAPTER 11

THE ELEVEN LIFE LAWS OF DUPKEEING

Dupkee (n. and v.)—The *dupkee* is our cultural line dance. When we *dupkee*, we basically dance around in circles for hours. We hold hands. We sing. It's *waaay* fun, and we never get bored! It's just like a serveece ride but without the car!

The *dupkee* is common to all Arab nations, so basically, everyone who is Middle Eastern grew up doing it. Unfortunately, there really isn't an American equivalent. For example, not everyone knows how to do one identical type of dance here. The Electric Slide, the Macarena, and the Bootie Call don't count because not everyone knows them, but all Arabs know how to *dupkee*.

<u>Ahhh ... The Dupkee.</u>
Why exactly we dance around in circles for hours, holding hands, and yet never seem to get enough of it is a mystery. Even if the body is screaming in pain, the inflicted, upon hearing the first note of what they know will be a really damn good song, will be dragged up by their aching feet to go for yet another round of circles. This is a very freakish thing and those of us who have experienced it know we are hopeless. It's like a bad addiction. And we abhor the mere thought of rehab.

I didn't realize how messed up I was until one time when I was at a *hafli* in the mid 1980s. I was dancing the whole night, and, not to be gross, the skin on my feet was rubbing against my shoes so badly that they began to bleed a little. I sat down for a second to give them a break, but when the singer hit the first note of one of my favorite songs, I don't know what happened to me! I grabbed my *mesbaha*,[58] flew off my chair, and headed to the front of the line. I think I even knocked over a kid or two on my way up.

Another, rather personal, story that I really have no business sharing with you occurred back when I was a 19-year-old sophomore in college. It was a Saturday night and we were at the grand *hafli* at the Sheraton Hotel. All of us girls were looking particularly beautiful for the event and the boys were looking rather hot. The music was incredible and I was dancing hard. At one point, I led this really long *dupkee* line, and, let me tell you, we were on fire! It was sharp, tight, and fierce! You couldn't wipe the smile off my face, I was so happy! I was totally in a different world. Then, out of nowhere, this hot, sexy guy grabs my hand, looks me straight in the eye, smiles, and pulls me out of the *dupkee* line. You gotta understand, I liked this guy. A lot. We were really good friends and got along very well. Chemistry, attraction, and an intense connection—it was all there. I am ridiculously picky about guys and this one was special. He was tall, had dark brown hair, a nice, strong, masculine physique, sharp bone structure, sex appeal, and a wicked sense of humor.

I had been hoping this time around that he would notice me in a more mature, womanly way. And I was really flattered because he began to express that kind of interest in me. Things were developing quite smoothly between us that weekend. And I was liking it. A lot.

So, anyway, this guy pulled me right out of the *dupkee* line. He wanted to talk. All I remember is me loving the whole idea but insisting that whatever it was that he needed to say could wait until later. He's dashing through the crowded banquet hall, holding my hand nice and firmly. I'm right behind him, clasping his hand and thinking, "You know, this better be good! I like you and all, but I mean what could be so urgent? And where are you taking me, anyway?"

So blond ... so naïve.

And so damn passionate about dancing.

But I've learned. These days, I tell guys upfront that if they want to go kissing, it has to be *after* the *hafli* not in the middle of it!

---

58. Beads. (A more detailed explanation is coming up.)

You see, I know myself. One freakin' note of the *mijwez*, and all my girly-girl femininity goes flying out the window. Every single ounce. No matter how hard I try to control it, my sexy-cool barometer instantaneously shatters into a thousand pathetic pieces. There I am at a *hafli* lookin' all fine. I got my sexy, backless gown on, slit up the side, and I'm having an intimate conversation with some hottie. I'm playin' it up, making strong eye contact, flirting, and letting the sensual energy ooze on out. I'm like ...

"Oh really? So, how do you like being an international top secret pilot for the CIA? Wow, that sounds so exciting *(twirling stirrer, slowly sipping Bacardi)*. How interesting, flying secret missions all over the globe *(flipping hair over exposed shoulder, tilting head to the side)*. Really? *(batting eyelashes.)* I bet you go on all kinds of spontaneous, wild, exotic adventures, don't you? It must be so thrilling to just pick up at the last minute and jet wherever you ...

"OH MY GOD! DID YOU HEAR THAT? That's Najwa Karam! This is my favorite song! Oh my God! I love this song! I gotta dance! Where are my cousins? Did you see my cousins? Where's my *mesbaha*? Where's the line? Here! *(Slam!)* Hold this drink! Damn it! Someone beat me to the front of the line! Son-of-a-b**ch!

Oh ... oh ... I'm sorry ... Did you? ... uhhh ... Did you wanna dance or something?"

I am so messed up.

And so single.

I'll never meet a guy.

At least not at a *hafli*, I won't.

I know where I have to go.

A place that is completely opposite of a *hafli*.

Yup.

To the *Muktabee*. [59]

---

59. Library.

No wonder all the girls in Chapter 4 go there. They know better.

❄ ❄ ❄ ❄ ❄

The fact of the matter is that we love our *haflis,* and we love to *dupkee;* it's just in our blood. Sadly, though, there are those few among us who think that *haflis* are all out *ho-downs.* They are, but not really. *Ho downs,* my dear, are for our missing-tooth, ign'rant, unshowered for-weeks, barn-happy, plaid-wearin', stinky-*I-haven't-washed-my-clothes-in-a-month-here-smell-them-if-you-don't-believe-me*-shirt, old hand-me-down-jean wearin', burly, straw eatin', wannabee counterparts. They are for the people who inhabit some other mountainous terrain that we don't associate with. They are not refined nor is it our responsibility to refine them. They are who they are, so let us leave them at that, shall we?

Good.

Now, there is simply no reason to kick your feet all over the dance floor. None. It's simply not necessary and it makes the rest of us look bad. It looks like you've never left the barnyard, and we don't want that. Refine it a little or go up to the previous paragraph where you belong. And please, don't go *hootin'-n-hollarin* on your way up!

For the rest of you who understand that *dupkeeing* is not Dance Fever, please continue reading.

Do you remember the kid in the third grade who picked his nose? Well, no matter if he turned out to be some hot-shot lawyer, you'll always remember him as the kid in the third grade who picked his nose. Well it's kinda the same thing with the *dupkee.* Social taboos and *dupkee* taboos are one in the same. And your reputation will follow you for the rest of your life. Break the rules, and you'll always be feared as the one person who will screw up even the most sleek, hardworking, disciplined *dupkee* line.

People may not see you for 30 years, but somewhere, someday, in some city that you're visiting, they will immediately spot you from all the way across a large banquet hall that is filled with thousands of people. The instant they recognize you, their hearts will start racing, their palms will begin sweating, and they will become short of breath. They will attempt to scream, but their voices will be frozen, paralyzed, due to the trauma that you inflicted on them decades earlier. Some will even experience a full-blown panic attack. You don't ever want that to happen. Trust me, it's a bad thing. I still wake up with cold sweats in the middle of the night from incidents that happened when I was a teenager.

The most important thing you need to understand is that there is a strict pecking order in the *dupkee* line. And when that order is broken, there are problems. Big problems. A lot of it depends on how good the music is. Recent studies by the American College of Imakngthisup have shown that the degree of tension associated with breaking a *dupkee* chain is directly proportionate to the quality of the music being played. The more awesome the song, the greater the tension when the rules are broken. And it's further compounded by long-standing tribal rivalries. It's a serious thing, I'm telling you. Like a *coup d'état* in a third world nation.

Intense disputes over leadership have broken out with residual effects lasting decades, i. e. , Allentown versus Pittsburgh, Holiday Inn, Labor Day Weekend *Maharajan, circa 1979*. To this day, certain factions don't speak to each other. We're not sure if they even know *why* anymore. *We're not even sure if they know that they're really not even a real faction in the first place.*

Some modern historians speculate that the origination of the Lebanese Militia and Hezbollah were born out of these *dupkee* clashes. Being a leader is a very serious thing. It's about respect and honor. It's about blood and loyalty. It's about a really freakin' tight a** *dupkee* line.

In order to maintain a peaceful Arab world order and create long-term stability in Middle East circles, we must recognize the fixed eternal laws that govern our cultural dance and pledge ourselves to abide by them. Remember, these laws are scientifically-based like the laws of motion in physics. We are dealing with absolute geometric truths: straight lines, perfect circles, and precise timing.

Therefore ...

WHEREAS RESOLUTION 1979, HEREBY CALLS FOR THE IMMEDIATE MULTILATERAL ADHERENCE TO AND IMPLEMENTATION OF:

THE ELEVEN LIFE LAWS OF DUPKEEING

Rule #1—Only Leaders May Lead

Leading a *dupkee* line is tantamount to leading troupes into battle. It is not a task to be taken lightly nor is it for the fainthearted. It's an enormous responsibility and carries with it a lot of pressure. Never assume leadership of a line until you have earned the right to do so. Just like the military code R. H. I. P. *(Rank Has Its Privileges)*, the *dupkee* has its own special elite code. Great leaders emerge by overcoming tough challenges, and that only happens with wisdom and years of experience. Think: Roosevelt, Lincoln, Churchill … *Mirwan.* [60]

Rule #2—Children May Never Lead

No matter how cute they are, how darling it looks, or how much they kick, scream and cry, children may never lead. Ever. Unless, of course, they demonstrate outstanding ability. And, then, only for a short time. The adult leader has paid his/her dues and is entitled to enjoy dancing up in the front with the best. They have suffered in the back of the line for years, garnering painful bruises from some clowns who, after a couple of beers, suddenly discovered they had some roots and wanted to learn all about *being one of them, there, Aaaaay-rabs.*

The child will eventually earn his right to lead, but he must be groomed for years prior to making his debut. When his time finally comes, it's crucial that he have the support of his adult relatives because it's a rite of passage. When he is sanctioned by the elders, he will feel accepted in the eyes of the community. And he deserves that because leading a *dupkee* line requires a tremendous amount of responsibility, maturity, and a really keen sense of navigating multiple crop circles … *I mean … dupkee* circles.

You should start learning when you're young. Begin at the end of the line, work your way up to the middle, and hope for a future spot in the front—next to your aunt or something. Slowly begin your journey from the person, who is next to the person, who is about 30 people away from the actual leader.

Unless of course, you're Greek, then just throw this entire rule out the window. If you're Greek, get a bunch of your teenage male cousins and hook it up at the annual Greek Orthodox Church Festival. As an observer, sit back and watch in amazement as these Greeks do some crazy dance that has them literally flipping all over the place. It's amazing! About 10 teenage boys hold hands in a line while one kid repeatedly spins upside down, holding on to nothing but a damn handkerchief—and two very trusted friends on either side of him.

---

60. Common male name.

After the festival, head out to the Greek nightclub and watch them do the same thing except this time with grown men who've drunk lots of ouzo. [61] Just keep away from the dance floor. Oh yeah, and watch out for flying plates. Greeks like to break them when they're having a good time. It's just how they celebrate. I know some guys who still have china shrapnel wedged in their heads since 1986. They haven't been the same since.

<u>Rule #3—Always Have Your Own</u> *Mesbaha*
The *mesbaha*[62] is a short string of beads that leaders twirl around when they are dancing in the front of the line. You could say that the *mesbaha* is to a leader what the Terrible Towel is to a Steelers fan; it's both their ultimate weapon and symbol of pride. Don't be deceived by its small size though; the *mesbaha* holds enormous power. It establishes your legitimacy as the emir and grants you absolute sovereignty over your little kingdom, of course, validating you as the right and true leader of your little line. Most importantly, though, it defines territorial boundaries. The *mesbaha* is like the official seal of a nation that all other "states" recognize.

A *hafli*, therefore, in which there are multiple *dupkee* circles, is almost like the United Nations. It's a slew of little "countries" dancing around doing their own thing while, at the same time, trying to achieve their agendas in a peaceful manner. But, just like the real UN, that's not always the case. At times, the *dupkee* platform can be dangerous, hostile even. Every now and then, a couple of no-good thugs like to stir up trouble. These tyrants intimidate and threaten everyone else. As commander-in-chief, you have the responsibility to order your line to attack or to defend itself against invading factions. Even if you only suspect—you know, without any real solid evidence—that you might be attacked, then you must take action. And if that means a preemptive strike, then so be it. The *mesbaha* is your ammunition. When the opportune moment arises, the great leader will raise his strong, mighty *mesbaha* high into the air and, with a thunderous roar, charge his fearless troops straight into battle. Fast and swift!

You must hold on to your *mesbaha* at all times, and at all costs, this is to secure your seat of power. Furthermore, as any long-standing ruler knows, longevity depends on how well you stabilize your future line of succession. It is absolutely

---

61. Greek version of *arak*.

62. Technically, they're really worry beads, but we like to use them when we dance.

imperative that you have a solid heir in place and ready to go at a moment's notice in order to sustain any kind of dynasty, and that requires excellent tactical skills.

When a leader feels that it is time to pass the torch, they will, in secret code, signal one of their own to take over. He'll make strong eye contact with his right-hand man, give a discreet nod and, with laser-sharp precision, toss the magic *mesbaha* across the dance floor. The second-in-command catches it with fascinating accuracy. He now has his orders and knows exactly what to do. He bolts across the dance floor confidently twirling his *mesbaha as if to claim his territory for all to see.* He storms to the front of the line, takes his place and steps in as the new legitimate leader. He's in control, now. It's like the entire inauguration ceremony took place during the two-second *mesbaha* toss.

Now, in the event that something goes wrong and someone accidentally walks off with your *mesbaha*, don't get nervous. Remember, a great leader is always prepared for the worst. A great leader will always have a spare tied-up handkerchief handy to use as a backup *mesbaha*. And, if he is really in a jam, he'll grab a banquet linen napkin, tie a big knot in the center, and go reclaim his territory!

Rule #4—Never Break Up The Guys
Never. Never. Never break up the guys. The guys are amazing. They're not like the girls. They're *"the guys,"* you know? The guys have this incredible synergy when they dance together and it's cool as hell. When you've got like seven guys dancing in the front of the line all you can do is sit back and watch. The way they move, the way they stomp their feet, is so slick. You get chills from the sound their shoes make when they snap the floor. It's sharp. It's hard. And it's tight, especially if they're really good dancers. Plus, if they're really good dancers, their collective sex appeal automatically shoots up an additional 30 points.

The guys are the best; they're young, they're free, and they're having the time of their lives. And it shows.

Never break up the guys.

Rule #5—Learn To Identify Alliances And Don't Break Them Up
It's a fact: People like dancing with their own people. There is a certain rhythm going, a nice energy, a smooth flow. They know who is a strong dancer and who is not. Who compliments their particular style and who kills it. When you see a strong alliance, don't break them up. You're just asking for trouble.

You can usually identify popular alliances after about the second or third *hafli*. Actually, by that time, you'll be able to spot them a mile away, blindfolded. These people are tight, loyal, and they always got each other's back, no matter what. Semper Fi, baby! Semper Fi![63]

And let me tell you, with some alliances, even if you *tried* to bust in, you couldn't. They won't let you. The mean ones will smile right in your face like you're old pals but, underneath, their hands will be locked in a human barricade. You're not getting in. And, in worst cases, the embarrassment falls on you. Depending on how cliquish some women are[64] they'll squeeze their hands real tight, shake their heads, and flat out tell you, *"Mabisseer."*[65] Not only will they tell you *"Mabisseer,"* but they'll release their locked hands just so they can point their fingers to redirect you elsewhere. Talk about rejection. In front of everyone, too. Ouch!

Attitudes aside, they're just doing their own thing, so do yourself a favor, and don't bust in. Forge your own alliance with some other people. If you encounter a group who are inviting and nice, then you just made some new friends. But, if they're acting all stuck up, well then, who needs them anyway, right?

Rule #6—Never Attempt A Coup Without A Loyal Army To Back You Up

Imagine this: you think you're a way better dancer than the person who is currently leading the *dupkee* line, so you, Ms. *'Thang'* bust out completely unprepared and run up to the front of the line, waving your little, silly, dollar store-bought handkerchief like you own the damn place. Your girls follow you ... *well* ... *because they're your girls* ... and the next thing you know, you look around and it's you, your sister, and your one cousin. That's it!

Can you say *hu-mi-li-a-tion?*

Good girl.

Now you won't have to wear blush for a whole week.

Honey, you deserve to be humiliated. Come on, now! You tried to overthrow a legitimate *dupkee* leader and you weren't even prepared! That's like having a revo-

---

63. Semper Fidelis (Always Faithful)—U.S. Marine Corps motto.

64. Women are generally fussy about these kinds of things. Guys are totally cool about it.

65. It ain't happenin'.

lution without informing the guerillas! What? You just showed up at the town square expecting a show down? How stupid! If this were real-life *dupkee* combat instead of just a drill, you'd be out. Gone.

Coups involve a lot of work. There's coordination, strategic planning, logistics; it's just not something you do on impulse. There's a lot to consider: training, artillery, communications, ground operations, back-up support. Where were the rest of your girls? Didn't they know you were invading another line? Didn't they get their orders? Why did they go AWOL on you like that? And what happened to your reinforcements? What about intelligence gathering? Was someone in your line working undercover? Where exactly was your second-in-command just prior to the strike? Who was your lookout? And where the hell was your *mesbaha*? You went out there with a dollar store handkerchief? You started a major revolution with a freakin' dollar store handkerchief?

Unbelievable!

Don't let the press get a hold of this one. If they find out, it's all over.

Look, failed coups just don't exist in the *dupkee* world. Is that understood? From this point on, make sure that if you are going to bust in and take over a line that you secure a strong army to back you up. Read over Rules #7 and #8. And, while you're at it, reread Rule #3! That's an order!

Rule #7—Beware of Dissenters
There's a lot of pride that comes with being in the best *dupkee* line on the dance floor. When you're in the best line, all "eyez" are on you. And let's face it, some women would just die for that kind of attention. I don't know what it is but it's like people take it as a personal victory or something. All you girls are on the dance floor, laughing, having fun, and acting like best friends. But watch your back, babe, for real. Once that ship starts going down, take a step back and count how many of your friends are still around.

It's true, a loyal crew will never abandon their beloved captain, but there are always gonna be opportunists looking for their next fix. These people commit treason all the time and eventually become enemies of the state. These low-life, good-for-nothing traitors jump from one *dupkee* line to the next, until they find the most slammin' circle. And they never look back. B***ards!

<u>Rule #8—Create An Emergency Plan For Catastrophic Collisions</u>
Red Alert! Dupkee Line Down! Repeat! Dupkee Line Down! Mayday! Mayday!

You're leading a fantastic *dupkee* line, and, all at once, out of nowhere, *BAAM!* It's a head on collision! And it's a bad one. You manage to regain your balance and look around; people are scattered everywhere! You see only a few survivors struggling to emerge from the dance floor. It's utter chaos as refugees scramble to seek asylum in neighboring *dupkee* lines. Your line is completely destroyed. Your once massive military battleship is sinking right before your very eyes.

You can't let this happen.
What do you do?

Commence Rescue Operations, immediately!

Quick! Pull one of the survivors out from the wreckage and get her up to dance solo! Throw her in the middle of a circle and surround her with the other survivors. Start clapping! Fast! Look like you're having fun! Look like the change was intended! Hurry! Now, switch girls, get another one! Somebody, make a *zalghouta!* Quick!

Stand tall. Chest out. Chin up. Smile!

Hurry! Gather up the prettiest survivors of the crew! Get the ones with the biggest hair and heaviest makeup. Throw them all in the circle. Now, all together, discreetly and smoothly edge your way to an open area of the dance floor and make strong eye contact with the band's singer. Flirt! Flirt hard! Quick! Get him to come off the stage with his microphone and sing to your group. Get the *tabal* guy, too! He's even better! Make him come over to your circle with his *tabal* and play hard!

Keep that going until the song ends.

Whew!

You made it!

Close call!

Look, you gotta understand; this is war, for real. You can't lose face. Not in this crowd, you can't. You gotta do whatever it takes to get through. That's your reputation on the line, you know? Just go sit down and take a break for a couple of songs; you'll be all right. Have a drink; you need it.

Rule #9—Get Certified In *Dupkee* Traffic Control
You've just witnessed a severe head-on collision right in the middle of a hafli. The National Dupkee Transportation Safety Board is conducting its own investigation into what happened. They're performing toxicology tests and looking into possible foul play. This didn't have to happen. Fortunately, there weren't any casualties, but it could have been worse. Next time, we might not be so lucky.

Traffic control is critical in preventing accidents like the one you just read about. The latest projections show that by 2025, there will be a whopping 35% shortage in qualified *dupkee* leaders. This will put enormous pressure on already weakened *dupkee* lines and increase the likelihood of even more serious accidents. We need experienced leaders for the future. Therefore, it's essential that we recruit our finest and equip them with the best possible training.

Uma Samir Wants You!

Candidates must have a winning attitude, a willingness to take risks, and a really strong sense of direction. As a *Dupkee*-Leader-In-Training, you will learn how to command your line to accurately change course from its present coordinates to any given direction. You will gain the confidence necessary to make solid decisions when you see dangerous oncoming traffic approaching. As a Master Drill Sergeant, you'll holler *"Left Flank!"* and your line will instantly turn left. *"Right Flank!" BAMM!* They're charging right. *"Forward March!"* And it's full speed ahead.

Such elite training is particularly critical when switching *dupkee* variations in the middle of a song. A recent study by the University of Urstupidifubelivethiz has shown that the number of accidents caused by changing *dupkee* styles are doubled when a commander fails to effectively warn his troupes ahead of time.

Upon successful completion of the program, you will be assigned a small *dupkee* line to manage under the direct supervision of a top, International *Dupkee* Queen. Don't worry about making mistakes at first; dexterity comes with experience. In time, you will have mastered your particular expertise and instinctually know when you are prepared to go out on your own. In due course, you'll know how to steer your line through the most ferocious, shark-infested waters. It will become as natural to you as applying lip liner without a mirror.

Together we can make the dupkee floor a safer place for everyone.

Rule #10—Boost Morale

A good leader always looks after her girls. She temporarily leaves her position in the front, goes out into the field, and checks on her troupes to see how they're doing. The number-two in charge keeps order while the leader dances down the line, personally saluting each warrior, bestowing upon her gratitude and recognition for a job well done. She does this by twirling her *mesbaha* as a gesture of applause. She does this to boost their morale and inspire them to reach for greater heights.

But the leader never goes down the line for selfish reasons. Never to show off her fancy footwork—*you know, too much.*

Rule #11—Keep Your Line Polished

Just because the music is pumpin' doesn't mean you have to look like a candidate for the next *village idiot* position. Keep your line tight, straight, and disciplined. Do your part to make it the most envied one out there. Don't allow your people to get sloppy with waves of tight squishy spots followed by large awkward gaps. And, by all means, make sure everyone is doing the same step—*at the same time.* Remember, you're their coach; they're counting on you.

Knowing when to fire your line up and when to pull back is the difference between brilliance and disgrace. It can give you fame or leave you lying in the gutter being pitied by passers-by. Dancing well means dancing with integrity and purpose. And this is called having class, style and grace. It's everything we, at the Institute, strive for.

All of this might sound overwhelming to you, and that's certainly understandable. The laws, in and of themselves, are extremely rigid. And, trust me, it's not easy leading a *dupkee* line. But just think, if you work hard at it and have consistency and style, you could be cherished for generations to come. Or your reputation might gain you a very small, insignificant cult following; maybe even a little fan club with a teeney-bopper or two. It's worth somethin' though. It's more than what you had before.

Chapter 12

The Much-Envied Zalghouta Queen

Zalghouta (n. or v. —still debating that one.)—A *zalghouta* is a very loud Arabian expression of excitement and joy. And when used in other contexts, it's an expression of strength, unity and/or fervor. It's also a really cool battle cry. [66] In fact, it sounds very much like Hollywood's portrayal of an American Indian battle cry. It's a high-pitched, rapid, tongue-firing sequence that goes something like this:

La-la-la-la-la-la-la-la-la-la-leeeesh!

Zalghoutas are also widely used in rap songs and within current news coverage of the Middle East. Arabs use it on various occasions and in a variety of different contexts. [67] However, because it can be used at both joyful occasions as well as, in some cases, *not-so-joyful* ones, it can create some confusion.

For instance, a *zalghouta* will always be used at weddings and baptisms, but they can also be used at political uprisings and the like. Unfortunately, there isn't a universal governing body to establish standards and codes for determining the nature of the appropriateness of events. Therefore, one may not know for certain whether they are celebrating something good or something *not-so-good*. You just have to use common sense. If you don't, disastrous and irreversible consequences may result.

---

66. At least it was back in the day.

67. Mostly happy ones, though.

For example, you may *zalghet* because you think you are celebrating a wedding, which is most likely the case. However, if the circumstances are not crystal clear and, unbeknownst to you, some other rather serious event is going on, another villager may misinterpret that *zalghouta* for what they mistakenly think is a mockery and an outright provocation. In which case, the offended family, erroneously taking the original *zalghouta* as a direct insult, might then send out yet another *zalghouta* as a tribal call to revive a centuries-old vendetta. By that time, everything's outta control and before you know it, you've got the whole village *zalghouting* all over the place without anyone really even knowing why! And, on top of that, they don't know if they should be happy or sad or what. It's an emotional mess!

So, try to be as clear as possible about what event you're attending. After all, it could mean your life.

For those of you who are stuck on the definition and still don't understand what exactly a *zalghouta* is, just turn on CNN. You're bound to catch a *zalghouta* somewhere in any given half-hour segment. Better yet, turn it on during the *Situation Room* you know, when "breaking news happens."

Speaking of CNN, indulge me for a moment, please. Is that okay? Thank you. I need to get this out of my system. I just have to say that Wolf Blitzer gets on my nerves so bad. He really does. I can't stand him. Great reporter, but just too much, you know what I mean? His voice, his mannerisms, his seriousness—it kills me. He could turn the most mundane, boring story into this urgent, breaking news crisis with devastating global consequences.

And everything has to always be so damned official with him! It's irritating! It's like he drops titles around just to impress people. Like it suddenly makes the story more important or something. *"High ranking officials. … Top security administration officials. … Senior administration officials. …* Blah, blah, blah!

That man can turn a freakin' Dr. Seuss story into a national crisis. You listen to him and the next thing you know you're boarding up windows, stocking up on bottled water, buying generators, and loading up a rifle or two. I've never done it myself, but I did check around once or twice to see how we were gonna barricade ourselves in, you know, in case we ever had to. Thank God he wasn't working as a reporter when the *War of the Worlds* came out. Nobody would have made it out alive after his telling of a martian invasion.

I swear I'm not kidding. My blood pressure literally soars at the sound of his voice. I get chest pains. Anxiety attacks. He scares me too much. His style is so fearful that you think at any given moment he's gonna break the news about Armageddon. I just can't watch him anymore.

"CNN has just learned that senior White House officials secretly met with key Homeland Security officials in emergency talks to address a possible bio-chemical attack on the U.S. in the rare form of liquid green eggs and ham. Such a disaster would threaten the US water supply. How prepared are we as a nation to handle a disaster of such magnitude. Who is guarding our dams at this hour? Is the water you're drinking right now already contaminated?"

How the hell did that man read fairy tales to his kid at night? Think about it. How scary did Wolf Blitzer make the Big Bad Wolf sound to his four-year-old? You know he took it over the top; he's the type who enjoys that kind of thing. He even looks like he could be the wolf dressed up like granny. He's already got the beard and glasses—just put a nightgown on him! And a bonnet! Knowing Blitzer, he probably shut off the lights and used freaky scare tactics like saying, *"This Just In! Breaking News out of the Black Forest! We've just received word that …!"* He probably got two inches away from his kid's face and opened his eyes real big and scary. The kid was probably s**tting bricks the whole time. He wet his bed. He didn't sleep. Poor guy is probably living as a recluse somewhere, suffering from post traumatic stress disorder.

He's a sick one!

And you know who else drives me crazy?

Larry King.

He's another one. Oh, I cannot stand him. Let me just say for the record that Larry King has gradually transformed from a skilled veteran talk show host into an old, loud, scatterbrained, south Floridian Jewish woman. I don't know *how*. I don't know *when*. But he did *(damn Welch's grape juice)!*

Thank you for indulging me. I'm done now.

Let's continue on with business, shall we?

Bonus Tips On How To Get A Zalghouta Queen For Your Village

The *Zalghouta Queen* is in a class of her own. This woman, who is both revered and envied, has the most important job in the village. She, like the Lebanese hairdresser,[68] is the one who holds power.

Her job is to attend every village occasion and belt out the best possible *zalghouta* that her vocal cords can handle. Although she is a *"Queen"* of sorts, she maintains a professional presence and takes her job very seriously. It's up to her to set the tone of that particular event and she can really mess it up if she's not prepared.

For example, just after the priest announces, *"Man and wife,"* she's ON!

"LA-LA-LA-LA-LA-LA-LA-LEEESHH!"

A fraction of a second too late and the whole wedding's shot—reception and all. It's just a downer after that.

The same deal with the *tabal*. The moment the *tabal* comes out and the bride starts dancing with the groom, she's ON! The *Zalghouta Queen* can't be in the ladies room touching up her lip liner, you know what I mean?

So, how do you go about recruiting a reliable *Zalghouta Queen* for your village?

You hold a *Zalghouta Challenge*. That's right, a *Zalghouta Challenge*, a tournament, if you will. Post decorative flyers all around your village asking for qualified contestants. Make sure your applicants include relevant experience, training and a brief essay on why they feel they are the best candidate for the job. Skip personal reference requests all together; they're useless.

Set aside a full day to host preliminary trials and make sure there aren't any other scheduled events taking place that day. (Remember the warning about confusing joyful and no-so-joyful events.) Gather all registered applicants, check their qualifications, do a few quick interviews, and begin your eliminations. Continue until you have the top 10 finalists.

---

68. See Chapter 16.

Then—*and here's where it gets good*—climb up to the highest point on the mountain, bring lots of spring water (for dry throats) position the judges at the base ...

AND LET THE GAMES BEGIN!

Your final champion *Zalghouta Queen* should be chosen with the utmost care. She must demonstrate the exceptional ability to reach a range extending from one end of the village all the way to the other end, and everything in between. Her *zalghouta* must be strong enough to be heard over all other noise including fire trucks, police sirens, ambulances, black hawk helicopters, and tons of crying kids.

Bear in mind, however, that being a *Zalghouta Queen* is about more than just having supersonic vocal cords. It's also about character and integrity. Not only must your champion have the fastest whipping tongue, but, like *Ms. America*, she should be chosen on her ability to best represent your particular village.

Ask yourself: if we were to enter into the nationals tomorrow, would this person be the most qualified to speak for us? Is she the embodiment of the best model citizen our village has to offer? When we present ourselves on the world stage, would we be proud to have her as our ambassador? Will she be there when the priest says, *"Man and wife,"* or will she be in the ladies room with a lip liner in one hand, a cell phone in the other, smoking a cigarette and gabbing away?

You gotta weed out the bad ones, you know?

Once a champion has been selected, she must be ordained. The committee should have a crowned coronation in the town square to make it official. It should be an all-day affair, a massive celebration for the entire village. You can call it, *"The Wedding of the Zalghouta Queen to Her Subjects."* Pull out all the stops. Kill the fatted calf! Bring out the merry dancers! The *Tabal!* The hairdressers! The *foo-foos!* Let the champagne flow! Celebrate with a feast and all-day, interactive festivities!

The *Zalghouta Queen* should be rewarded for her exceptional qualities and tremendous sacrifices by being granted a lifetime appointment. After all, job security is the least we can offer her. And it's critical that she have the full backing of the village council because some knucklehead, somewhere, is bound to come out of the woodworks and try to knock her off her throne. Being a *Zalghouta Queen* can be a precarious thing, and we certainly don't need pockets of rebels popping up all over the place.

The only time a *Zalghouta Queen* should ever be replaced is if she has a medical problem that would render her unable to perform her duties as such. And, all right, if someone just happens to pop out of the woodworks and is *really, really, I mean really, good,* then, hell, kick the prima donna out.

Look, it's just gotta be done. If you're one of those people who feel guilty about firing a dedicated, loyal employee, just change the way you think about the process. For example, start to think of the whole thing like the order of succession of queen bees in the natural world. Every so often, a pack of ungrateful, spoiled rotten, little backstabbing, worker bees sneak some special royal jelly into the hive and feed it to the chosen future queen. A future queen, mind you, that *they* chose and conspired with behind their current "beloved" monarch's back.

At a certain point, after little *Ms. 'I'm-the-new-diva! Who's-in-charge-around-here? Where-are-my-wings? I-need-my-wings! I'm-on-in-five-minutes! Can-somebody-please-get-me-my-wings! This-is-the-third-time-I-had-to-ask!'* Queen Bee has developed enough strength, she challenges the reigning Queen Bee. And they fight until the best queen wins. And then a new dynasty begins.

Nature's weird.

Finally, make sure that your first round draft pick understands that nobody is indispensable, not even her. And as the newly inaugurated *Zalghouta Queen,* she is responsible to show up for all village occasions—on time and prepared. No exceptions. No excuses. If she can't handle the pressure, she's out!

※ ※ ※ ※ ※

For those who are interested in organizing such an event, I have enclosed my very own personal *Zalghouta Queen Challenge* contest flyer to help you get started. [69]

In case you're wondering about my credentials, you should know that I am a professional *Zalghouta Queen.* In fact, I am *the Zalghouta Queen, thank you very much!* I have been the *Zalghouta Queen* for my particular "village" in America, ever since I was a kid, so I speak with the utmost authority. My village loves and respects me very much. Truth be told, they adore me. However, lately there have been a few jealous, little, spoiled brats who are conspiring to overthrow me.

---

69. Contest flyer is located at the end of the book.

That's okay, though. I've been in this business long enough to know how to deal with them. Excuse me, just a second, while I pull this ... *this dagger ... ouch! ... Out of my back ... Ahhh! ... That feels better now.*

Chapter 13

Um Kalthoum

Um.
Just saying her name gives me chills.
Honestly.

People worshiped *Um.*
People still worship *Um.*
I worship *Um.*

Next to the universe itself, *Um Kalthoum* is the greatest creation.

Um Kalthoum is unquestionably the most gifted Middle Eastern artist of all time, bar none. This traditional, classical vocalist commanded more respect than some world leaders of her day. At her peak, she was practically revered as a goddess. Adored by the people. Loved by all. Her death shocked and devastated the entire Arab world. The city of Cairo, Egypt, shut down for three days to mourn her death. Some committed suicide. Her funeral was one of the largest gatherings in recorded history, with roughly four million in attendance. [70]

She is the consummate artist of all artists.

---

70. It was not just her music that they fell in love with. It was her. Her spirit, her passion, her soul. She gave much of her wealth to the poor, the suffering, the forgotten, and the orphans. She was a powerful symbol of Arab pride and nationalism. Critics blame her for losing the Yom Kippur war as Arabs were cast under her spell, drugged by her intoxicating voice.

Her voice is not of this world. Her music is not of this world. It transports you to that secret place buried deep within your soul. The one so sacred, private, and powerful, that you dare not visit alone. She takes you to that place where you cannot breathe without your love. Your emotions overwhelm you, consume you, and swallow you up. You are at their mercy.

Um Kalthoum lures you into her world. Like a thief in the night, she creeps quietly and grabs hold of your heart, rendering you helpless, unable and unwilling to be released from her intricate web. She will take you.

Her voice, possessed with power and strength, emanates from a place deep within her own soul. And, once unleashed, will own yours. It makes you yearn for love that you cannot find. Hunger for love you cannot taste. Reach for love you cannot hold. Die for love you cannot have.

She is Um.

She sang about love between a man and a woman. Not ordinary love but deep, profound love. That rare, passionate, once-in-a-lifetime love. That intense, forbidden, suicidal love. That eternal love that only one in 10 thousand lifetimes knows.

That Guinevere and Lancelot love.

That love.

She sang of love forgotten, received, lost and unrequited. This woman had an amazingly powerful presence. From the moment she stepped on stage, she possessed her audience. At the very first resonance of her voice, they were hers.

She captured the very heart of the Arab world and held it in the palm of her hand.

When she sang, she started out slowly, gradually increasing in intensity before bringing the emotional energy to a climatic peak.

And then, she released it.

She brought the Arab world to its knees.

Her concerts lasted for hours.

When you listen to *Um Kalthoum* you will feel something deep inside that cannot be expressed in human language. You will feel emotions that remain in the spiritual realm. If you have ever truly been in love, you will understand.

Personally, I'm all about taking it over the top and surrendering to the whole experience. I mean, if you're going to listen to *Um Kalthoum,* there's no question about it, you have to do it right. And in order to really feel it and achieve the best dramatic experience possible, it's critical that you create the right atmosphere. Everything must be perfect.

You must have with you the following: your true love, your very close friends, your very close family members, high-quality cigarettes—actually, several cartons of high-quality cigarettes—*bizzer,* an *argeelee* with only the finest tobacco, lots of time, strong Arabic coffee, a bottle of Prozac, five boxes of Kleenex, a phone nearby that is pre-programmed to dial emergency 9-1-1, and lots of *arak.*

When you listen to her, close your eyes.

If you are an especially sensitive or highly emotional person, make sure that you have a trusted and responsible friend sitting in the chair right next to you, holding your hand, particularly when she is singing songs about unrequited love or you just might end it all right then and there.

She's that good.

I tried my best to portray *Um Kalthoum* as I believe her to be and, as I said, I worship her, so you know where my heart is. But you really have to listen to her for yourself to understand what I am talking about.

I originally wanted to include a small portion of her masterpiece *Inta Omri* ("You Are My Life"), but after reading it translated, it lost so much of its intensity, depth, and meaning that I decided against it. Having said that, go find a copy of *Inta Omri.*

Shut your eyes.
Shut the lights.
Light the candles.
And make a night of it.

Surrender to *Um.*

Chapter 14

Why We Spend So Much Time Hanging Out

Lunches are serious business in the Middle East. They can last an average of three to four hours. When you go out to lunch, plan to be gone for the entire day. Be prepared to sit. And sit some more. Then get up and dance. Then sit. Then dance. Then sit again. Smoke some *argeelee*. And sit and dance again—but don't eat too much! Remember girls: it's only lunch, a bite here and there will do.

Until now, I could never understand why all my cousins made such a big deal about going out to lunch. I hate lunch. I really do. It interrupts your business day and your productivity. And, worst of all, it makes you feel slothful. I'd rather go out for dinner; it's much more efficient. That way, you get everything you need to get done during normal business hours so that later on, you can relax and treat yourself to an enjoyable evening.

Well, the day after I arrived in Syria, we were invited to lunch. I thought, "Okay, it's the first day; no big deal; we'll go out to lunch." We got there at 12 p.m. and left at 4 p.m. I found myself in the middle of the day, at exactly 3 p.m. in the afternoon drinking *arak* and dancing. There was a live singer, a five-piece band, a dancer, and the place was packed. Dumbfounded, I turned to my sister and said, "What the ^*$# is wrong with these people? What the hell are they doing? How come they're not working? What's going on here? Don't they have jobs? Get to work you guys! It's three o'clock in the freakin' afternoon. Get up and go to work! Now!"

Exactly seven days later, I found myself suffering from some kind of weird lunch withdrawal syndrome. That is, if I wasn't dancing, sipping *arak,* and eating with at least 15 other people, something was wrong.

In America, we don't do that. We can't. We're too neurotic.

You see, over there lunch is an all-day event. It's special time that you spend together with those whom you love. As a guest in the Middle East, you will be invited out all the time by lots of different people. And you can't refuse an invitation because that would be insulting. So, now that you have this information, don't get all fussy when five hours have passed and all you did all day long was just "have lunch."

That's not the only thing that is likely to get on your nerves. There are lots of other things that we're not used to in this country. For example, when you go out to a nice restaurant, you will undoubtedly feel like Don Corleone in *The Godfather.* The formality is a bit much. All of the male servers look and act like mafioso, I swear. I'm not lying. It's intense, man. I feel like if I signaled a waiter to come over and gave him an order to assassinate a rival family member, it would be a done deal. *BAMM!* You know? It's scary. They intimidate you so much that sometimes you're afraid to eat.

About 10 masculine waiters will stand at attention around your table like personal bodyguards. They'll take three hours to serve 20 culinary masterpieces. These men don't even allow you to put the food on your own plate; they do it for you. Imagine, 10 dashingly handsome Antonio Bandares-type waiters constantly watching over you, attending to your every whim, waiting to fulfill your every desire, anticipating your every need. *Oh my!*

The whole ordeal is a bit nerve wracking and much too high maintenance for this chick. I'd rather just kick back and have a *shawarma*[71] and a beer—and put my own food on my own damn plate, you know? Like, "I'll take 12 chicken wings sir; not just one, *thank you very much! And where the hell is the hot sauce, anyway?"*

When you're out, you'll also notice that there are no tables for two. Instead, most restaurants set up their massive dining rooms "banquet style," with tables that seat roughly 30 patrons at a time. They don't play that quiet, intimate dinner-for-two thing. It's you, your family, your husband's family, your friends, your neighbors, your neighbor's friends, half the village sometimes—*and sometimes the other half, too.* You're all going out together in huge numbers. Intimacy? *Ahhh* ... not here. Sorry, babe, wrong country.

---

71. A popular delicious sandwich.

You might be asking what the big deal about lunch is, anyway. Nothing really. It's just that they enjoy a party *all* the time. And there's nothing wrong with that. In fact, it got me thinking, Americans need to stop working at 1 p.m. and go have some fun. We're too stressed out and overworked here. Yes, we're productive, but we're paying a big price for it. We wait for the weekend to relax, and, by that time, we're too burnt out to enjoy anything, anyway. America needs to establish a little siesta.

And Visiting?
Honey, if you thought lunch sucked up your time, you haven't gone visiting.

Middle Eastern people visit each other—a lot. That's just what they do. They visit you. You visit them. Then they take you to go visit someone else. Then that someone else comes to visit you. And they insist that you come back. Then you visit an entirely different family clan, and the cycle starts all over again. You will hear these funny little words over and over again: "*Tfadlaay*[72] … *Taa'h, la unday, shrab Ahawee!*"[73]

A nice cup of coffee? Yeah, right. Don't kid yourself, there's a hidden agenda in there somewhere. Look, marriage deals are sometimes made over an innocent cup of coffee. Trust me, I know. But in all fairness, most visits are actually designed for your own benefit.

You see, the average villager knows that you'll visit at least 10 different households on any given day. So, they'll serve you Arabic coffee in a little demitasse cup, along with a small piece of sweet in the middle of the afternoon. There is a very specific and deliberate purpose for this and the whole country is in on it. They truly understand how exhausting it can be to visit so many people, and they know you will need a little caffeine perk up and a sugar surge to get you all ready for your next visit. Otherwise, you'll never make it. You'll be completely worn out and totally spent. Consider it a community effort; people helping people.

You know what else is gonna work that last nerve of yours? Hearing the word, *mishtatlek*.[74] Oh, man! You'll hear it over and over again. *Mishtatlek, ya inaay, mishtatlek!*[75] They say

---

72. A warm expression of hospitality.

73. Welcome, come over to my house and drink coffee!

74. Literally translated, "I miss you."

75. I miss you, sweetheart, I miss you!

it to you all the time, even when they first meet you. That's kind of odd, you know, especially when you guys just saw each other a couple of hours ago.

Americans would have a hard time comprehending that kind of hospitality. It would be a little too strange for us. We would naturally think, "What are you talking about, lady? I just visited you for five straight hours yesterday, and then I saw you again for three hours last night over *Umtay Bedea's*[76] house. I'm going to see you the day after tomorrow at *bint Khaltay's*[77] wedding. You can't possibly miss me yet. There's no way. On top of that, we just freakin' met for the very first time the day before yesterday. And why are you asking me to visit you again? That's weird. That's really weird. Aren't you sick of me yet? You know what? I'm starting to get a little sick of you!"

You *think* it. But you don't ever *say* it. And you know what burns the worst? You *have* to go back over to their house again, at least one more time before you leave. If you don't, it's a big insult. And in case you haven't noticed ... *oh, I don't know ... say, over the last millennium or so ...* Arabs aren't real good at brushing off insults. It's just not one of our fortes; you know what I mean?

And God help you if you're caught hanging out over someone else's house a lot more than theirs. Been there, done that. Won't do that again. Oh, and don't forget, when you're all done visiting for the very last time, make sure you extend that hospitality right back to them and invite the family over to your place. That would just be the polite thing to do.

You know the *"h"* in hospitality?
It also stands for headache.

> *Important Secret Bonus Tip:* This advice is especially valuable to the truly commitment phobic. If you ever want to get out of visiting—or really anything for that matter—there is a secret loophole. Just repeat these words in response to every invitation: *"Inshalla! Inshalla!"*[8] That's your only hope because what it does is take the responsibility off of your shoulders and puts them directly onto God's. And come on, I mean they can't go around blaming God or anything; that would be

---

76. Aunt Bedea's house.

77. My cousin's. (Technically, my aunt's daughter).

78. God willing! God willing

bad. So, they just have to accept the situation as it occurs, as it would be God's will if you somehow weren't able to make it. And then you, my friend, get off scott-free.

Example:

(Them) "You have to come back to my house again, tonight for coffee!"

(You) "*Inshalla! Inshalla!*"

(Them) "We'll see you in an hour again, at lunch, right?"

(You) "*Inshalla! Inshalla!*"

Visiting wouldn't be such a pain in the a** if they were short and sweet. But they aren't—ever. Once you step inside, you're pretty much stuck there for a real long time. And it's not like you can make an excuse to leave or anything. I mean, what are you gonna say? You're in the middle of the village, for goodness sakes! Where could you possibly have to go? *"Ahh ... I just remembered ... I have to go to the store."* Yeah, right. Forget it. Either your hosts have what you need or they know someone who has what you need. And if that doesn't work, they'll send someone out to the store to *get* what you need. Baby, you just ain't leavin'! You're trapped. And the village is so small that everyone knows your business anyway, so trust me, whatever kind of grand concoction you think you can come up with, isn't going to work.

Except for this:

At one point, I was going to pull my hair out. Literally. I needed a break so bad that if I didn't get one, I swore I was going to destroy every living thing that stood in my path—infants and children included. It was that bad. All I needed was one freakin' minute to myself. Alone. Away from everybody. Just to breathe. Just to think. Just to stop. To take a walk alone. To *be* alone. To shut down for a second. And I tried everything. I mean *eve-ry-thing!* And they wouldn't let up. None of them. Not for a second.

Standing on the brink of insanity I was just about to take that one last critical step and cross over. But God is truly gracious; He saved me. In the end, the only thing that worked was when I flat out lied to my hosts. Nerves shot and blood boiling, I looked them straight in the eyes and told them that I needed to climb the mountain alone to talk with God—to be near Him and to pray quietly in His holy presence. *Oh My God!* Then! Then they finally let me go! Then they understood!

Arabs and religion.

Unbelievable!

I wasn't prayin' though. I was cursin' the whole way up!

Look, it's annoying and it's frustrating, but it's our way. We have a hard time letting go, even if it's just for a little while. We're just always hanging out with each other. It's how we show you that we really love you.

Besides, what the hell would Arabs do with quiet time? Think about it. Seriously. Down time? Arabs? We'd be totally lost. We wouldn't know what to do with ourselves. It'd be way too weird, you know? Imagine … complete silence. Nobody around us for hours. No distractions. No chaos. No obligations. No drama. And we had time to ponder. To sort out our thoughts. To hear our own voice. To discover our own unique individuality. To question why things are the way they are …

What are you nuts?

Dude, you okay?

Hey you? Hey!

Open your eyes!

Dude, I'm so sorry about that! I didn't mean to traumatize you. I won't do it again, I promise. Look, it's okay, calm down. We'll just keep on visiting each other. We'll visit a lot, all right? I swear. Look, don't we all live right next to each other, anyway? Okay, then. See. Everything will be just like it was before.

All joking aside, I just have to say one last thing about all that visiting we do. It's a given, every culture has its good and bad points but, as Americans, we pretty much have everything we could possibly want to create a fabulous life for ourselves but we're paying a big price for it.

We work so hard, we stress out, and then we go home to even more stress. We stand over the kitchen sink and chow down processed foods before we run out the door to make it to work on time. Some of us haven't seen a vegetable in years. We're thousands of dollars in credit card debt and one paycheck away from foreclosure. Reality TV has become our own *personal* reality because our brains are too fried and our attention spans are too shot to handle anything else. Cell phones, laptops, and BlackBerrys keep us connected to the office, but not to ourselves.

We get a couple of weeks vacation a year and, when that's over and done with, we get right back to the grindstone. We eat fast food like there's no tomorrow and then we have to get gastric bypass surgery to fix it all up. We're depressed, so we pop anti-depressants to make us feel good. We turn on the 11 o'clock news and then we get depressed all over again. We go to sleep, wake up the next day, and once again stand over the kitchen sink chowing down our processed foods before jumping right back into the rat race.

Unfortunately, our lifestyle in America is so fast-paced that it doesn't allow for much time to just kick back, unwind, and truly enjoy each other's company. There is so much loneliness in this country and that's a serious issue. Of course, one can be in a room with thousands of people and still feel alone, but I'm not talking about that. What's missing here, I think, is a sense of closeness and intimacy—a sense of togetherness, of community, and of belonging to a greater family. We are so isolated from each other here, that it is negatively impacting our already neglected souls. When we are unable to take care of our most critical needs, we try to numb the pain with the addiction *du jour*—food, drugs, alcohol, possessions—anything, anything, to make the pain go away. We need nurturing.

Overseas, by and large, your cousins, sisters, brothers, aunts, uncles and friends are always around you. There are so many people with you, that you're never really alone, which helps you not to be so lonely in the first place. In Arabic countries, you get absolutely no privacy whatsoever. None. But other than that minor nuisance, you generally feel warmth and closeness with others. And it's not just Arabs who enjoy such a relaxed way of life, either. Italians, Spaniards, Greeks they're in all the cafés drinking coffee. In India they're sippin' chai. In Ireland, they're chuggin' beers. And since the stress level is much lower, they're usually having a nice time.

There is definitely something different over there. I'm not sure what it is, but I know *that* it is. Don't get me wrong, America is great. I love our respect for privacy, individuality, and personal space. There's nothing more lovely than when you're off doing your own thing, and nobody's in your business. But we need to balance things out a little more.

In Syria, it's not unusual to have a house full of company sitting around laughing, talking, and then witness a beautiful, unexpected thing happen. Out of the blue, some 13-year-old kid will burst out and start singing *ataba*[79] or play the music of *Um Kalthoum* on the *oud*.[80] How many teenagers do you know who would sing classical music from his heart, just to delight his aunts and uncles? That would be way too uncool. Besides, they'd be too busy downloading music on their iPods anyway.

The soul is rich when it is filled with human intimacy and it is in distress when it is empty.

When you're sitting in your cousin's house, surrounded by your relatives and friends, talking, laughing, and singing, and the sweet mountain breeze is gently blowing through the window, you feel like you are living life as it was meant to be lived—purely, naturally and simply. You begin to understand why God made the trees, and the stars, and earth, and people. How He created those beautiful things for us, for our pleasure, so that we can experience heaven on earth.

You begin to see how far removed the artificial world that we live in is from the one we were originally created to inhabit. You wonder how it came to be that your natural existence was somehow stolen from you, without you even knowing it. It's an ugly feeling. But when you once again hear, the sounds of birds, of wind, of song, and of laughter, your spirit will forgive you because at least now it's happy that you've come back home.

---

79. Traditional a cappella music.

80. Arabic string instrument.

And every soul is always looking for its way back home.

Bizzer: Sewing the Seeds of Gossip

Bizzer.

Bizzer serves a very critical function in Arabic culture. You know all that ooey-goey, lovey-dovey togetherness I just got done telling you about? Well, love isn't the only reason we get together. We also get together to gossip.

Now, there are many types of *bizzer*, but, for our purposes, we will stick to the three most popular ones used in the Middle East. In order of importance, they are pumpkin seeds, watermelon seeds, and Egyptian melon seeds.

As an Arab-American female, the most fundamental question you must ask yourself is: *"Is you is, or is you ain't a bizzer-crackin' h**?"* Because, if you are, then great! You're set. But, if you're not, you need to get yourself a yellow highlighter and start taking notes.

You might be asking yourself what's the big deal about *bizzer*, anyway? I mean, they're just seeds for goodness sakes! Well, it's really quite simple. *Bizzer* is to Arabs what cell phones are to girlfriends. You can't gossip without them.

It's impossible.

Go ahead, try.

See?

You can't, can you?

It's like the words won't come out right. The sentences don't flow properly. You don't know what to do with your hands. In fact, the whole hand-to-mouth operation gets all mixed-up. And then the main characters get switched-up, the plot's in the wrong order. It's really bad.

And, honestly, what's the Arab culture without gossip? Nothing. It's Blah! *Boring!* What would we do with our creative storytelling skills? What would we do with our infinite imagination? What would we do if we were to mind our own business? And don't forget, those little powerhouse proteins are packed with essential nutrients—just the thing you need to keep the gossip flowing!

In all fairness, though, that's only one reason why *bizzer* is important to Arabic culture. But, as far as you're concerned, just know that *bizzer* is critical to your legitimacy as an Arab-American, therefore, it's vital to understand everything you can about it.

The most important thing you should know is that people crack *bizzer* all the time. Everywhere you go, people are crackin' *bizzer*. When people visit each other, the first thing they do is break out the *bizzer*. When you go to a restaurant, the first thing they put out on the table is the *bizzer*. When you sit for hours on end with your friends and family and BS all night, *you crack bizzer*. When you're driving in the *serveece, you're crackin' bizzer*. When you're sitting around doing nothing, *you're crackin' bizzer*. It's a social food—even if you're just socializing with yourself.

Aside from the three main types of *bizzer*, there are also nuts in the mix, but they don't count since there's no challenge to actually *crack* them. There's no real work involved. Essentially, you just pop them in your mouth, and then you're done—very anti-climatic. I don't even acknowledge them as being relevant. "Filler food" is the term I prefer to diminish their value. Except for pistachio nuts because they require some work to crack, so they qualify, but that's about it.

Real Arabic people crack *bizzer—well*. And you can always spot an imposter because the authentic ones are brilliant multi-taskers. You see, true Arabic persons can hold a conversation, drive a car, smoke an *argeelee*, feed a baby, carry lots of plastic bags, argue about a phone bill with the customer service representative, and do laundry—all while *cracking bizzer*.

And let me tell you, it's *how* you *crack the bizzer* that makes or breaks you.

All my life, I always just grabbed a handful of *bizzer* and shoved them in my mouth—shells and all. I never knew how to *crack bizzer*. Actually, I never knew you were *supposed* to. I saw other people do it, but I guess I just never really cared. That wasn't a problem until I went overseas and saw first hand the fastest, most swiftest *bizzer-cracking* folk this side of the Nile.

Then, it mattered.
It mattered big.

You just can't be in a room full of company and have the shells all explode and get stuck in your mouth. It gets too embarrassing. Because, when that happens, you have to take them apart by putting your fingers way in the back of your mouth. So you're all up in there, trying to get them out of the tiny, unflossable spaces near your wisdom teeth, and it just doesn't look right. And sometimes they get wedged back in there pretty tight, too. Plus, sometimes, you might accidentally swallow a really salty shell or you might choke on a fragmented sliver. It just gets all messed up. It's awkward and not very ladylike. And on top of that, you feel totally uncomfortable when everyone in the room is doing it the right way except you. You're fumbling the ball. And you're fumbling bad.

And you can't just give up and eat the shells like you did back in America. Not over there you can't. Besides, what would be the point then? There's no challenge, no individual growth, no progression—no nothing. You've gotta earn your validation. Otherwise, in this game, it doesn't count. That's how strongly I feel about being able to *crack bizzer*.

When I was in Syria, I felt very warm and welcomed by the people. I felt that I belonged to a very special kind of club—one big, happy club where all the people loved each other. I felt accepted as one of them. It was a lifelong dream come true. But, I have to confess something. And I hope you keep my secret safe because I'm trusting you as a good friend.

You see I have this fear and it scares me really bad sometimes. When I think about it, I start to get sick in my belly. You know that feeling you get right before there's gonna be a big extended family explosion in which *you* are the primary subject of discussion? Yeah. That one. Well, I kinda feel like that sometimes. See, my greatest fear is that no matter how much these people like and accept me as one of their own, no matter how much they hug me, kiss me, and tell me, *"You are my sister! I love you!"* No matter how much fun we all have together, laughing and talking, I'm gonna be kicked to the curb. Flat out rejected, and treated like a red-headed step-child. And the worst part is that I feel like a complete fraud. I'm cheating right in front of their faces.

At some point, they're going to see right through me. They're going to get suspicious, at first, and then, secretly talk amongst each other. Whisper. Then, glance over to me. Whisper more. Then glance over, again. Then, they're all going to gang up, back me in a dark corner, and confront me. The entire village will come together, jitney drivers and all, in a high village council meeting and demand that I undergo an examination to see if I can *crack bizzer* the right way.

The Syrian way.

I feel in my heart that I will be subjected to three strenuous tests: one for each kind of *bizzer*. I will have to prove that I possess the natural ability to crack *bizzer* in the same manner that blue-blood royals are tested in fairy tales. Remember the *Princess and the Pea?* In the story, the queen put a tiny, little pea under 20 thick mattresses in order to find out if the mysterious girl was a real princess as she had claimed to be. Well, as it turned out, the princess had the purest, most bluest blood running through her royal veins. It is my belief that I will be subject to the same scrutiny just to prove that I am a true Syrian.

If I pass all three tests, I'll receive my official membership in the club. With processing and shipping, it should take roughly three to five weeks. But, if I fail, well then, my visits overseas will be restricted to very short periods of time, during the slow season and only by invitation from a bona fide sponsor—until I learn to *crack bizzer* the right way.

I have to pass the tests!

I've been practicing very hard for the past six months and now can crack the pumpkin seeds very easily. As a matter of fact, I've gotten so good that I can even do it while I'm driving *and* changing a CD in my car. In fact, I'm so good that, half the time, I don't even have my hands on the wheel! But the other two seeds are still a problem for me.

I'm terrified.

I have nightmares about being denied membership. I have nightmares about someday receiving a registered letter in the mail …

> *Dear Ms. Khalil,*
>
> *We regret to inform you that your application for membership has been denied. Although you have demonstrated outstanding progress with regard to cracking the pumpkin bizzer seeds, you have not passed in the other two bizzer categories. Therefore, you have failed to meet the overall necessary requirements established by the high village council.*
>
> *We thank you for your interest and wish you the best of luck in all of your future endeavors.*

Thank you,
Local Village High Council

Sometimes I wake up in the middle of the night with cold sweats.

I gotta become a *bizzer crackin' h**!*
I just have to!

Why We're Like Royalty

Let's face it, we're like royalty in many interesting, yet disturbing, ways. Disturbing because we're really not officially royalty,[81] not by any stretch of the imagination. Although, I must say, there are those among us who believe that they really are royal and act like it, too. But if you think about it, almost every single thing in our lives parallels theirs except that we're not as rich and we don't use the taxpayer's money to pay the mortgage. And we're not as stiff. And we're certainly not alabaster-colored. Oh yeah, and our parties are a whole lot different from theirs. A bit unrestrained, I'd say. Plus, we do our own laundry. And we take out our own trash. But other than that, I think we are uncannily similar in a number of ways.

After glancing over to their life every once in a while and then reverting back to ours, I've come to the conclusion that their so-called privileged life … well … *pretty much sucks*. I think it sucks much worse than ours because the basic assumption is that they are able to have whatever they want and do whatever they want but they don't or they can't. I mean, they're crowned heads for goodness sakes. *"As you wish your Highness." "Say but the word, my lady, and it shall be done."* Here they are with all this sovereignty, you know, over the whole land and everything, and they're downright slaves to tradition. That's just gotta suck. I don't know any monarchs personally or anything, but I'm thinking, they gotta be pissed on some level.

As Arabic girls, we have to deal with a lot of irritating nuisances as well, and I think that's what makes us so similar. It has to do with a number of things such as impossible expectations, the constant glare of being in the spotlight, demanding

---

81. Excludes Arab Kingdoms, i. e. , Jordan, Bahrain, Saudi Arabia…*ahh…because they really are royalty (dah!).*

family obligations, demanding social obligations, extraordinary responsibility, the pressure of always having to be honorable and noble, knowing the consequences of deviation, having to follow stringent protocol, understanding your position in the community, understanding that you can't go around indiscriminately kissing too many frogs before finding your prince, understanding that you can't go around indiscriminately kissing too many frogs before relatives/paparazzi find out, the annoying formalities of finding a proper suitor, the pressure of always having to be pleasant, hospitable and gracious (even during those times when you just want to punch somebody in the face), of being scrutinized and condemned over the tiniest of mistakes, of having to say "yes" because it's the right thing to do, rather than saying "no" because you damn well feel like it, of having no privacy whatsoever, of having everybody and their mother involved in your business.

You know, those kinds of things.

It's not easy being a princess.

Chauffeurs and caviar don't sound all that glamorous now, do they?

That's a lot of pressure. Most people don't have to deal with all that, at least not to the extent that we do. Take Prince Charles and Camilla, for example. They went off and married people they didn't love while deep inside they were yearning for each other. For what? I don't get it. Aren't castles, princesses, knights, passion and true love, the ingredients that make up all that romantic stuff, like in Camelot? Boy, they screwed up big time! With dysfunctional relationships like that, how do they expect us to believe in fairy tales? What, nobody ever heard of Cinderella? *Hello?* I'm really not sure what went down with Prince Charles, but I'll betcha a buck the queen mom put her two cents in. Oh yes, the Queen Mother *and her royal mouth*. All I know is that when you find your true love, you should be together from that moment on, regardless of who disapproves. You know what I mean?

This all sounds uncomfortably familiar, doesn't it? I know; I'm sorry. But it just goes to show how much we have in common with royal folk. Granted, our crises may not be as exciting or catastrophic as the ones that take place in a *real* kingdom, but we do have the same kinds of issues that authentic princesses have to deal with in our own little *pretend* kingdoms.

Wouldn't it be great to sit down with a real princess and just talk, you know? I would love that. We'd be up all night gabbing away about the stresses and drama we gotta deal with. That would be so cool. Just us girls. Kicked back, feet up, and just chillin' with some Coronas. We'd be like, *"Girl, don't even start! Believe me, I understand. They got me stressing, too. I can't take it no more!"*

"Oh dear friends, you'll not believe what just happened to me. My presence was requested to attend the Royal House of Windsor's Christmas Ball at the Imperial Gardens and His Majesty, the King, demanded that my escort be the Honorable Prince of Wales. *(Girl, listen to this s**t! We got tickets to the Fares Karam concert in LA, and my dad says, you're not going unless you take your brother with you!")*

So, during the event, the wicked Duchess of Gloucester was in a fit of rage and summoned the paparazzi to catch a false glimpse of my affection for the Duke of Kensington in order that she might create a devastating scandal and sabotage my engagement to Prince Phillip. Ghastly! *(Hanna, my jealous cousin was causing me all kind of trouble! She threw a hissy fit and called my aunts, uncles, cousins, and everyone else in the whole damn village talking s**t! The b**ch set me up and tried to make it like I was playin' my man, so that she could ruin my engagement to Jozeph!)*

Now, clearly all of my subjects are outraged at such a fabrication —a concocted happenstance that never occurred! And now my engagement to Prince Phillip may possibly be terminated. Oh, how dreadful! Furthermore, if I do marry, the Queen Mum warned me, in no uncertain terms, that I shall be completely responsible for producing an heir to the throne, immediately. She said, "We are the House of Windsor, you do realize that?"

(See, now all the people are talking! You see that?! She caused all kinda problems for this family! I told you she was no good! Now, he's gonna buttel (break off the engagement), Alla Ye'Saaidnee! (God help me!) And the s**t never stops! If we do get married, my mother-in-law is already on me about making a boy! She says, "If you marry my son, you better make a boy, fast! You're the woman, it's your fault if there's no son to carry on the name!"

See what I mean?
We're just like them.
Scary, isn't it?

In the event that this alarmingly striking comparison just put you into total shock by mirroring your own tormented life, I suggest that you immediately delude yourself into thinking that you really are royalty. Pretending is an extremely useful psychological tool that will help protect you from completely cracking up. Just close your eyes real tight and begin the brainwashing process. Train yourself to believe that you really are a blue-blood member of the Royal House of *Whatever You Like*.

Soon, you will begin to feel differently about yourself and your role. You'll feel a sense of duty, entitlement and responsibility that you have never felt before. You will feel special, as if you were specifically chosen among all the elite in the kingdom to marry your prince. And if you succeed in producing male heirs, you will be adored by all. Then, you can bestow countless blessings upon your subjects from your second floor window ... *uhh* ... *I mean* ... from your palace balcony. And you can take long, early morning strolls in the secret garden of *"La-La Land."* Because honey, if that's what it's gonna take you to get through this thing, you better get to it 'cause it ain't gettin' no easier.

So there, pretend you're a royal princess, and everything will work out just fine.

I promise, your majesty.

I promise.

Why We're Always Late

We are always late because we have no concept of time.

None. None, whatsoever. And why should we? Our culture is lost in time. People from all over the world gravitate to our region because they feel a sense of timelessness. They feel like they can lose themselves in an exotic world so far removed from their own. They want to soothe themselves in the cool waters of a mirage. They want to melt away into the romance of the desert. They long to feel the magic kiss of Qais and Leila.[82] They want to indulge themselves in the rapture of the Middle East.

Time is suspended.
And we have no concept of time.

This is our culture.

---

82. Arabic story of forbidden love (along the lines of Romeo and Juliet).

With every breath, you lose your ability to remain grounded. You are not in this world at all. You are laughing, dancing, singing, enjoying. You are living. You are up all night, smoking *argeelee*, drinking, and just being with your friends. Dawn breaks. The Great Artist Himself has painted a breathtaking sky. And you all greet morning together. You don't feel a minute pass you by. It just slips away.

Before you know it, it's the end of August, your vacation is done, and it's time to come back to America. And you ask yourself, *"wayn rah elwa'et?"*[83] You are sad and crying a week before your flight even takes off. You want time to stand still—forever.

You don't want to wake up from this beautiful dream.
Alla ykhaleekay, lat Fay'ihnay.[84]

We have no concept of time.
And why should we?

We're always late because it's more fun that way

We're late for stuff. You know the story: we say we'll be there at one o'clock; we come at three. We say we'll be *just one minute;* we are *just one hour.* Our *haflis* don't even start until midnight. The main singer graces the stage at 1:00 a.m., and we dance all night.

Think how long it takes for us to cross the desert. If you take a car, surely you'll get there faster, but if you take an old fashioned caravan and do it the hard way how much more meaningful will the celebration be when you finally meet up with your loved ones? You appreciate your blessings so much more that way. You see, we have a certain mentality. We think, *"What's the big deal? We'll get there, eventually!"*

Besides that, Syria is like seven hours ahead of us; therefore, *theoretically*, they're actually *early*. Think about it. They're like almost *a half-day* early, so they can afford to hang out and wait. They've got all the time in the world. And us Arabs in America? What's our excuse? Well, we're here back in America, and we're

---

83. Where did the time go?

84. God please, don't wake me!

like seven hours *behind*. So we're thinking, "*Hey! We're seven hours behind. We're already late. There's nothing we can do about it now! Why fuss and get all upset? We'll just try for tomorrow.*"

It's been operating like that for centuries.

So, don't try to change it. You won't be able to anyway. It's like trying to fill in a black hole—you'll be swallowed up by its gravitational pull.

There is, however, one thing—actually, it's the only thing—that we're never late for, and that's getting married. It kinda seems that we do that one ... *well ... particularly early.*

Oh, and what am I thinking? Jeez! That's not true! We obey time. We watch clocks. Of course we do! Just the biological one, though. Yup! We count the seconds on that on that one, baby (Ouch! Sorry about the pun).

<u>Being late is not such a bad thing</u>
Come with me and let's take a short trip across the Atlantic to the western world, shall we?

We are so blessed here. We have everything we could possibly want, including the opportunity to get it, if we don't already have it. In America, anyone can walk off the street with little or no education, work hard, use their God-given talents, and become a millionaire. We've seen it happen over and over again in this country. These are truly blessings. The downside, as I've already talked about, is that most of us are stuck in a horrible rat race.

One of the things that resonated with me so strongly while visiting Syria is that, by nature, I'm pretty natural. And I've always gravitated to that which is natural. Like, I could *drink* olive oil—in fact, I think I have. Eating fresh spinach and olive oil makes me happy because they are good for my body. Eating those foods means I am giving my body what it needs. And my soul needs its own nutrition, too. I need to sing, laugh, drink *arak*, and tell jokes with my cousins. I think I might be some sort of hippy-chick underneath, I don't know. But anyway, it's natural. And I'm natural. And that's so much of why I felt like I was home again when I visited Syria.

I believe, in America, we've gotten way off course. It's a blessing not to suffer, but having life too easy ... *well* ... kinda makes life hard. What we need to do is turn this thing around a bit. Don't get me wrong, work is good—*very good.* We just need more balance. More playtime.

See, paradoxically, that extra play time is found when life is a bit harder, because it can be fun to *get through it together.* For example, if we're both waiting two hours for the *serveece*[85] to come, we can hang out, drink coffee together, and talk. In a spiritual way, it makes life more meaningful. Logistically, it stinks, but you get my point.

Or, if you're waiting for the water to come back on, and I'm waiting for the water to come back on, we can go *mishwarr* to the mountain spring and fill some empty bottles until it gets turned on. You know, that kind of thing.

Plus, their whole work day is scheduled differently than ours, too. For example, they work at like 7 a.m., and stop at 1 p.m. to break for lunch. And, then, sometimes, maybe if they feel like it, they'll go back in the evening for a little while. Or maybe not. It just depends, you know, like on how they feel at that moment. It's no big deal. I mean, it's not like they're going anywhere. Jeez, relax! Come on, they're gonna be there tomorrow for goodness sakes!

Try that in America.

I am getting a little concerned, though, because I heard from a very reliable source that in some parts, they're now implementing weekends. So, you know what that means, don't you? Structure. And that's not good. They're going in at 9 a.m. and leaving at 5 p.m. and having two consecutive days off. I don't like it. I don't like it one bit! The next thing you know, they'll be pushing for restricted sick days, time cards, and reduced comp days. Job productivity is going to replace fun as the number one priority. It's sick. And it's only going to get worse from there. If we don't put a stop to it now, some braino is gonna come up with the bright idea of implementing one-week vacations instead of month-long holidays! Then what? Then where will we be?

---

85. The jitney.

I don't like it. I don't like it one bit.

"B'tehkay Arabay?"[86]

Like most foreign languages, Arabic is divided into two categories: the formal and the familiar. For example, in France, when speaking with friends, one would use the word *"tu."* However, when conversing with the president, the appropriate term would be *"vous."* Us, Americans just get straight to the point, and only use one language whether we're talking with our boy or the prez. Unless of course, you're from South Central, then you have a whole different set of linguistic possibilities.

Suffice it to say that each individual Arabic country has its own distinctive familiar dialect that sets it apart from all others. The language itself is basically the same, but the particular accent is what gives it its unique twist. Much like a Texan can be easily distinguished from a New Yorker, the Syrian can be easily differentiated from the Egyptian. However, *all* Arabic countries use exactly the same *formal* language. Standard Classical Arabic, as it is called, is universally recognized by all Arab nations as the official language and does not change from one country to the next. It is also the one that is used for the written word.

Now that you understand all that, speak Arabic. It's vital to your legitimacy. If you were blessed enough to have an adult teach you the language when you were a child, then good for you. For those who weren't, learn it. It's not going to be that easy, either, because it's not just about using the proper syntax. You have to know the customs, phrases, and cultural behaviors that go with it as well. You also need to know when to use them appropriately and in the right context.

Speaking Arabic connects you to your rich heritage. It also allows you to understand when someone may be talking about you behind your back—or, in some cases, right to your face. What's more, it empowers you to respond to all kinds of insults. Hell, if you get really good, and you're up for a little fun, you can throw out a few of your own (first timers don't try this!). Just make sure that you're pronouncing your insults correctly, otherwise you'll look like a buffoon. *"Your mother was a hamster, and your father smelt of elderberries,"* just doesn't have the same effect, you know?

Go find someone to teach you Arabic, and make sure they know what they're talking about. If for some reason, you can't find anyone in your area, then my best advice is to take a trip to the motherland, and spend some quality time over there. Live

---

86. "Do you speak Arabic?"

amongst the natives, eat the *falafels,* take long *mishwarrs,* and, before you know it, my friend, you will find yourself being able to *"tehkay Arabee!"*[87] Now, all you have to do is learn what it is that you're saying. And more importantly, what it means.

Another thing: No matter how hard you try to conceal the fact that you are a non-native speaker, you should know that you'll be a dead giveaway the second you open your mouth. As I stated earlier, there are many different national and regional dialects. And then there is *yours.* Your dialect says, "Hi there. My name is so-and-so. I'm a foreigner. I'm trying to fit in." And believe me, your introduction speaks just as loudly as someone speaking broken English to an American. So, whether you like it or not, when you speak Arabic, you're gonna have an accent. And that cute little accent of yours is going to be your involuntary verbal resumé. It's going to reveal where you come from, your status, your level of education, and everything else you might want to keep confidential. Standard Classical Arabic, can be slightly less revealing (not by much, though.) So, if privacy is an issue, I'd stick with that.

Remember, Standard Classical Arabic is the official language used in formal settings. If you are speaking with somebody really important, like an ambassador, use that. On the other hand, if you want to call your brother a big *jahish*[88] colloquial Arabic would be the better choice.

One final bit of advice: Some people in the Middle East, particularly *sitos,* will just straight-up talk to you to in Arabic. Even if you tell them—in Arabic—*"Please stop, lady! I don't know what you're saying!"* they will continue rambling on with what they were saying—without missing a breath. And at the end of 10 minutes of torturing you, they'll look right in your eyes and ask: *Fhimti Alayee? Mazboot, saa'h?*[89]

Just nod your head.

---

87. Talk Arabic.

88. Jackass.

89. You see what I'm saying? I'm right, right?

Chapter 15

The Sperm in the Air Theory

I touched on this a bit back in Chapter 1, but it's such a fundamental part of our socialization—and such a damn hyper-sensitive topic—that it requires closer examination. Overseas, generally speaking, traditional Arabic women don't openly, casually or carelessly date. They date, but it's a different style of dating. And it's certainly not anything like the way Westerners go about it. Not by a long shot. In the Middle East, women are not exactly encouraged to go off traipsing about with every Tom, Dick and Harry that she finds attractive. In other words, she's generally not going from guy to guy to guy. Nor would she be open about it if she were. Essentially, she is not *freely* dating, as a Westerner might understand it. I'm not talking about hanging out with guy friends or just plain going out. I'm talking about openly and publicly dating as a bona fide couple, casually, and without any serious future marital plans.

Sex-and-the-City girls they are not.

Albeit, things are changing, but, for the most part, it's still a very different dating game over there. But that's not what's shocking. What's shocking is that this is not just true for women who reside in the motherland—it is also true for many traditional Arab-American females who live right here in the good old U.S. of A. It's true for those whose parents left the hot desert sands for the even hotter, steamier South Beach sands. The problem is that the dating game is a lot more confusing on these shores than it is over there. A whole lot more. And again, there are consequences.

And if you're a guy?

Well ...

Let's just say, if you're a guy—make that any guy, regardless of nationality—you pretty much get to do whatever you want, wherever you want, and with whomever you want, you know, without any serious repercussions. I'm not saying this to attack men; I'm saying it because it's true. Hey, whatever you do is your business, babe, not mine. But we all know that a guy can impregnate a loose chick during a drunken one-night stand and still come out smelling like a rose. Am I right? Thank you. So, right or wrong, fair or unfair, good or bad, that's just the way it is.

Now, you don't have to get all bitter about that double standard, and you certainly shouldn't think negatively about guys. They're just doing their part to ensure the survival of the species. It's a big responsibility. Good job, men! Evolutionary arguments aside, there are very good reasons for these rules and now that I am mature and wise, I fully support them.

You see, back in the day when I was young, naïve and impetuous—and didn't have a clue in the world—I would scream at my father for his antiquated idea that good Arabic girls were not to date. What was up with that? There I was, a teenager, trying to figure that one out. My American friends were openly dating, but why couldn't we? What was wrong with having a boyfriend? Of course, there were loopholes you could go through, like sneaking around to meet your man, but I wasn't into all that. Not this girl. I'm a strong-willed, fierce, independent chick, and if I was going to date, dammit! I was going to be normal about it!

Actually, I didn't have to sneak around, but as a fiery teenager I was just trying to make sense of the insane rationale. I was trying to sort out all the cultural confusion and spearhead the Arabic Equal Rights Dating Crusade. Plus, I thought not being allowed to openly date was really stupid.

At any rate, there I was at 15 years old dealing with this crazy mentality. My American brain was at war with my Arabic brain. And I was losing the battle on both sides. So, I, in natural, feisty Syrian-American *femme-fatale* fashion, would scream at the top of my lungs to my father, "What's wrong with you backwards people? Why the hell aren't we allowed to date? What are you people? Crazy? You're ridiculous! You old-fashioned farmers! It's the 20th century! Wake up! We're in America!"

To which my father, in natural, feisty Syrian *farmer-fatale* fashion, would scream back just as loud and say, "Whatchu tink? You crazy! You tink you date for fun? *La'net-ellah-ala-Sheetan!*[90] What matter wit' you? *Yaharek ...!*[91] You date for marriage, kid! Damn this generation! The end of the world is comin'! Damn kids, wanna go with a boy—just any boy, like nuthin? Technology gonna ruin this world! Damn technology! Gonna make the world end! You'll see! The world comin' to end! *Allah yela'n ...! Sheetan ...! Jahshee ...! Kaleb ...!*[92]

There was just one problem, though. For the life of me, I couldn't figure out how you went about marrying someone if you weren't allowed to even date him in the first place. It just didn't make any gosh darn sense to me. Some things are just naturally supposed to go in chronological order. You know: Step 1, *then* Step 2. It's like, you wash your hair, *then* apply the conditioner. Or you remove the old nail polish, *then* apply the new color. Or you get a medical degree, *then* practice surgery. That kind of thing, you know? Maybe I was overreacting, but I just couldn't get it. But silly me. Now, I understand.

Dating to them simply meant: Pick one! Any one! He's good enough. Good! There! Now you're done! The wedding is tomorrow! We'll pick you up at 2 p.m. *Matt towley?*[93] And that's it. You're married. Simple isn't it? I always complicate things. I do. Seriously. How easy is that?

Nowadays, not only do I understand my father, but I kind of agree with him, too. I mean, come on, why all the fuss? Dating is just like a really long, drawn-out, two-year interview, where you never really know if you're gonna get the job in the end, anyway. Besides, at any given moment, you might be laid off, your guy might be outsourcing your job without you even knowing it, or worse yet, you might even be flat out replaced by an inexperienced colleague much younger than yourself. So, I agree with his idea, except for one minor detail—that "love thing." You see, it's just that, that "love thing" keeps getting in the way. Aside from being a hopeless romantic, I am the type of person who doesn't fall in love easily, and when I do, it's hard. Real hard. See? See, how Syrian I am? It's always about love.

---

90. Cursing the devil.

91. Another common curse.

92. A rather complex curse somehow involving the devil a donkey, and a dog.

93. Don't be late, you hear?

Listen, I'm well aware that at times I can be overdramatic, unrealistic and way too romantic, but I just keep thinking about that thing that makes your life worth living and your soul fulfilled. That thing that makes you want to wake up every morning because he is with you, in your life. He is your breath. The man who finally brings you home to yourself, and with whom when you are together, experience intense spiritual energy. Even if the world is falling apart, when you are with him, everything is fine. That's when you should walk down the aisle.

And not a moment before.

In order for you to fully understand the difficulties that Arab-American girls have to face with regard to dating—and eventually finding her true love—you have to understand the complexities of living in the middle of two diametrically opposed cultures.

And you have to understand a little bit of history.

When many of our parents left the village decades ago, some of them just forgot to progress with the rest of the world. Hey, it happens. However, many of the villages back in the old country, even the ones with limited running water, kept moving forward. [94] As a result, ironically, some actually came out light years ahead of their American counterparts. The problems occurred because some of our people here clung on far too long—*and way damn too tight*—to their old ways. They retained a very "village" mentality, while simultaneously living (and planting roots) in a progressive, new American city.

So, after many decades of examining and re-examining this issue—and banging my head against a brick wall—I have come to a simple conclusion that basically boils down to one thing: bad timing.

That's it.

Nothing else.

Let me explain.

What happened was, when those immigrants set sail for the new world ... *all right, I'm sorry* ... when they boarded the plane at the airport, they truly had legitimate

---

94. Relatively speaking, of course.

reasons to protect their unmarried female children. So, they did everything in their power to ensure that their girls wouldn't fall victim to the dark side and evil temptations running so rampant in America. You know, like talking to boys and stuff.

When they arrived here, America was just wrapping up its own sexual revolution. Smoke was still rising from the bra burnings of the 1960s. The '70s were way too psychedelic for anyone, let alone a disoriented Arab immigrant. And the '80s ushered in AIDS, drive-by shootings, and crack. They were scared. And rightfully so. Think about it. If you came from such a conservative culture, you'd probably be scared, too.

But life in America wasn't always like that. You see, back in the day—during the 1930s, '40s and '50s—things were very different. Arab-Americans lived much more balanced and free lives. I personally have many photographs of young women all respectfully, tastefully and openly intermingling with real nice hottie Italian boys. It was no big deal. Everyone pretty much understood, accepted, and abided by the general social rules of the day.

But after JFK's assassination, America lost its innocence. Society spun way out of control, and nobody knew what the hell was going on, including Americans. Civil Rights riots, Woodstock, Vietnam, LSD and bad strobe lights—this place was crazy back then. So, those immigrants had their reasons, even if they were a bit extreme. I like to call it their own little culture shock. And boy, were they shocked! Things just got way too confusing for everybody. Cloudy and confusing. Just a big cloud of purple haze. Of course, until disco finally came along and straightened everything out. At that point, everyone just stopped analyzing and hit the dance floor!

Interestingly enough, life in the Middle East was more or less similar to life in America, before America hit its rough spots. Both cultures were nice and conservative, relatively speaking. Strangely enough, however, it just so happened that that was the exact same time when some villagers had the bright idea that it was finally time to cash in on those frequent flyer miles and head on over across the pond to find out what all the fuss was about.

Bad Timing.

Bad, Bad, Timing.

And that's why the younger generation can't appreciate this book. They just can't get it. They can't get it because they live a lovely life now. They have great timing.

You see, America had about two good decades to straighten things out for itself. We went through big hair in the '80s, and you can see where that got us. Grunge in the '90s—a direct, rebellious reaction to the '80s. And now that we're in the 2000s, we're finding out that we don't really need all that make-up and hairspray. Nor do we need to look like we haven't bathed for a month. And that it's okay to relax and just be ourselves. We're settling into the middle ground, if you will.

Much like an acne-prone, awkward, braces-wearing teenager who blossomed into a knock-out bombshell, we've had a lot of time to get adjusted and fill out, so to speak. Just growing pains, you know? The shock from both the Arab and the American sides is pretty much over. In addition, as we've learned from our *foo-foo* friends, the birth of the Internet and the satellite dish made it possible for everyone to look outside their windows and find out what their neighbors are up to *(and, heck, if they're getting away with it, then hey, why not, right)?*

Essentially, the immigrant's original flight to America foreshadowed the whole assimilation process of the early 1970s: like a real bad airplane ride with lots of unexpected turbulence and all kinds of unidentifiable things flying out of overhead compartments—oxygen masks automatically releasing and barely lit aisle lights to direct you to the nearest emergency exit. It's been a bumpy ride. But now, finally, we've got clear skies ahead of us. The captain has just turned off the seat belt sign. You are now free to move about your life.

It is important to understand however, that this was not the case with those Arabs who *remained* back in the Middle East. In fact, it was quite the opposite. There were no in-flight worries to concern yourself with or any sudden losses in cabin pressure. Since the flight plan remained practically unchanged since the dawn of time, it was a guaranteed smooth ride all the way. Non-stop direct service meant no long layovers in obscure places while waiting to make the right connection. Express arrival to your destination prevailed over the uncertainty of wandering around aimlessly in a labyrinth of empty gates and confusing terminals. Confirmed advanced reservations guaranteed a secure spot, eliminating the unpredictability which comes with standby status and experienced travel agents ensured a smooth transition. And that still holds true today. Because things are pretty much just as conservative as they've always been, girls over there don't have to deal with all the discombobulation and disorientation that girls in America have to deal with.

Thanks to a whole new generation of brave, adventurous test pilots, we in America have pushed the envelope and basically broke the sound barrier. *And let me tell you, it's always fun pushing envelopes and breaking barriers!* Unfortunately, however, all of the progress that's been made makes little difference anyway, because the fact still remains that the American boy may, or may not, know how to interact with an Arabic girl. And that, in and of itself, is still a threat—especially since those test pilots all have very different training backgrounds, various instrument ratings, and few qualified first officers who know how to accurately navigate the skies.

The primary difference is that overseas, gender roles are much more clearly defined and strictly adhered to, in part because "proper, appropriate and acceptable" socialization starts very early in childhood and is not only embedded, but also reinforced, in every single aspect of society. Therefore, since everyone is basically on the same page, there is very little, if any, room for behavioral confusion. For example, an Arabic boy knows exactly how to interact with an Arabic girl, i. e. , how he should behave, what his boundaries are, and what his boundaries *are not*, etc. (as well the consequences for violating them.) The boys learn to respect the girls like sisters; they protect and watch over them. It is their duty. There's even a phrase for it: *mindeer balna aleke* [95]

Likewise, girls enjoy the comfort of knowing that their male relatives and friends are looking out for them. Like any small community, everyone's keeping an eye out for each other, and as a result, it's really rather safe. [96] Keep in mind, however, that the village is one thing and the city is another. Having said that, alone at night, in overpopulated cities and far from international hotels, is not the best time for a single female to take an adventurous, fact-finding evening stroll by herself.

I know this from experience. During my first trip to Italy, back in 1989, a group of us girls got chased down by some hottie Italian guys on the hunt for loose American chicks. And we weren't even on a fact-finding anything. The only thing we were trying to find was food. Five guido-type guys jumped out of their car and chased us about a half a block before we ran screaming into a café. We weren't in any serious danger or anything; I think they were just out having some fun, but, for a minute, though, it was a little scary. Obviously, you gotta use common sense wherever you go. No walking down dark alleys letting everybody know you're the new tourist in town who's come to check out the place.

But as a general rule, in the Middle East, your cousin, your friend, your neighbor, or anyone who has a connection to you, will always be watching out for and

---

95. To watch over someone. We're watching over you (lookin' out for you).

96. Relatively speaking, of course.

protecting you. You, as their guest, are under their protection. It's like the Law of the Desert. It's honorable. Admittedly, it does get on your nerves a little and can sometimes get outta hand. Like when me and my male cousin walk into a camera shop, and the guy behind the counter is checking me out, and my cousin gets all up in his face: *"Aay! Whatta you lookin' at? Huh? I axxxed you a question! I'm talkin' to you! Look at her one more time, and I'll kill you dead, ya' hear? Now beat it, kid! Scram!"*

It's kind of a little ego booster in a sick, twisted way. Like, he'll get into a fist fight, just for you! You kinda get that *ooeey-gooey* girly feeling, like some big, hottie, macho guido-guy will beat up another guy just because he looked at you the wrong way. Or, in your opinion, looked at you *the right way*.

Anyway, it's taken me forever and a day, but after decades of unscientific analysis, I finally understand and accept the previous generations' conservative ways. Not necessarily *agree*—but understand and accept. However, as a 15-year-old, I didn't understand. I couldn't have. Sometimes they made the biggest deal out of the most stupidist things, like walking up the street in broad daylight—you know, at a time when boys are known to be roaming around. What the hell was that about? What? We needed to be escorted? To make sure we were protected? Protected from what? This is America, you whackos!

Well, one particular time—actually, the only time it ever happened—my female cousins and I ventured into dark and dangerous territory—we took a casual, summer stroll to the convenience store up the street. Unbeknownst to us, we were followed by an over-protective male member of the Arab community. And let me tell you, girl, when we found out, all hell broke loose! That was it. The final seal in the Book of Revelations had just cracked. Big, big mistake! Now, you have to understand that we were 20 typical, hyper-emotional females, with all the normal, erratic adolescent hormones that every girl possesses. One diva even more dramatic than the next.

We were furious.

FUR-I-OUS!

All at once we all marched on over to Aunt Aggie's front porch (my mother's house, which was the designated War Planning Room and official crisis meeting place for high-level emergency talks).

This was the big one.
We were fuming. We were livid.
And we were ready to kill!

And the boys in the family? They were smart. They hid. They were scared. And rightfully so. Their heads would have just been ripped off. No mercy. I'm telling you, it was fierce! I swear I saw fire coming out of one of the girl's mouths! It was that bad. Of all the fervent, heated, impassioned arguments we have ever had—this one topped them all.

And then.

All of sudden, a very strange thing happened.

About five-and-a-half hours later, after we completely exhausted ourselves from screaming our lungs out, everything suddenly just calmed down. A strange, yet beautiful, peace came over us. It was surreal. It was as if, all at once, the heavens opened up and the light from above shined down, breaking the dark clouds and ending the ferocious storm. I swear, what I experienced that day, was the gift of divine wisdom.

Upon careful examination, lots of chocolate, Doritos, and Diet Pepsi, we decided that the insanity wasn't insane after all. It made perfect sense the whole time. We just couldn't see it. Our minds—infected. Our hearts—deceived. Contaminated by evil Western logic. After about 2,800 calories per female, we decided that the only possible, logical explanation for such an absurd, irrational and asinine idea as to why we couldn't walk up the street without being followed by an overprotective male who had nothing better to do in his life was because there must have been Sperm In The Air!

Do you see now?

Imagine, just imagine, if one of us helpless, vulnerable girls would have been in the wrong place at the wrong time (*translation:* anywhere outside of the house), we could get inadvertently and indiscriminately hit by one of those little evil sperm thingies! Can you imagine? And if that would have happened, we could have—No, silly! Not died! Worse! Yes, worse than death! If one of us got accidentally hit, we could get pregnant and disgrace the family name! We would have, in a short trip to pick up a gallon of milk, a box of Juju Fruits, and some garbage bags on sale at half-price with a double-coupon, destroyed everything our family has ever sacrificed for their entire lives—other people's opinions!

Silly me!

Now, I understand!

They were just protecting us.

Better. Much better to walk in groups escorted by strong, overprotective males, rather than to fight one of those evil, little spermy thingies all by yourself.

And wouldn't you know it?

As a result, the most coveted, most guarded secret since the dawn of time has at last, been revealed:

Sperm has invisible wings, and does not die when it hits the air!

*****

<u>Other Ridiculous Widely Held Misconceptions</u>
There are simply too many absurd ones to list, but let me just share this one true story. I was telling my Arab-American girlfriend that I was writing a book about the difficulties of living in the middle of our two cultures. And this young, bright, 24-year-old doctor looks up at me and says, *"Dalel, I'm a doctor. I just gave a complete rectal exam to 36-year-old male patient the other day, and I get home, and my dad is giving me a hard time because I want to go out, and its 11:00 p.m. I mean, I'm in the exam room, checking for lumps in private parts of this guy's anatomy and I can't go out because it's 11 p.m."*

Sir, at this time, I would like to enter my plea of insanity.

Thank you.

I rest my case.

*****

(All joking aside, brace yourself, babe. Because whether you realize it or not, we're on the brink of a massive worldwide explosion and it's headed our way. Like a category five hurricane silently brewing offshore, all the conditions are right to create the perfect storm. And, like FEMA, nobody's paying much attention; even though the warning signs couldn't be any clearer. In case you haven't noticed, the Middle East is setting

itself up for its very own, long overdue, and unavoidable sexual revolution. And due to extreme radical elements, this one will have unprecedented global consequences. The levees are simply not capable of withstanding such a powerful psychological storm surge—they're gonna break.

Inch by inch, "perverted" Western culture is infesting conservative Arabic societies and poisoning its youth. Daring Iraqi girls are boldly, yet discretely, eyeing handsome American soldiers. Frustrated Arabic teenage girls are watching scantly-clad superstars shake their thangs in increasingly provocative Arabic music videos, and questioning why they can't do the same. Robust teenage boys are listening to 50 Cent with no viable way to express, or release, their own tumultuous energy. And young people are asserting their sexual independence with a rebelliousness never seen before in that part of the world. The desert heat is dizzying, the pressure is building up, and the new generation is ready to thrust forward. I'm telling you, the s**t's gonna hit the fan! Real hard. Real soon.

Just thought I'd give you the heads up.

CHAPTER 16

THE LEBANESE HAIRDRESSER—YOUR NEW BEST FRIEND!

"Queer Eye" has nothing on this guy.

Let me tell you about the Lebanese hairdresser. He is pure, raw talent. Forget everybody else; he is all you need to transform your life. Don't underestimate the Lebanese hairdresser. If you could bottle his talent, you, Bill Gates, and Oprah would all be neighbors. This man is the only human being that you could trust enough to say, *"Here, take my head. Do with it, as you please."*

He is an artist in the truest sense. A sculptor. The Michelangelo of hair. He is brilliant. Genius. And always on the cutting edge. He is a creator, a gift bestowed upon him by the great Architect Himself. With his priceless hands, he designs masterpieces of hair from nothing. Coiffure runs through his blood and in ever fiber of his being right down to his fingertips. His intuition is fierce. His style unparalleled.

And you?

You are his canvas.

The Lebanese hairdresser is like a world-renowned surgeon who performs rare, high-risk operations. He works with fascinating precision and laser-sharp focus. His instruments are straightening irons, scissors, and diffusers. And his operating room is his salon. His specialized training lies in reconstructive surgery, and correcting severe malpractice. To him, the definition of emergency medicine is

L'Oreal Professional Revitalizer. And his prescription for therapy is Redkin Anti-Snap Intense, Leave-in Conditioning Treatment.

The Lebanese hairdresser also has advanced training and is certified in Emergency Disaster Response Relief. When accidents happen, he's the first on the scene. He's the one working out in the field, providing rescue and recovery to tragic hair victims. And he never compromises his artistic integrity, either. He loves his job and finds the challenge of transforming a badly-colored head of over-processed damaged hair utterly exhilarating. It gets his adrenalin pumping.

He examines his subject. He studies her. All her vital information instantly pours into his brain. It's downloading data at lightening speed. Angles, cheekbone proportions, eyebrow symmetry, facial tones, eye color, hair color, personality, nose length. Every detail is considered. Any other human being would combust having that much data rush in so fast, but not him. He was born for this. The thrill. The adventure. The pathetic-looking creature sitting in his chair! He grabs a cigarette. And then another. He studies some more. You feel his eyes pierce into you. You feel his intensity. You feel his scissors coming towards you!

Nothing can break his concentration. He is thinking. He is analyzing. He is perspiring. His assistant wipes the sweat from his forehead. He thinks some more. Then! At last, he decides! *Yes! That's it!*

Slash! Go the Scissors! Slash!
Slash again!
(Your head spins!)
Breathe. Just Breathe.

(Whoa! ... I need a cigarette!)

Calm Down.
Count to 10, backwards.

Nine ... eight ... seven ... six ...

Cut here!
Cut there!

Twist!
Quick pin up!
Twist again!
Fast Clip!

Ouch! Sharp wet bangs slice your cornea!

His salon instantly transforms into a war zone! You find yourself hunting for trenches, fearing for your very life! You're crawling on all fours, trying to make it out alive! Bobby pins are flying everywhere! Above your head, it's a sea of flying hairpins! Big clips, small clips—everywhere!

Quick! HIT THE FLOOR! There goes another one!

Combs, brushes, styling tools—coming in from every direction! You're dodging them all!

INCOMING WOUNDED! (helicopter sound)
REPEAT. ...
INCOMING WOUNDED!

The hairspray fumes overwhelm you. Oxygen levels are rapidly decreasing. You can't breathe! You can't see anymore! It's all become a thick blanket of aerosol fog. You try to run for cover, but the sparks flying from the shorted-out curling iron wires are the only things lighting your path. And they're barely even visible! The reflection from the sparks hitting up against the sheets of highlighting foils temporarily blinds you. Bottles of conditioner fall and splatter, creating a slick, oil-like spill on the floor.

Chemicals, toner, bleach—flying everywhere!
You're caught in the crossfire. You're fighting for your life.
You're dehydrated, disoriented, and desperate!

Slash!
Slash!
Slash!

Four hours and three packs of Marlboro Reds later. ...

Voilà! He's done!

Whew!

You made it!

The masterpiece is complete.

And it's breathtaking.

You look absolutely stunning!

You need a cigarette.

Tonight, when you go to that *hafli* that you paid a *kazillion* dollars for, you will look divine. You'll wear that red, dramatic, off-the-shoulder, Oscar De La Renta gown. Your Harry Winston diamond necklace will lie ever-so naturally upon your neck. Your makeup will be flawless. Your hair will be in an updo, accented by tight swirls, and caressing your glowing face.

It's Oscar night, and you're ready for the red carpet.

When you walk into that room tonight, every head will turn. And every jaw will drop.

Who IS that?

You have arrived.

That man, the Lebanese hairdresser, created you.

You are his magnum opus.

He will be so happy for you, beaming with pride. Because, when you walked into his salon *(or his living room on the seventh floor of his ninth story walkup)*, you looked like hell. You almost sent him running screaming through the streets (right passed the gay guy who was startled to death by the *foo-foo)!*

But now?

Now, you look like royalty.

This man holds the ultimate power to your beauty. You should appreciate all that he has done for you. Remember, though, power is a sacred thing. It may be used for good. It may be used for evil. It may be used to make you look absolutely horrific!

One must be wary of those who hold power. Have we learned nothing from Frodo Baggins? Nothing? Three *Lord of the Rings* flicks, and we come out no wiser? Remember the ring? The ring controls you, and, when it's on, you are at the mercy of the Dark Lord Sauron—same thing with the Lebanese hairdresser. When you're in his chair, you are at the mercy of the Lebanese hairdresser. And don't kid yourself; everyone's got a dark side, even him. So, whatever you do, don't get on his bad side. Remember the *Orcs?* Do you want to look like that?

❈ ❈ ❈ ❈ ❈

Another word of caution: be extra careful. Illegal hairspray trafficking is on the rise, particularly in Southeast Asia. Aqua Net Extra Hold and the pharmaceutical-grade form of Super Hold are considered among the deadliest and most traded on the black market, with an average of two million kilo tons being smuggled in per day. It's a known fact that *foo-foos* are on the FBI Watch List for using unlawful amounts of hairspray.

Who do you think is supplying them?

Chapter 17

French Women Aren't The Only Ones Who Don't Get Fat

As a woman, it's critical to take care of yourself—physically, emotionally, mentally and spiritually. It's your responsibility and nobody else's. When you commit to yourself in a healthy way, you will discover that you can't help but feel fantastic about yourself. And it will show. You will feel such enthusiasm for life, whether you have a man in it or not. Because we all know by now that happiness lies within. And we all want happiness, don't we?

So, condition yourself to eat fresh vegetables everyday. Not fried vegetables hidden under some genetically-engineered sour crème or under some mysterious cheese-food product that can be used to caulk your bathtub. I mean fresh spinach salads, greens and the like. Take care of your mind. Do what you need to do to achieve clarity and strength. Put God first. And try to keep your emotions in check. Exercise. Smile. Be grateful. And enjoy your life.

Now, given that, know this ...

You cannot be overweight and go to Syria. You just can't. And don't even think about Lebanon. It's completely out of the question. You can go to Egypt though, and I hear Jordan is quite forgiving, but that's about it. Actually, Egypt for some reason tends to find thicker women slightly more attractive. But the truth of the matter is that most others don't really see much appeal in a large, plus-size single woman. Sorry girls, I know it hurts, but I'd rather you know up front.

But don't take it personally, it's a cultural thing. You see, Arabic women, like most other Mediterranean women, value appearances—a lot. It's just in their nature. Men are visual creatures. And, by now you know that the whole country is pretty much all about getting married. So, you should look your best if you're in the market for a husband. And basically every female in the country is in the market for a husband. My advice? Reinvent your image, shed those unwanted pounds, and forgo the humiliation.

Unfortunately, women living in the Middle East have a slight advantage over the rest of us. It's called *metabolism*. You see, they are naturally thinner simply because of their lifestyle. In the summertime, for example, they dance in the middle of the afternoon and sometimes, again, in the middle of the night. They climb up big mountains in four inch heels, and they don't drive. They walk everywhere, all the time. They eat fresh fruits and vegetables. Every morning local farmers drive truckloads of their newly-picked produce and sell them right in the villages. And since their food is, for the most part, unprocessed, a peach actually tastes like the peach God intended it to. The milkman is at the door no later than 9 a.m. because that's when the cow has just been milked. It's that fresh. So, given their circumstances, of course they're going to be thinner.

Look, I'm not telling you that you can't enter certain Arabic countries if you're overweight because I want you to feel bad about yourself. Not at all. It happens to be the truth. And … It's the law. As I stated before, in Egypt, you're fine, welcomed even. But I think that back in March of last year Lebanon's National Assembly issued a government decree stating that all visitors, regardless of citizenship status, will be denied entry visas at the border if their BMI (Body Mass Index) is above 22%. Yup. No kidding. They won't let you in the country. You will politely be asked to leave and escorted out if necessary. Much like the strict anti-pollution laws in Singapore, they don't play around. And honestly, can you blame them? I mean they worked hard for their reputation; they have every right to protect it. Even their *sitos* dress sexy. I even heard they wear bikinis and such. *Oh, I'm sorry. You're right. I forgot about that.* There are no *sitos* in Lebanon only *taytas*. [97]

Now Syria, I understand, allows for a slightly larger BMI range. I am told that customs officers there will allow a person to enter the country if they have a BMI anywhere up to 23%. And if I'm not mistaken, I believe that, under certain spe-

---

97. Just a chic way to say *sito*.

cial circumstances, you might be able to get that extended up to 23. 5%. Again, I'm not completely sure, so you will want to check with the embassy beforehand.

The reason that I am emphasizing this whole weight thing is for the sake of your own dignity. Believe me; you don't want to experience what other women have described as nothing short of mortifying. Not that they were denied entry, but they were shamelessly put on the spot and embarrassed. The sad truth is that some undignified and unrefined women will look you straight in the eye and tell you how fat you are. Not all, but some. Most really don't mean any harm. And others? Yup, they mean harm. They can be downright cruel and make you want to cry. But hey, every culture's got their share of wicked women, right? If, however, you speak fluent Arabic, you are automatically exempt because you can defend yourself by pleasantly telling them to kiss off and informing them that you are happy just the way you are. Regardless of their motive, these women will, in a room full of company—and during a rare moment of silence—loudly say …

"Honey, you too fat! You too fat is no good *(she'll squeeze your left thigh real tight to show you).* See! No nice for you *(point finger in your face)!* You make diet, okay? Zis one cabbage diet. Yes, you eat cabbage everyday for one month and you lose one hundred pounds. Do zis one she call him Souws B**ch."[98] And in two octaves higher than her natural voice she will screech, *"la taakly khibbiz!"*[99] Then she will smile and grab your chin as if you were six years old and issue you a blessing: *"Inaay, dakheelic! Alla ykhaleekee!"*[100]

Remember that special word we learned back in Chapter 11?

Yup. That's the one. Let's say it together this time. …

Hu-mi-li-a-tion?

Good girl.

---

98. South Beach (Diet).

99. Don't eat bread!

100. Sweetheart! God keep you!

(Note: In order to simplify things, from here on in—all future *inaays, dakheelics, habeebees,* and other affectionate terms will be generally referred to as "sweetheart" and/or "angel" [the Arabic language is just too poetic, and I don't have time to explain everything])!

Listen to me, darling. If there were ever a moment when you needed just the right jump-start to motivate you to finally lose those extra unwanted pounds, that, I'd say, would be the one. Bear in mind, sweetheart, that the secret to successful weight loss is not to make a big ordeal out of it. Keep it simple. Just don't eat. That's it. Oh, and try not to exercise. But if you must, don't break a sweat. It doesn't look very nice.

Even if you aren't currently in the market for a husband, understand that appearances are very important in Mediterranean cultures. That's just the way it is. Both men and women from that part of the world take a great deal of pride in looking chic and stylish. Whether it be Italy, Greece, Spain or France, fashion is top priority. Come on, even the Pope wears *Prada*.

I'm convinced it's the Mediterranean lifestyle that makes one feel so sensual. The sun, the climate, the wine, the desert, the romance, the dance, the sea itself. The sea is open, vibrant and all-embracing. It is seductive. There is an indescribable, powerful sensual energy that stimulates and awakens one's raw primal instincts, making one feel natural, uninhibited, alive and free. Living in an environment where you feel so candid, natural, open and sexy makes you feel different inside. It makes you feel special. It makes you feel like a woman. Like Sophia Loren.

When Mediterranean women step outside, generally speaking, they look good even if it's just to get the mail. Their fashion sense is very feminine and they know how to play it up. Unfortunately, many of us American females have lost that very precious part of ourselves that makes us feel womanly. And we need to get it back. Fast. We don't have to give up our inner-strength, independent spirit or anything else that makes us who we are; we just need to give that inner goddess a little breathing room. In the States, it's just fine to pull your hair back, throw on a pair of old sweats, and walk out the door before your morning coffee. Not good. Not good, at all.

Ladies, in the interest of full disclosure, I have to tell you I'm an ex-con. Yup. A repeat offender. Like a pathetic heroine addict, I've been in and out of fashion prison for the most heinous crimes. Maximum security, too. Sad, but true. And, believe me it ain't a pretty place to be. No pun intended. So, I speak to you from experience. I'm in recovery right now, working a 12-step. It's not easy. I take it one day at a time.

Look, please don't misunderstand me; there's nothing wrong with walking out the door in sweats. And it certainly doesn't mean that you can't feel sexy in them. You can feel quiet sexy in sweats. Think J. Lo. Even when she's dressed down, she's dressed up. That's the great thing about America, though. Here, you can wear a sports bra with your midriff fully exposed, baring your toned back, and take a three-mile run in a public park. Can't do that everywhere. Nope. No ma'am, you can't. Freedom. Now, that's *real* beauty. Let me just say for the record, that Angelina Jolie took the words right out of my mouth when she said, "I don't feel pretty when I'm all made up. I feel beautiful when I'm out in the middle of nowhere, and I'm sweating and working really hard. That's when I feel beautiful." I'm right there with her. Throw me in the middle of Africa in the hot desert sun and let me feel the raw earth with my bare hands, then I'll feel beautiful.

All I'm trying to say is that it's nice to feel sexy and feminine, you know, even if you have to take out the trash all by yourself. You don't have to wear a stitch of makeup; it's just about who you are: how you carry yourself, how you live your life, and what you believe. It's about your inner spirit. It's about conviction, confidence. It's about presentation. When asked about sex appeal, Sophia Loren replied, "50% of sex appeal is what you have and the other 50% is what people *think* you have."

Sophia Loren, Tina Turner, Lauren Hutton. These are all spirited women who never gave up on themselves. They look fabulous. I mean come on, I'm leg pressing 190 pounds at the gym, and Tina Turner's legs are in better shape than mine will ever be. And she's like 70-years-old! That's sick. That's what gets me. They're like freakin' senior citizens or something. Retirement, my ass! That's bulls**t! They're cashing in those social security checks and buying Dolce & Gabanna stilettos.

We need to learn from them.

They've got personal style. And you know the best part about having personal style? The best part is that you don't have to bust your bank account to get it. That's right. Just ask any Arabic girl; she knows. Because bargains, my dear, are an Arabic girl's best friend. You know exactly what I'm talking about, too! Oh yes, you do!

It's New Year's Eve. You're all at the Grand *Hafli* dressed to kill. Glitter and sequins are blinding the elderly. The combination of a thousand different perfumes is suffocating the banquet staff. And all you girls are primping in the bathroom during the band's two hour break. You're all crammed in there, all 300 of you. Each doing your own thing. Touching up your lipstick, mending the runner in your pantyhose with clear nail polish, fixing your bra straps, comparing nose jobs, swapping hairpins, massaging your aching feet and gossiping about who's wearing what, and just how slutty they look in it. And you're all complimenting each other. Oh, let me tell you! It's a complimenting festival in there! There is just so much BS going on that you have to come up for air every 10 seconds.

You're all in there telling each other how beautiful you look. Even from within the stalls your mouths are running, "Oh, you look so gorgeous! Turn around!" "Oh you lost some weight didn't you? Nice and skinny. No, I'm serious. You did. I could tell right away!" *(Thank you. I'm on this new diet. You just eat one grapefruit in the morning, and you can have all the fat you want, all day long, and you lose like 10 pounds in the first day.)* "Are those *new* blond highlights? Oh, they're gorgeous! No really, I mean it, because they look so different from your *old* blond highlights. Who does your hair, anyway?" "Oh, you look like a queen! Doesn't she look like a queen? Where in the world did you get that gorgeous dress? I absolutely love it!"

And like a kid on Christmas morning, their eyes light up! They are so relieved you asked. They have been waiting. Waiting for somebody—anybody—to ask that very question.

"Do you know how much I paid for this diamond-laced, backless, strapless, turquoise, hand-stitched, sequined, French Chiffon, slit-up-the-side, designer gown?"

"Guess!"

"No guess! Come on! What do you think?" (She twirls around with a great big smile.)

Can't you just take one lousy, stinking guess?

"JUST GUESS!"

"$5.00!" *(smerk)*

"Can you believe it?"

"$5.00!"

"It was originally $4,978 and 52 cents—plus tax without the store coupon—and I got it for $5.00!"

"*Walla! An Jad!*"[101]

---

101. Really! Seriously (I swear)!

"You can barely even buy a McDonald's Happy Meal for $5.00!" (Comparison shopping—it's one of our obsessions). It's a little tight here around the waist, I mean it's not perfect. And it's kind of hard to breath, you know, when I sit down for more than five seconds at a time. But you can't really tell, right?"

They are just so proud of themselves. They secretly think, "I am so good. I'm the bargain queen! They all wish they had my shopping skills!" We get really excited about those kinds of things. It's not about the dress at all. It's about the bargain, itself. I guess all women get happy, but us Arabs take it to a totally different level. It's like a personal victory or something. It's embarrassing sometimes.

Chapter 18

Takin' the Jitney to Homs

Nobody in Syria owns a car. All right, that's not true. Some do, but most don't. So, how do people get around? They take the jitney. Or, rather, *"the serveece."*[102]

The importance of the jitney driver to Arabic culture cannot be underestimated. They are an extremely valuable resource. In fact, they are so important that the Ministries of Tourism would do well if they implemented a program devoted entirely to the sole development of the Arabic jitney driver. They could assign it a nifty name, like "The Service for the *Serveece.*"

For instance, if they were to take any jitney driver and offer them the basics—free unlimited use of showers, lots of free soap, free deodorant, free mouthwash, classes in hygiene management, plus medical and dental (because some need teeth real bad)—and, then, polished him up a bit, you know, refined him a little, groomed him, trained him in proper social skills, instructed him on how to contain his saliva while conversing with paying customers, and gave him a free copy of *The Proper Way to Handle Foreigners While In Your Cab*, countries would see a massive surge in economic growth. Tourism would explode, business would skyrocket, and, best of all, those countries would attain so much economic power that they could turn around and apply sanctions to nations that weren't very nice to them before.

---

102. Pronounced *"ser-veece."*

The Serveece

The *serveece* is the fun way to go. Actually, most of the times, it's the *only* way to go. Literally. Everybody crams in the van. And, usually, it's a not-so-new, non-air-conditioned, no-shock-absorbers-of-any-kind, highly-possible-to-break-down-at-any-given-moment, gas-guzzling, black-smoke-diesel-fuel, environmental-emissions-nightmare, 15-seater van. There are no designated, scheduled stops. No specific, predetermined routes. No backlogs to fill out. No quotas to meet. It just picks you up and takes you where you want to go, if it has room.

And it always has room.

Designed for the budget traveler in mind, the *serveece* has a "general admission policy" so generally everyone's admitted. You see, with no annoying fire marshal codes or maximum capacity seating limitations to comply with, everyone is welcome to just pile on in. And the savings get passed on to you.

But cheap fares aren't the only thing that keeps customers coming back. I'm convinced it's the rush.

Safety belts? No way! You're on an adventure, baby! Speed limit? For what? Stop signs? Get over yourself, already! And that's just in the cities. Wait till you drive up in the mountains. That's when it gets really fun. A seven-thousand-foot drop three feet from the edge on a one-lane road with drivers coming in from both directions. Oh, and did I mention no guard rails? Or street lights? Or reflectors of any kind? No mile markers. No emergency road pull-offs. No emergency phone lines.

And let me tell you, those mountain villages have the steepest, most curvaceous, tiny, little streets you ever saw! Spin here! Spin there! Spin! Spin! Everywhere! *Round the corner here we come! And round the corner there we go!* At really fast speeds, too! Every straightaway is a raceway! Everyone's a Jeff Gordon!

Nobody uses their signals to switch lanes, either. That would just be way too weird. Actually, you might even *get* a ticket for using one. There are only three traffic lights in Syria's third largest city, Homs. I know; I counted them. And nobody pays attention to them, anyway. I think they're just there for decoration, you know, to impress tourists or something. But, hey, we're still better than Cairo; they only have one. *And nobody pays attention to that one!*

When you're traveling on the highway, you'll get to see all kinds of neat stuff that you never saw before in your whole life and probably that you *won't ever see again* in your whole life. Only hours after I arrived in Syria, I witnessed something I had never seen or even imagined possible. Upon our arrival into Damascus, my uncle had arranged for a big magic bus to transport us from the airport to our hometown village, which was about three hours north. I was astutely aware that I was completely exhausted. After all, none of us slept for two days straight because we were traveling non-stop. We were totally sleep deprived and beyond jet-lagged. I dozed off a couple of times during the ride, but once, when I looked out my window from the big magic bus, I thought I might have been hallucinating. Yes, I was on a trip. Yes, I was on a magic bus. Yes, there was lots of smoke. But I assure you, I was not hallucinating. I did a double-take because I could not believe what I saw.

I glanced out of my window, and, in the very next lane, right below us, I saw a two-year-old girl driving a motorcycle. She was the most adorable little thing you ever saw in your whole entire life! She had on a cute little pink dress, with soft, lacey frills at the bottom. She was wearing little baby white socks and teeny-tiny shoes and a little pink elastic band around her bald head. *And she was burnin' rubber!* Her dad was behind her, actually *doing* the driving, but she was right there steering! I swear on my life, I saw this!

Unbelievable.

You'd think her dad would have at least remembered to strap on her Little Mermaid helmet or her Elmo motorcycle goggles! After all, she was the one weaving through all the traffic!

I'm just warning you right now if you go there, you're gonna see lots of crazy things.

And, you're gonna smell them, too.

I'm not sure if they think that black circular clouds of smoke dissipating into the air is visually fascinating or what. But I do know one thing for certain, no one seems to have ever heard of the English words "State Emissions Vehicle Testing." Nope. Not even the concept of it. Diesel fuel? Yes. Air quality? Sorry, no.

Trust me, nothing quite captures the feel of a Middle Eastern country like a long drive down a highway on a blazing, hot summer day. There is … *how shall I say* … a tantalizing aroma that fills the atmosphere. One which hints of a bouquet of toxic exhaust fumes, mixed with a dash of scorching, dry desert heat, and more than just a slight whisper of low grade asphalt. This unique rough and crude fragrance is a refreshing change from the usual clean, floral mists often found in the rural mountains. I personally feel that the gritty combination brings a certain authenticity to the whole experience and completely eliminates any shred of doubt that you are in the heart of a foreign country. It's as raw as it gets, babe. It's totally real. And I love it.

I suggest that you embrace the entire experience to the fullest. Take it all in. Roll down the windows. Put on some good Arabic music. Sing, clap, and dance. Let the warm breeze blow in your hair. Feel the strong desert heat. Drink cold bottled water. Bask in the glow of the sun. Let the sun kiss your face. Stare up at the clear blue sky.

Then you'll really experience the Middle East.

But, like I said, the drivers are what make it all so much fun. Get a fun driver, and brace yourself for an adventure because a *serveece* ride is like a rollercoaster ride at your favorite amusement park. Turns here! Turns there! Sudden stops for sheep crossing the street! Sudden stops for children crossing the street! Sudden stops just to say "Hi" to whoever is crossing the street! The ride is jumpy and bumpy! And full of surprises! Plus, they have the cutest, most funnest sounding horns, ever. But, just like any rollercoaster, there is a certain risk you assume when riding in one of these. And that risk is the possibility of losing your life.

Let me explain.

"Hamdillassalamee" and "Allay Selmek"
Upon my safe arrival from an out-of-town trip (while I was still in the States), my cousin gave me a big hug and said, *"Hamdillassalamee!"* I replied, *"Thanks. You know it's only a five hour trip from D. C. to Pittsburgh, so it's no big deal. But thanks, anyway."* She looked at me rather strangely and asked if I actually knew the meaning of the saying. And I casually told her, *"No. Not really."* So, she explained to me that it means something to the effect of *"Thank God you have arrived safely from your journey."* So, I said, *"Oh, well, isn't that nice,"* and then shrugged it off.

Then I went to Syria.

Now I know why they say, *"Hamdillassalamee."*

You don't know if you're going to make it off the freakin' mountain alive or not. It's true. A seven-thousand-foot drop three feet from the edge on a one-lane road with drivers coming in from both directions—and not a rail in sight.

If, by chance, you were lucky enough to get off the mountain alive, then it's a miracle! Then one says with conviction to the traveler, "Thank God you got off the mountain alive!" And since Arabs truly understand how dangerous the feat was and how fortunate you are to have escaped this near-death experience, you respond with gratitude by saying, *"Allay Selmek,"* which is loosely interpreted as *"You ain't lyin', girl!"*[103]

Hamdillassalamee!
Allay Selmek!

Get it now?

In some parts of the country the roads are truly that dangerous. No lie. Especially with your *happy-go-lucky* jitney driver. And trust me, babe, it's not like there are Search and Rescue Teams readily available 24/7 up in them mountains, you know what I'm sayin'? *CSI: Syria* is not yet available in all areas. Two whole days might pass before someone realizes you haven't arrived at your destination. Let's also factor in that your jitney driver more than likely had a couple of glasses of *arak* during lunch that day. And, who knows, maybe even during dinner that evening.

So, my friend, when someone says, *"Hamdillassalamee"* to you, respond with the utmost appreciation and gratitude by saying *"Allay Selmek!"*

"Khidnee"
Khidnee is another rather important term that I learned during my trip to the Middle East. It's so important that I think you should learn it, too. *Khidnee* literally means "take me with you." I've always known the translation, but I never really knew what the word *meant*. I'm talking about the true, underlying significance and *deeper meaning* of the word *Khidnee*.

You see, the thing about the mountain is that not only do you not know if you're going to get off of it alive, but even more than that, you honestly don't know *if* you're going to get off the mountain at all. Ever. And, in the event that you actually do, when roughly, that might possibly happen. You really can't get off by yourself; I mean, you need a ride because there's just no way without a car. I guess, technically, you could walk, but that will take a couple of days—and nights—and that rigorous trek will most likely just lead you to another mountain,

---

103. Really means God keep you safe.

anyway. Because all there are up in them mountains *are basically, other mountains.* They tend to show up in ranges, you know?

That's why, when they see you, they all ask, *"wayn rayeh?"*[104] Because they're thinking, *"I've been trying to get off this mountain for three days now, and it's a really long walk downhill. Plus, last time, I got lost for a month. I'm not doing that again! If you're going down the mountain, you could to take me with you!"*

"Khidnee"—"Take me with you."

Which, of course, brings me straight to *Khaltay Selma*.

Khaltay Selma,[105] *dakheel, inaa,*[106] has been trying to get off the mountain since 1956. Literally. The woman is still hoping and waiting. She's 93-years-old, and she's been packed and ready to go since 1956. She's been wearing the same black dress, the same black scarf, the same black pantyhose, the same black shoes, and she's got the same plastic grocery bag she's been carrying with her which contains her soap, her teeth, and about seven bobby pins. She's all ready to go.

In 1956, she told my father, *"Khidnay ma'ac, ya inaay, ya Michael. … Khidnay al America! Inaay, Dakheelak!"*[107]

During this last trip, we made it a point to visit *Khaltay Selma*. The instant she recognized my father, her eyes swelled up, and she burst into tears. It was truly a beautiful moment. Mind you, this was my father's second visit back to Syria since leaving for America nearly 50 years earlier. And only his first visit back to see *Khaltay Selma*. There, standing in front her, was her favorite nephew whose face she hadn't seen since he was a young man. My dad had told her—like any young, brave pioneer headed for America—that he would be back for her soon.

They sat with each other for a long time, talking, looking at old photos, and crying. Afterwards, we took her into the *serveece* with us so that we could all go and visit other family members, together. This sweet, frail, old woman was so happy to be with us, and, of course, we were so happy to be with her. Finally, we arrived at our destination, but she wouldn't get out. We kept telling her this was the right

---

104. "Where are you going?"

105. Aunt Selma.

106. Sweetheart, angel.

107. Take me with you, my sweetheart, my Michael…. Take me to America! Sweetheart, angel!

stop, but she didn't believe us. Needless to say, she had this mistrustful look on her face, real suspicious-like. And she wasn't budging. It took some coaxing, but, after a while, she eventually emerged from the vehicle. I think she thought she was finally going back to America with us. *Yaharam!*[108] Poor *Khaltay Selma*.

I blame my father. I really do. That wasn't right.

Khidnee.

I, personally, have a deep, profound appreciation for that word now. You see, I, too, like *Khaltay Selma*, was stuck on the mountain. Only for a day—but let me tell you, girl, that's all it took!

1956–2004. That's a *long* time.

Believe it or not, however, there are some people who don't ever want to come off the mountain—at all. They see no reason to. They just like to ride from village to village to village. But they take the *serveece,* you know, just for the fun of it. Like I said, it's one big party. The driver's always got his *imseglee*[109] blasting the best music, and everyone's clapping, singing, and dancing.

It's like a mini-hafli in a mini-van!

And no matter where you're going, who the jitney driver is, or where he's from, they all have this one particular song playing all the time. I call it *The Jitney Song* and it's *slammin'!* I don't know who sings it. I don't know its real title. I don't even know how long it's been around. But all the drivers have it, and they're all playin' it. It's like the official anthem of the National Association of Consolidated Jitney Drivers, and it's mandatory that it's played every time a new passenger enters the van. It's kinda like the official "Welcome" song. To welcome you. *"Welcome into my humble serveece. Welcome! Welcome! Welcome!"* The song is very upbeat and happy! It just makes you want to get up and dance. Actually, you *do* get up and dance.

Then, of course, everyone's got their *bizzer.* And they're crackin' *bizzer* all over the place—shells are all over the floor. All the women have their plastic grocery bags filled with their *garaad,*[110] and they all carry little tissues in their hands. They always have little crunched up tissues in their hands, but only the women. Which

---

108. What a shame!

109. Cassette player.

110. Stuff.

brings me to an entirely different subject. I don't know the answer to this, and I'd sure like to find out, but I have no idea why there aren't any napkins over there. No napkins. No paper napkins what-so-ever. Tissues? Oh yeah! Tons! Puffs, Kleenex, generic brand—you name it. But napkins? Not one.

I want to go and open up a napkin factory and see if it catches on.

The Jitney's Got the Hook Up

Jitney drivers in the Middle East are totally hooked up. He is your man when you're in town. He knows everybody and can get you anything. He's your own all-inclusive Home Shopping Network. Your personal concierge.

And that's exactly why they should be managed by the Ministries of Tourism.

Say, for example, that you want to get from Point A to Point B, and you call a jitney driver to take you there. By the end of the day, you will have gone from Point A to *Point Z*—without ever having planned to. You see, he'll take you to the *souk* to get all your shopping done. But, say, you need a certain item that you can't find there. Well, of course, he knows someone who sells it. And if that person doesn't have it, he'll know his competition. And, it goes without saying, *his competition's, competition.* And so on and so forth. Whatever the case, he'll keep driving you around until you get what you want. Guaranteed.

Need a hotel in Damascus? He'll find you the best (it's his cousin's). Need a good restaurant to entertain friends? He'll take you to the finest (it's his buddy's). Need a document translated? He'll drive you to a lawyer (it's his uncle). You see, he knows where everything is as well as all the stops in between. Want to buy a souvenir? His brother-in-law has a roadside stand, just over yonder.

He'll even negotiate for you.

That's right. He'll wheel and deal to get the best price for you. And, if you think that isn't enough, he'll do all the interpreting for you! Yes ma'am! In addition to being a transportation engineer, he is also, by trade, a trans-lingual interpreter, as well as a financial broker. He may not have any particular certificate or anything or any official document authorizing him as such—or for that matter any formal training—but he'll do just fine.

He'll translate whatever the seller is trying to tell you. Or, in some cases, what *he* wants the seller to tell you. And he'll tell the seller what you want to tell him. Or, in some cases, what *he* wants you to tell him. *He'll even answer for you.* Sometimes, you might not know it or anything, but, still, that's nice of him to be so accommodating.

Yes, this man will not only *think* for you, but sometimes he'll weigh out all the options and *decide* for you! You know, based on his particular mood at that particular moment. Nice, huh? He'll let you know if it's a good price or if the guy is ripping the shirt right off your back. In fact, a good jitney driver—a solid and honorable one—will never let you pay more than *he thinks* the merchandise is worth.

> *Traveler's Extra Bonus Tip: If you discovered during your trip that you've somehow become strangely addicted to all the disorganization and chaos, and find yourself craving one last, good old-fashioned anxiety attack, then by all means, take the jitney to the airport to catch your departure flight. Your driver just might wait to the very last possible minute to leave, but somehow, someway, he'll get you there right on time.*

Chapter 19

Why Kids in the Middle East Drink and Drive—and Why it's Okay

To say that kids are important to Arabic society is a huge understatement. Arabic children are the very lifeblood and pulse of the country. They have a critical and tremendously difficult role to play—a role most Westerners wouldn't be able to even begin to comprehend. I'm not talking about the *value* of children because all children are equally precious. Nor am I talking about *having* children. I am talking about *them, themselves*—the *importance* of Arabic children.

Kids in the Middle East are vital to the economy, social structure, and basic way of life. In fact, they are so vital that, without them, whole economies would just collapse, governments would go bankrupt, and civil war would break out.

You see, over there, children are taught from a very early age to be extremely mature, responsible, and independent. They're like "little-big people." Kids over there do things that kids over here would never dream of. But keep in mind, Arabic society is conducive to that. Actually, it's strategically designed that way. For instance, it's not uncommon in the Middle East for kids to be playing out in the street on a summer night unsupervised at 11 p.m. It's completely safe. I mean, who's gonna snatch your kid away? Your uncle? Yeah, right! Then just march right on over across the street, and get him back! It's no big deal!

As I explained earlier, it's safe over there, and everyone watches out for each other. Remember the phrase *Mindeer balna aleke?*[111] The community sees your child as their own. It's like the whole *It Takes a Village to Raise a Child* thing. I actually never read Hillary's book; I'm just referring to the catchy title because in the Middle East the whole village really does raise your child, whether you like it or not.

At any rate, kids are very important because they do all kinds of things that help the adults out tremendously. Take shopping for example. Overseas, you can give a kid five bucks and send him to the store to pick up two packs of Marlboro Lights, an international phone card, a prescription, and a pound of fresh ground coffee. You'll have no qualms about it. And neither will anyone else.

Imagine sending your six-year-old to the supermarket in America. To pick up cigarettes? Or legalized drugs?

With cash?

Can you say C. P. S?[112]

You'd be slapped with so many child endangerment charges your head will spin.

But over there? No problem.

And just like the jitney driver, the kids know everything. In fact, I think they know *more* than the jitney driver. You know what? On second thought, forget the jitney driver all together, he's overrated. The kid is your man! He'll hook you up. He'll take care of you. Except for one thing. He can't drive. That can be a bit of a problem. *Oh no ... wait ... forget that, too. Yes he can! I'm sorry, silly me! What am I thinking? They can drive. Ahh ... they do drive (they just don't have licenses yet, but more on that in a moment).*

Envision having your very own eight-year-old personal assistant without ever having to worry about violating child labor laws. Amazing isn't it? And let me tell you, they're rated number-one in efficiency, on-time delivery, and overall customer satisfaction.

Designer gown needs hemmed before five? No problem. This kid won't just *tell* you where the seamstress is located, he'll personally take your priceless garment to

---

111. To watch over someone. We're watching over you (lookin' out).

112. Child Protective Services?

his aunt's shop down the street. He'll even pick it up and deliver it to you by mid-afternoon the same day. Need a manicure? Tell him to go to the shop up the road and inform the lady that you need your nails done by eight. He's off and running! Laundry detergent prices getting you down? Don't worry, he'll shop around and get you the right price for your hard-earned dollar.

Sometimes, they'll offer the extra-added personal touch of 24-hour service, without you even asking for it. Yup! They'll come and ring your doorbell every half-hour just to see if you need anything—anything at all. And they'll come by randomly. Unexpectedly, you know, while you're taking a desperately-needed afternoon nap, so you can gear up for tonight's big all-night celebration. Yes, it's a little intrusive, but, hey, it's the price you pay for good help. One thing's for sure though: they get the job done. By the end of the day, you will have gotten everything you needed. Those little guys are so reliable and so multi-talented—I bet each and every one would make fine Lebanese hairdressers.

I'm telling you, scratch the jitney driver all together—go with the kid. They're cheaper, anyway. Same quality as the driver, but a lot less hassle, a lot less ego, and a lot less aggravation. They're just so much easier to deal with, and you get so much more for your money, you know? Plus, kids are so eager to please. They want to help out in any way they can, so they're always willingly go that extra mile. They'll take you to the store, translate for you, bargain, and seal the deal. They want to make you happy. *Because it makes them happy.*

Just buy them a toy or something. Really, they don't ask for anything in return. And they don't expect it, either, but you should be nice and buy them something. A Tonka Truck is good. Or a soccer ball, even. They'll appreciate it. It will make them feel important. It will make them feel like the little 'big shot' in the neighborhood and they'll get mad respect from their peers. Plus, you'll totally lose it when you see their big, beautiful eyes light up with joy! And their great wide smile stretched from ear to ear! It is so worth it!

You see, kids are such an integral part of society that they're often overlooked, overworked and underappreciated. [113] And being short doesn't help, either. So, the slightest bit of recognition from an adult makes them feel special. As with any loyal employee who is rewarded for their hard work, it gives them a sense of confidence, pride, and a feeling that they've somehow contributed to the greater good.

---

113. In the employee/employer sense, of course, (not as a precious child to their parents).

Frankly, it's the kids who get stuck doing all the grunt work. Their parents make them do everything. Not because they're mean or lazy, but because it's practical and necessary. For example, a mother will send her son George to walk all the way to the other side of the village to get *Mart'amay Hanna*[114] from the apple field so that she can come and get the phone because *Khalo Bassam*[115] called her, and he's over *Beit Jose Umtay's*.[116] And he needs to know if there are any *zaytoons*[117] there or if he should go pick some up from *Umtay Miriam's mahal*[118] before she closes and goes over to *Khaltay Ibtesam's*[119] house for coffee.

They're busy little guys.

The mother can't go herself because she's busy making food, entertaining visitors, and watching the baby. And, of course, there are no phones in the apple field. So, after that whole ordeal, *George*, will come back and play with his friends in the street for a little while longer before he hears a loud screeching voice call out once again: "GEORGE! YA GEORGE! TA'ALA HONE! YALLA TA'A! AJJIL!"[120]

And so, our sweet little George, with his big, piercing blue eyes, will look up to the roof top where his mother is hanging clothes out to dry, and he'll get his orders.

"Go take this shirt to *bint umaac's*[121] house and wait for her to fix it. When you're done, bring it over to *Khaltac Samera's*[122] house, so Shadi can try it on. Then go run these four cartons of chicken eggs to *Umtac Rhanna's*[123] house, and, on your

---

114. Aunt Hanna.

115. Uncle Bassam.

116. (My) uncle's house.

117. Olives.

118. Aunt Mariam's store.

119. Aunt Iptesam's.

120. GEORGE!...GEORGE!...COME HERE!...HURRY COME!...MOVE IT!

121. Your cousin's.

122. Aunt Samera's.

123. Aunt Rhanna's.

way home, pick up a bottle of *arak*[124] from *Beit Umac Jamil's*,[125] and bring it over to Dareen's house before she gets ready to go to the *Amadi*[126] tonight. *Yalla, ajjil!*"[127]

They're like Fed-Ex Ground.
And just as fast, too!

Given their hectic lifestyle, it's hard to imagine how they stay so damn cute! These little guys don't get a break, you know?

And those are just the *village* kids.
Then you've got your *inner-city* kids.

Whoa!

These guys are a totally different breed all together.

Streetwise. Savvy. Slick.

These guys are the *real* backbone of the economy, you know what I mean?

Want to talk business? Lay down your terms.
Want to invest in markets? He'll broker the deals.
Want to go global? He'll run the tightest worldwide distribution network out there.

The kid's on it.

They're running the show over there. They're in the *souks,* and they're wheelin' and dealin,' babe. And it ain't no kiddie stuff either. They're not just some little kids helping out; they're straight-up hustlers. They're managers, owners, buyers, traders, brokers, CEOs, CFOs, board members, financial advisors, senior accountants, department heads, regional managers, senior vice presidents, secretaries of

---

124. 100 proof alcohol.

125. Uncle Jamil's.

126. Baptism.

127. Hurry, go right now, move it!

commerce, secretaries of the treasury. They're everything. And to them, business is business.

There's some big action going on there, especially in the major cities. Damascus, Aleppo, and Homs are like New York, London, and Tokyo. Straight Street is like Wall Street. Opening Bell and they're live on the floor buying and selling in all sectors—financial, agricultural, metals and energy—you name it. They've got their own S&P Composite Index. They're trading, babe. Stocks. Bonds. Treasury Bills. Mutual Funds. Olive Oil. Light Sweet Crude Olive Oil. Sugar. Wheat. Grain. Corn. Coffee. Tobacco. Live cattle. Textiles. Sequins. Bonds notes. *Maté. Bizzer.* Bridal Gowns. Incense. Lingerie. Silver. Brass.

And gold.

Tons and tons of gold.

The *souks* are packed, and thousands of people are shopping. Every day is like Black Friday. Customers swarm everywhere, and they're demanding, too. Retailers gotta be fast, sharp, and quick!

And they're good. Very good.

These little guys are so good that, if they organized, they could restructure the economy of any third world country and turn it all around. They alone can get the country to a point where they could underwrite loans, provide military support, and distribute billions of dollars in federal-aid packages.

The countries need them.

Somebody tell Bono.

And even though they're rougher than the village kids, they're just as cute. Honestly. They are so cute that you *have* to buy something from them, anything. You've got like this sweet, little four-year-old angel holding out a bag of peanuts and asking you if you want to buy them. He's so adorable, how can you refuse? Then his older brother, you know, the five-year-old, has some gorgeous serving trays that he's selling for a buck a piece. And if you're buying one of those, you might as well head next door to his 12-year-old cousin's—he's got a stunning sequined gown that will be just perfect for tomorrow night's *hafli.*

And, hey, come on, you're shopping in the Middle East! How often does that happen, right? For goodness sakes! Go ahead and splurge! I mean, you can't buy a brilliant dress and just leave it at that, now can you? You gotta walk two doors down to see Ahmed, the 10-year-old. He sells the best gold in the entire *souk!*

I'm telling you, the countries need them.

Why Kids in the Middle East Drink and Drive—And Why it's Okay
In the Middle East, kids drink.
And kids drive.

And it's okay.

I've seen it with my very own eyes.

Kids drink *arak*. Yes indeed, they do. They may only take a sip here and there, but they're drinking, all right. Openly, you know? They're at the table, sitting right next to their parents and holding their very own glass. There's none of this infantile *"let me take a sip of daddy's arak while he's not looking, crap!"* They've got their very own drink. And it's not in a cute, little, Barney sippy-cup, either; it's in a regular adult-size glass. And they're sippin' away. Just enjoying the moment. It's relaxing for them. And they seem to really *need* it at times, you know? You kinda get that feeling. Maybe it's because of all the stress and work they have to deal with.

"Whew! Boy, I could really use a drink right now! That Umtay's house was so far away. And she took forever to sew up that shirt! I mean come on! Hurry up lady, will ya? Jeez! And the eggs were flyin' all over the place. Plus, I almost got run over by a reckless Jitney Driver! Jerk! He shouldn't be allowed to drive! What does he know anyway? Besides, he's stealing my business! You know what? I am so glad I had to go pick up the bottle of arak from Uma Jamil's house. Whew! What a day! What a lousy freakin' day! I need a drink!"

I'm not gonna deny them a little time to unwind. Hell no! For all that they do?

"Relax kid, take it easy. Here, have a drink; you deserve it! You're one helluva, kid, you know that? What are you, ten? Eleven? Well you look ten, I'm sorry, when will you be eight? Oh, seven? I'm sorry, seven. When will you be seven? Next Christmas? Oh, that's quite a bit away! Hey kid, you all right? That sure was a harrowing day for you. I'll tell ya, if I ever see that jitney driver again, I swear, I'll just ….!"

Honestly, I really don't think it's a bad idea for kids to drink—you know, in moderation and all. It's very common in European countries. In France, Italy and Spain, parents give their children wine to drink all the time. Hell, those kids are always loaded! And Ireland? Forget it! The wee lads are practically runnin' the pubs over there. Because drinking is socially acceptable overseas, the kids generally don't have an issue with it. They're not all hung-up and obsessed with the idea of sneaking out and drinking behind their parent's back because they never *had* to sneak out and drink behind their parent's back. Since it's not forbidden, there's no fear, mystery, or real cause for rebellion. It's basic psychology, really.

Generally speaking, drinking is an enjoyable past-time, a part of relaxation, and pretty much always done with friends or family. People over there really don't drink *to get drunk*. They wouldn't understand that concept. It just wouldn't make any sense to them. And because they cannot understand it, they'd think it is stupid to put yourself in such a situation. For what purpose? Unfortunately, it's a different mentality on many American college campuses today. Not all, but enough. Social drinking, okay. Drinking to get a buzz, okay. Having a drink alone by yourself to relax and unwind, okay.

Drinking to get totally blasted out of your mind? Weird.

Just for the record, I intend to start my future children out with only the finest: Cruzan Estate Dark Rum from St. Croix happens to be my drink of choice. Smooth, medium-bodied, rich … *mmmm* … *c*an you say *Mojito, Senorita?* How about *Bahama, Ya Mama?* What about *Marmarita*[128] *Margarita?* Anyone up for a *Syrian Slammer?*

Now, the other very unusual thing that I saw kids do over there was drive. That kind of blew me away—more than the *arak* thing. The little girl I told you about in the jitney chapter who was driving the motorcycle truly threw me off. It happened during my first day there, so it was one of the very first memories imprinted on my brain. I was exhausted from the trip, but I eventually managed to put the image that I saw somewhere in the back of my mind. But then, later on, the weirdest thing kept happening. I kept seeing it over and over again—but not with her—with other kids. Lots of other kids. Kids were driving everywhere. In fact, by the end of my trip, I was kind of used to it. It seemed pretty normal. Part of me even wanted to hitch a ride at times when I found myself stuck on the mountain.

The kids were *physically* situated behind the wheel, but the parents were *really* behind the wheel, if you know what I mean. They were just kind of sitting there on their parent's lap, hanging out, and holding on to the steering wheel. So, they were kind of driving, except that their feet were too short to touch the gas peddle or anything. They were just "play driving," I guess. But you know what really

---

128. Marmarita is the name of a village.

impressed me? The cars were all manual transmissions! Now, that was somethin' else because those are even harder to drive. Stick shifts? Come on! You got the clutch, the gas, the brake, the emergency brake—all that plus the steering? *Jeez!* It's one thing when an eight-year-old is driving an automatic, but an eight-year-old driving a stick? *I'm impressed!*

Now, let's see that boy in a Hummer.
Now, we're talkin'!

You know, there's a part of me that is tempted to say that I would probably trust a little Arabic kid driving a car more than I would trusting a lot of other people who actually have valid, state-issued licenses. DUIs, road rage, senile Floridian drivers—it's dangerous out there!

You do know that the whole "kid driving" thing is very common around the world, and not just in the Middle East, right? Kids like nine-years-old are driving in Zimbabwe, Laos, and Vietnam. Oh yeah. They are. In fact, they make up about 45% of the driving force over there. They're exceptionally skilled at driving on four-lane highways in the major capitals—not those silly, sissy-gumball European roundabout circles so common in Paris and Rome. That's like Kiddyland in Disneyworld to them. *Please!*

The kids are little Jitney-drivers-in-training, I guess. Just something to fall back on, you know, when business in the *souks* gets slow. They just don't have licenses because they're too short and need to sit on a phone book to get their photo I. D. s taken. And, the poor little things; they can't change the system either because they're just too little to understand how to get organized right. They need to unionize, and no one will show them how to do it. The good thing is that as a result of driving so young, the kids over there don't grow up with all kinds of irrational fears that some kids here, do. Think about it. If you're twelve-years-old, and you're driving a mini-van with 15 passengers up a 7,000-foot mountain with narrow, curvy roads, at 75 miles an hour—*what the hell could you ever possibly be afraid of for the rest of your entire life?*

"The what? The Boogie Man? Who is that? Is he a Mr. Minister of something? Mr. Boogie Man? Ahh. ... Yes, I know him! He is the Mr. Minister of something. I can't remember of what, but I heard of him before. Yes, he came to the embassy yesterday. Does he need a ride somewhere? I can take him. Where does he want to go?"

So, the next time you're in a taxi cab in New York City, and your foreign, non-English-speaking driver is swerving in-and-out of traffic right down Fifth Avenue—in the opposite direction—dodging pedestrians, and hitting crater size potholes at seventy miles an hour, just relax. He's from a third world country. He's got *years* of experience!

※ ※ ※ ※ ※

Look, don't make such a big deal out of "endangering the welfare of a minor." The kids are fine, trust me.

Have a drink with them.
Go for a ride with them.

Just don't let your eight-year-old *drink while they drive*.

That, my friend, would not be good.

Chapter 20

Restaurants, Real Estate and Retail: The Universal Language of Immigrants

<u>The Three R's</u>

*As understood by Americans: Reading Writing and Arithmetic.

*As understood by Immigrants: Restaurants, Real Estate, and Retail.

(Uhh ... how come the immigrants managed to get the three that actually start with the letter R? Hmmm... Interesting.)

<u>We're Business People, Straight-Up Entrepreneurs</u>
We don't like to work for other people. It's as simple as that. We like to be the boss and that's that. We're phenomenal when it comes to business. We're merchants. Always were, always will be. If there's something to sell, we'll sell it. If there's something you need, we'll find it and sell it to you. Sometimes we'll sell it to you, even if you're not sure that you want to buy it.

We're always hustling. And when it's our turn to buy, we never accept the actual price, either—that's just too insulting. It's insulting to our inner-selves, our families, our ancestors and our heritage. We feel like we've betrayed our entire race. We just don't do it. Actually, we *can't* do it.

You see, we haggle. And we haggle—*well*. We can't help but bring the price down lower than the seller's asking price, sometimes even if it's just one lousy, stinking penny. We just have to do it. It's in our blood. And you know what? If we don't do it, we feel like we just got ripped off. Like, we just got chumped. And nobody wants to feel like they just got chumped.

In rare cases, when we do accidentally slip off course (we all have those days) and end up paying more than we want to, we start to feel bad about ourselves and ugly things happen. It's the beginnings of a diva's inner rage. After running her mouth in a lengthy, unsuccessful attempt to lower the price, she'll throw her right hand up in the air, lift her head up proudly, and shout, *"Yalla! Khalas! Stifflay!"*[129] As if it's *your* fault that she spent more than she wanted to.

It doesn't matter if it was already a steal, if we don't haggle it down, we feel cheated. Don't ask me why. I don't know. I just know that we do. Trust me, it's not about the money. We got the money. The only logical theory I could come up with is that it might have something to do with control (just guessing, here). It's some internal issue that, when all is said and done, we need to feel that *we* were the ones who determined the final price of the merchandise, not them. Not the merchant who actually bought it wholesale. Not the guy who's been in business for the past 35 years. Not the man who makes a living from retail. Not him. But us.

And boy do we get pissy when that doesn't happen.

Our stiffee friends? They're a whole different breed all together. They just go right up to the counter, in a very calm and orderly fashion, politely present the merchandise with the $350 price tag, pull out their Visa card, and pay for it. Just like that.

Weird, isn't it?

They make it simple. But not us. That's way too uncomplicated a process for us to even *think* about.

Let me explain.

In the *souk* in Syria, I witnessed my sister Leila almost bring a grown man to tears. She bought merchandise from a shop owner probably valued at $500 for something

---

129. Loosely translated as a ticked-off, "Whatever! Forget you! Do whatever you want!"

like 25 bucks. She was in his store for two-and-a-half heat-sweltering, non-stop hours, trying to bring his price down for a bunch of gorgeous, hand-made serving trays, small mosaic end tables and intricately detailed gold-plated tea pots.

Unbelievable!

She wouldn't let up. Not for a second. And, neither would he. That man was just as fierce. He couldn't help himself either because, like her, it's in his blood to haggle. And he was goin' at it full force. He went right along with the game. Back and forth they went. Intensely. For hours. And not a point on the board. Tied 0–0. Playing hard. Fighting for the championship title. It was like watching the U.S. Open. Serena—Venus—Serena—Venus—Serena—Venus! But much sadder. More pathetic. And the guy just kept playing right into her hands. Finally, I just sat on a bucket, ate some pistachio nuts, waited and watched her crush this man. It was brutal.

Leila's good. *Leila's real good.* Poor guy, though. I don't even think he realized what happened until it was all over and done with. Actually, I think that's when it finally hit him. And it hit him hard. I heard the shop closed down. It's just a vacant hole in the wall, now. Broken bottles, empty cans, stray cats running around. Some say he had a nervous breakdown. So sad.

Addictions

It's a great thing to be an entrepreneur, but, for every up, there is a down. Self-employment has an ugly, dark side that few people talk about, but, believe me, it's real. If you're not careful about running your own business, you may find yourself battling the worst kinds of addictions. You see, some families don't balance life very well. And, when that happens, often times they end up becoming workaholics. And it's even worse when the cycle has been going on for a couple of generations.

Take *Jidu,* for example. Any *Jidu* will do. *Jidu* has been working since he was three years old. He started out by selling olive oil to nearby villages. Oh, go ahead and ask him; he'll be more than happy to tell you how he suffered. By the time he was nine, he was supporting his family. At 11, he was supporting his own village, as well as his neighbor's. At 25, he found himself in America with his wife and 12 kids. His life is completely changed, forever. A new country, a new language, a new life. He's a natural survivor, so what does he do? He goes to work, doing the only thing that he knows how to do—*sell.* And he's selling whatever he can.

In the process of all this, he's developed a very strong work ethic. Deep down inside he *likes* to work. A lot. A whole lot. He likes to work so much that 50 years have passed, and he's never taken a vacation. And he's not alone. According to statistics from the Department of Labor and Industry, some *Jidus* have been working since 1918—nonstop! And they're not gonna stop now. I personally think that *they think* if they stop, somehow, someway, they're gonna die—just like that. Flat on the floor. Right then and there. *BOOM!* So, no matter what you say, they're never gonna stop.

Besides, it's too much fun to give it all up just like that. You see, *Jidus* love to b**ch about how much they've worked. *Ohhh! They love it!* In fact, b**ching about it is almost as much fun as the work itself! And they're good. They do it, *well!* They wrote the book on it! Yup! *Twelve Simple Steps to B**ching About Working, by Jid-Jidu. Copyright©1923. Suffering Man's Press, ISBN 1-55920-216-0. U.S. Library of Congress, Washington, D. C.* Yes sir! They'll gladly tell you how they walked up the mountain in the snow, sideways, while they were temporarily crippled and blinded by a man who pierced their eye with a dagger during a wretched fight, when he tried to get bread for his 24 starving children.

Yup, *Jidu!*

Yup! Yup! Yup! I know. I'm listening. Go on, go ahead …

I know, Jidu I know! They were all starving until you came with the food. I know the story. You've been telling me for the past 30 years.

See why *Jidus* are such good storytellers? They make the biggest mountains out of the teeniest, tiniest, little molehills.

And what's good story without a little guilt, right?

No, no, no. You can't just go ahead and tell a story about personal suffering without making everyone around you feel bad about how good they have it. What good would that do? You gotta go on and tell them how it was *all for them.* How every last bit of *his* suffering was so that *you* could have a roof over your head. And there's no reason to stop there, either. Come on! *Jidus'* just getting warmed up! He's gotta go on about how ungrateful this generation is. It doesn't matter *what* generation it is, as long as it's *this* generation—*and not his.* Because kids aren't the same as they were when he was young. All because of technology, you know. Because technology ruined everything. It brainwashed the kids. Now, they don't listen to their parents anymore. And that's why the end of the world is coming.

Jidu logic. Go figure.

Look, all those *Jidus* really want is just some appreciation, that's all. They need to know that we still love them more than anything else in the world. They're so darned cute! What's *not* cute, however, is when the whole family has adopted his workaholic addiction, and everyone's buzzing around non-stop. Then, it's no fun at all. If you're not careful, you can burn out.

But even if you do, it's still better than working for someone else. You know exactly what I'm talking about, don't you?

See, that's where we're a bit crazy.

No matter how exhausted, drained, or stressed out we are, we would still continue to bust our a**es and work in our own businesses before we would ever go and work for someone else! *(Excuse me, why do you think I'm writing this book? Hello?)*

No matter how successful we are working in a steady job for a Fortune 500 company, we would give it all up in a heartbeat. It doesn't matter if we came to this country on a student visa back in 1970, studied engineering for five years, worked three part-time jobs, and ate dirt to survive. It doesn't matter that we delivered pizzas to pay the bills and lived in a bad neighborhood to save on rent. It doesn't matter that we drove a cab while working as a dishwasher on the weekends to save enough money to go back to school for a master's degree. It doesn't matter. It doesn't matter if we finally got a Ph. D. in quantum physics and have a great future with Boeing ahead of us. ... We will quit our jobs and open up a pizza shop!

IN A HEARTBEAT, MA'AM.

IN A HEARTBEAT!

Why?

Because we love business! It's our addiction of choice. And it's a bad addiction, you know, like a good/bad addiction. Any business is good for us as long as it's *our* business. We just tend to excel with real estate, restaurants, and retail.

Why these three, you ask? Read on ...

Real Estate
One word—cash!
Enough said?
Good.

All right, there's more. Real estate is fast, easy, and all yours. And when you're done the building automatically becomes your kid's. You are completely the boss. You can never get fired. And you make all the final decisions. You determine if you want to fix that leaky roof or just wait until it crashes right down into the first floor kitchen. It's entirely your choice *and that's a good feeling!*

We also have a tendency to rent to foreign students, especially from third-world countries because, quite honestly, a leaky roof kinda feels a lot like home to some of them. And, in some cases, it's actually a step up. They don't complain. Nor do they know much about laws, tenant's rights, or building inspectors. Plus, if it's the middle of winter and there's no heat, you can always blame it on the government and tell them that they ration the gas. Believe me, they'll understand. Another advantage is that foreign students don't have wild parties. And, besides, most of us have developed a genetic predisposition to handle a variety of nasty cooking smells that usually infiltrate the overheated, germy, stuffy, dimly-lit, narrow, dirty hallways.

It is, of course, your choice to be a slumlord if that's what you wish. Personally, I'm not. Call me crazy, but I like the idea of spending the money and getting the problem fixed once and for all—you know, the right way. But, please, don't tell anyone. It's just one of those quirky little *sane* things I do.

Restaurants
Same word—cash!

Restaurants bring in lots of cash. They're fun. They're exciting. And they keep us real busy. And we are a bunch of little busy bodies, aren't we now? I'm a restaurant kid. I grew up in it, and it's in my blood. The one thing that's so great about owning a restaurant is that it's kinda like having company over for dinner every night. What's even better is that you get money every time they come to visit!

How about that?

Cha-ching!

For that reason, you work really hard for them to like you the best so that they come back and visit you all the time. You don't ever want them to visit other people, though—just *you* at *your* place. Because *your* place is special.

Our restaurant truly was special. And we had fun all the time. My mother made Khalil's restaurant in Pittsburgh the friendliest place to be. Back in the 1970s, customers lined up for blocks to have dinner with us. And, when it was busy and the food was late coming out of the kitchen, my mother would stand in the middle of the dining room and make an announcement in front of everybody. She would say, "Hey, everyone, we're backed up in the kitchen! We're gonna have a party till the cooks get caught up!" Then all of my sisters, my brother, and cousins would come out, play the drums, and dance. She was so Syrian!

Which brings me to my next point. If you've got kids, exploit them. I mean it. That's free labor right there. And believe me, labor costs add up quick. That's right, make every day, "Take Your Daughter To Work Day!" Besides that, customers love the charm of eating in an authentic, ethnic, family-owned restaurant.

It's also a good idea to hire your extended family. In fact, your whole labor force can consist of all of your relatives. They're loyal, hardworking, and will truly look out for your business. The good thing is that they'll never steal off of you; however, they might just turn around and become your competition. You just gotta watch.

And let's not forget all the illegal help. Come on, there's a whole work force in just one family alone. Plus, think of all the money you'll save on group health insurance. And you'll have peace of mind knowing they'll never report you to OSHA,[130] the IRS[131] or to the INS[132] What more could you ask for?

So, here's a plan that will help get you started. It worked for us. Buy a building. There's your real estate venture, right there. Open a restaurant. Step #2 done! And live upstairs. You save money that way. Then when you've got all that under control, expand. Have your brother open up a 7-11 right next door. All the bases are covered now. Congratulations! You did it! Now everybody can all live together, and work together, and make all kinds of money together. Work and live together, pretty much everyday, all the time. "I'm gonna go home now, I'll see you upstairs."

---

130. Occupational Safety and Health Administration.

131. Internal Revenue Service.

132. Immigration and Naturalization Service.

"Okay, see you upstairs." "I'm gonna go to work, now, so I'll see you downstairs, okay?" "Okay, I guess I'll see you downstairs later on, when I go to work." "Okay." "See ya, then!" "See ya!" "Bye now." "Okay, later." "Later." "Hey, by the way, can you go next door to our brother's place because we ran out of sugar packets and coffee filters."

Nothing like a family business.

The best part of it all, though, is that your kids can come down in their pajamas in the middle of the busy dinner hour if they're having a nightmare. Or if they're having a fight with another sibling. Or if *you're* having a party—like my mom always did. Believe me, there's nothing more adorable as a cute little four-year-old girl all snuggled up in her comfy, cozy, babydoll pajamas, her long, curly, soft brown tresses, with a ragged, worn teddy bear dangling from her tiny, precious hand in the middle of the dining room—filling up empty water glasses, passing out menus, and seating parties of 12.

"Smoking or non? Right this way, ma'am. ..."

Aside from free labor, restaurants work out rather nicely for us because our food is so darn delicious, healthy, and popular. Within only the past 10 years or so, items like hummus and tabouli have found their way into the mainstream American diet, and supermarkets have continuously stocked our foods in their ethnic aisles. It's obvious, the Middle Eastern food craze is only going to get bigger. You know what I'm thinking, don't you? "Yes ma'am. Would you like fries with that McFalafel meal or do you just want to supersize the tabouli?" I'm betting five years tops. I feel it. The fast food industry is going to have to make drastic changes to provide a more seriously healthy menu because you sure as hell won't be "Lovin' It!" when you're hooked up to an IV in the cardiac arrest wing of the hospital. That's for damn sure! And they know that! Plus, their little active, exercise totin' Ronald McDonald clown won't be able to keep up much longer if he keeps eating them Big Macs *and they know that, too.*

Just make sure that if you do end up opening a restaurant that the food is authentic and fresh. We've got a reputation to uphold, you know. Oh yeah, and make sure you get health insurance because owning a restaurant will suck the life out of you more than any other business.

Retail

We love retail. Because we get it from wholesale. And then we resell it. And, in order to buy it, you gotta go through the middle man. And that's us. We're the middle man. And it's good to be the middle man!

We love retail in general, but, for some reason, we tend to excel with convenience stores. We just dominate in that area. And now I know why. You see, I was in the dollar store yesterday and, all my life, I could never understand why all ethnic people, especially Arabs, love the dollar store. I, personally, never liked it; as a matter of fact, I hated it. But I kept asking myself, "why does everyone love the damn dollar store?"

And then, all of a sudden, it hit me. It's because they're exactly like the stores in the Middle East except the stores in the Middle East are much smaller. But both are totally fun to shop in. They've got everything from a bar of soap, to Nestle coffee, to slippers, to nail polish and everything else you could possibly want *but only one of each*. Everything is crammed in on top of each other, all dusty and disorganized, just like the dollar store, so we feel right at home in either place. Clutter is king, wherever you go!

And in the Middle East, if by chance the shop is closed, it's not a problem, just step outside and holler up to the veranda; they'll be right down to open the door. They're really not all that different from small ethnic stores in America. Our little shops look just like the Korean, Indian, and Vietnamese stores right down the street from you. And they, too, will be happy to come downstairs and open up for business if you ask them. Funny how all of our stores look like *each other*, but none even remotely resemble Walgreens. *Hmmm...*

Convenience stores, especially the really teeny-tiny ones, suit us just fine. Because we're shop keepers and we like that. It's our shop and we'll keep it. *Thank you very much!*

Besides that, we can sell whatever we want, including videos, cell phones, phone cards, airplane tickets, gyros, electronic devices, walkie-talkies, tickets to upcoming *haflis*, tickets to upcoming *haflis* in other cities, tickets overseas, satellite dishes, stereos, henna, soap, baby eggplant, coconut oil, baptism certificate forms, bootleg CDs, bootleg videos, key chains of flags from your native country *(no matter what it is)*, marriage licenses, antibiotics, wedding invitations. We can fix your cars, rent you apartments, get you a jitney driver, give you a tattoo in the backroom *(but only tattoos of flags of your native country)*, book a band for a wedding, book a *bride* for a wedding, handle immigration problems, sell multi-entry visas, book a catering. … We can do it all. And we do *do it all!*

Now that's convenience!

Businesses That Don't Have the Slightest Chance of Success in the Middle East

Some businesses just won't work in the Middle East. No matter how hard you try or how many success stories you hear about in the United States, it ain't happenin' over there. Not a chance! Nada! Zip! So, before you apply for a loan to get a new business started, read over this list very carefully because the following are direct routes to bankruptcy court.

Telemarketing Business
You're joking, right?

Not a chance in hell this thing would even get off the ground.

As an Arab-American, you should instinctively know this, but, in case you forgot, this is how it will go:

"Allo? Mean am yehkee? Marhabba, keefik? Kifa Imik? Keef Bayik? Inshallah mlah? Keif sahtik? Slamtic ya inaay, salamtic.

Laykee, ana smieat eno khalik Firas bil mestashfa, saa'h? An jad? Ya waaylay! La! Walla? Yeeeeeh! Shoo hennee majaaneen? Laykee, metoolay whooey ma shaf el-serveece? Ya Waylaaaaay! Ya Rub! Ya Inaay! Tayeb, laykee, ana hall'a jai ala beitkone!"

("Hello? Who am I speaking with? How are you? How's everything? How's your mother? How's your father? God willing, they are well! How's your health? I'm sorry, sweetheart, I'm sorry.

Listen, I heard that your Uncle Firas is in the hospital, is that right? For real? Oh my goodness! No! Really? Whoa! What are they crazy? Look, you are saying that he didn't see the [jitney] driver? Oh my goodness! My goodness, my sweetheart! Okay, listen, I'm coming over to your house right now!")

You'd never get the sale.

Because you would just never get around to talking about the product that you originally called for.

Matchmaking Service
This would make number one on the Top 10 list of ridiculous business ideas in the Middle East.

A Matchmaking Service?

And you think people are going to *pay* for something like this?

You think people are going to actually pay a monthly fee for you to call their *uma*[133] to send their five sons over to meet you? It's your own *uma* for goodness sakes! Just walk across the street and right through the kitchen door!

Look, honestly, I'm a reasonable person. I'm willing to explore the flip side of the argument. Let's say that perhaps, for some strange reason, you might possibly be—hypothetically speaking, of course—interested in marrying someone *outside* of your own family. Why? I don't know? But, for the sake of argument, let's just say you do. Okay, I can see your point. But still, no way! Just go to your *sito's* house, and she'll pull out her up-to-the-minute international database of eligible bachelors. She's equipped from Tartous, Syria to Topeka, Kansas, she's got 'em all, darlin'! Besides, the entire Middle East has got to be interrelated by now, so, if you're marrying an Arabic guy, no doubt, you're marrying a cousin. It's unavoidable.

But a fee?

Actually *paying* someone money to find a husband for you?

Sorry, babe. Not on this side of the hemisphere.

Postal Delivery Service
Ha!
This one's funny, too!
Postal Delivery Service.
What a joke!

---

133. Uncle.

You mean *pay* to ship something over to the Middle East? You gotta be kidding! What? You can't find nobody going over? What? You can't find nobody's suitcase you can't squeeze clothes, shoes, and medicine into?

Money Wire Transfer Service
Let me be real clear about this one.

There is no way in hell that anybody is going to hand over cold, hard cash—from their hands or out of their bras—to anyone who isn't their trusted friend or relative. And who isn't actually going to be *physically* boarding a plane.

Period. The end.

Think about it. You're going to give a complete stranger—someone you have never seen in your entire life—*any* denomination of currency?

And actually pay them *even more money* to properly handle it? *Ahhh ... I don't think so!*

I don't care *how* bonded and insured the company is.

We ain't bonding, and I ain't sure!

Track it all you want, baby. It ain't happenin'!

Not with us, anyway!

Retail Bridal Gown Shop
Pay $2,000 for a dress that you're gonna be wearing for seven hours?

Right.

A dress, mind you, that you will never wear again in your entire life? Some white, fluffy, frilly garment that will sit in a box on the top shelf of your closet, forever? They're just not into that whole "Oh! I have a great idea; let me go into bankruptcy for the next 10 years of my life, so I can brag to all my friends, that I wore Vera Wang" thing.

Uh-uh.

Nope. No, thank you. They'll just pay the standard $75 bridal gown rental fee and ... *oh ... I don't know* ... maybe save the rest of the $1,925 dollars to buy food and clothes over the next several years, perhaps? It's just more practical that way.

My mom did it in 1956 when she married my dad.

See how much money she saved? She bought a whole restaurant!

Now that's making your dollar *streeetch!*

What You Won't Find in Abundance in the Middle East

Fancy French Toilets
Not too many of those in use at this point in time. The most commonly used ones right now are the ever-popular-holes-in-the-ground. Yup! Less plumbing work, you know? And less expensive, too. But things are changing. Western-style upright porcelain fixtures are beginning to become more and more popular.

High Prices
It's pretty cheap over there for us but not for the people who live there. For instance, you can feed a family of six for a dollar-fifty. That's right. How, you ask? Falafel sandwiches cost .25 cents a piece.

Cigarettes will cost you a dollar-forty.
An updo at the local village salon will cost about eight bucks. [134]
Dinner, drinks, and live entertainment for twenty people runs about a hundred and fifty bucks.

But a car?

A car will cost you, baby. In some countries, a car will cost you three times its original sticker price. Why? I don't know. Maybe it's because they want to keep the jitney drivers in business.

---

134. Price does not reflect Lebanese hairdressers', which are higher.

Phone Books

Don't be silly! Of course they have them in the Middle East! They're just not as in demand over there as they are over here because they just don't need them as much, you know? Because over there, if you need something, you can just ask around.

For example, if you need to buy a cell phone, you don't have to let your fingers do *any* walking. You could just ask someone, and they'll tell you, "Oh, Ibrahim from *Imabarra*[135] sells them." And then they'll take you to his *mahal*. [136]

Or, if you need a video, *Umo Elias*[137] will take you to *Khalto Samera's*[138] son because his *ibn umo*[139] is married to *Khalto Hanna's*[140] eldest daughter. And her second cousin has a video shop right next to *bint Umo Essa in Marmarita*.[141]

Or, say, you need a technician to look at the problem that your having with your satellite dish. You just go with George, remember him? The little kid who drinks *arak?* He'll take you to *Umo Joseph's mat'aam*[142] to get Rami[143] because he's having coffee over there. And, of course, Rami will drive you to *Kaymee*[144] because, there, Naif just came back from Lebanon, and he has a few extra satellite dishes laying around in his backyard. And he has a screwdriver and an old antenna too. So, if you want, he could just fix it for you.

That's why you don't need a phone book.

---

135. Name of a village.

136. Store.

137. Uncle Elias.

138. Aunt Samera's.

139. Cousin.

140. Aunt Hanna's.

141. Uncle Essa's daughter who lives in Marmarita (a village).

142. Uncle Joseph's restaurant.

143. Rami, the jitney driver.

144. Another name of a village.

Automation Technology
I hate it.
I hate talking to robots that sound like humans.

"I'm sorry ... I didn't get that ... I think you were trying to say Account Link PIN. ... Did you say account link PIN? Okay. Let's try again. Please say the number of the business you want ..."

I $*&%#^ hate it!

She's so fake, you can't even gossip with her!

And if they introduce automation technology, then you know something crazy, like Directory Assistance is bound to take off.

And what if Ibrahim doesn't have a phone yet? See? That's not fair.

Obviously everyone has a cell phone by now, but it costs like three times as much dialing Directory Assistance from a cell than it is calling from a land-line phone. Plus, you gotta understand that old *Jidus* have a hard time understanding how they work and all. They get confused with the numbers, text message options, and all the multimedia choices. Some inadvertently record videos while trying to dial out. It's hard for them. And it's frustrating. I must admit though, they do seem to enjoy their little electronic gadgets. They just don't fuss with that many menu options like automatic redial. They like it the old fashioned way where you just punch the numbers in—one by one—and talk. Or rather, punch the numbers in—one by one—and shout real loud.

Napkins
We touched on the subject of napkins, earlier.
No napkins, no big deal, right?

Except when you have to go to the bathroom. In a public place. Then, it becomes a big deal. It becomes a *really* big deal.

You see, the problem occurs when you're all out having lunch at a restaurant somewhere, and you have to go to the bathroom. And you have to get the Kleenex tissues. The Kleenex tissues that are situated on the lunch table. The 14-seater lunch table. The 14-seater long, banquet-style lunch table. On the opposite end. Where all the *guys* are sitting. So, in order to get them, you have to impose on ten men to pass them *all the way over* from the other side of the table. So, now, *everybody* knows that you have to go to the bathroom. And then you don't want to take *too many* tissues with you. Because ... *well ... you know why.*

It's like a wide-open statement.
It's just too weird for me.
Like everybody knows and all.

Apple Pie
For the life of me, I can't figure it out. Everyone and their mother owns an apple farm. There are apple orchards everywhere. Literally. Acres and acres of apple trees. But what do they do with all of those apples?

Nobody makes apple pie. You can't find an apple pie anywhere in the entire country. Apple turnovers? Sure. Apple baklawa? Absolutely. Apple cake? No question. But apple pie? Not a slice. They're nowhere in sight. There is just no *Fitayer Tiffah*. [145] They always seem to have enough *Tiffah*[146] for the tobacco in the *argeelee*, though. There's no real shortage of that, anywhere. In fact, their most popular flavor is apple flavor. And do you know what the second most popular flavor is? Yup! Double apple flavor *(tiffahtan)*. [147]

Oh, wait! Hold on a minute!

Ohhh ...!
I get it now!
So ... that's where all the apples are going! That makes sense!

(Calm down! I'm learning! I'm learning!)

Before You Go ...

Here are some pretty important things you should know before traveling to the Middle East:

---

145. Apple pie.

146. Apples.

147. Double apple flavor.

Everyone smokes
If you quit smoking, you'll start again.
You just will. Trust me.

And most likely it will be Marlboro Reds, Winstons, or Camels. Either way, it'll be a *hard* cigarette. One that barely passes minimal federal regulation standards.

Another thing to remember is that it is perfectly acceptable for a girl to smoke an *argeelee* in front of her parents. However, it is *not okay* for her to smoke *cigarettes* in front of anybody. You could be married with nine kids, hold a Ph. D. in biomedical engineering—and it's still not okay to smoke cigarettes in front of your parents. Why? I don't know? It just isn't.

Guys can smoke.
Guys *should* smoke.
Seventeen-year-old *shebab*[148] had better smoke.

But girls?
No.

Girls "Clip-Clop"
You will hear a lot of *"clip-clopping"* all over the Middle East. That's right. *Clip-clop, clip-clop, clip-clop.* And you will not find that sound anywhere else in the world. [149] Do you know what that sound is? It's the sound a girl makes when she is walking down the steps and in the hallways of buildings all over the Middle East—in her feminine, four-inch high heels.

You see, over there, nobody really has carpet. We *make* really nice carpets—you know, oriental rugs and stuff—we just don't *use* them very often. Basically, all of the floors are made out of ceramic tile. And the shoes over there are manufactured in such a way that makes it conducive to making that sound. I think they secretly do it on purpose to enjoy a little joke or two on the rest of us. So, you'll be like on the fifth floor of a building, and, all of the sudden, you'll hear, *clip-clop … clip-*

---

148. Guys.

149. All right, that's not true either. That sound exists in other Mediterranean countries—but, still—no one clip-clops like us!

clop … clip-clop and you'll automatically know that some girl is walking up the steps. All over the Middle East, you'll hear *clip-clop, clip-clop* echoing everywhere all the time.

That's how you know you're still in the Middle East. You know, just in case you get lost or something.

<u>You will fall in love</u>
We've already discussed this earlier in the book.
This is just a friendly reminder.

<u>Always lie about your age</u>
It is absolutely imperative that you never reveal the truth about your age *if you are above 29 years old.*

Know this fact: If you are single, you will automatically be submitted into the national lottery as an available candidate for marriage whether you like it or not. Or whether you want to or not. Remember the whole national pastime thing? So, the very first thing people will ask you—after two other important criteria have been established—is your age.

1. Your sex *(dah! They can see that)*.
2. Your marital status *(they'll find out)*.
3. Your age.

Oh, and by the way, don't leave your passport or any other I. D. for that matter laying around.

I'll let you in on a little secret trick which makes it so that, either way, you can't lose. For instance, if you're not quite ready for the big commitment, add a good 10 years on to your real age then you will be too old to matter. And, conversely, if you'd like to tie the knot, simply subtract a good ten years from your real age. As you've already learned, the average turn around time for overseas marriage proposals is usually 24 hours from the time you step off the plane, but, if you are younger, you automatically jump the queue.

<u>You will become sad when you leave the Middle East</u>
I already discussed this in the Author's Official Disclaimer, but it's worth going over again.

When you leave the Middle East, you will become very depressed. It's as simple as that. You will cry. A lot. It happens to everyone. It's just the way it is.

You will begin to question many things, including your sense of purpose. You will begin to question *why* you have been doing *what* you have been doing for so long. You will begin to question the price you have been paying for trying to live the American dream. And you will be sad. Your priorities will change. Your life will change. You will be confused. You will feel angry that you let such a fundamental part of you slip away during your mad rush to success. But then you will feel happy because you finally found what was lost or forgotten for so long.

You will wonder what to do next with your life, now that you've found paradise. You will wonder *how* you will even be able to do anything at all, now that you found paradise.

It's inevitable. It happens to everyone. Just ride it out.

I have yet to meet anyone who hasn't suffered some degree of sadness upon leaving the Middle East. Trust me. *It ain't just about having a nice vacation.*

When you come back, you won't be able to function for at least a month. Your serotonin level will drop to record lows. Your mind will play tricks on you. Without even realizing it, your fingers will automatically motion as if they were still *cracking bizzer*. Your legs will start kicking the minute you hear the beat of a *tabal* on the new Arabic CD that you brought back with you. You will inevitably find yourself dancing around your kitchen table, in the middle of the day, listening to Arabic music, drinking *arak,* trying to have a *sahara,*[150] and pretending that you were back "home." And then you will look around and realize that it is just *you*. And that you are dancing around your kitchen table alone, in the middle of the day, drinking *arak* all by yourself.

And reality will hit like a brick wall.
And then you'll break down and cry.
It's okay; you're still in denial.

---

150. Arabic party.

Your sadness may not be as deep as mine was, but, hey, everybody's different.

The good news is that America will bring you right back to reality, real quick. Nothing like a past due mortgage statement to sober things up! *No Siree!* So, eventually, you will get better. Give it a couple of months. Get through the holidays, the snowy winter, and the New Year.

Blink your eyes. Then blink again.

Close them shut.

Blink once more.

Close them again.

And blink one last time.

Now open them.

Surprise!

Guess what?

It's summertime!

Time to go back, and do it all over again!

Chapter 21

▼

Shunkleesh and the Bush Conspiracy

Shunkleesh (n.)—So dangerous, that you might be arrested for possession. A pungent, horrific-smelling, aged cheese that can also be used as a very powerful lethal weapon and is frequently swapped on the black market. It is slightly less deadly than ricin and more abundant than uranium. The latest figures point to some one million lost and forgotten *shunkleesh* balls in remote locations all over the world. A government-issued warning suggests they are likely giving off toxic levels of radiation at this moment. This ghastly smelling cheese, however, is absolutely delicious to eat.

Legend has it that, in 1972, a Detroit-bound TWA flight returning from the Middle East was grounded because a staunch odor was emitting from the cargo area. The passengers were evacuated while agents and bomb-sniffing canines searched the craft. The crew initially suspected there might have been a dead body smuggled onto the plane, but authorities later confirmed that the foul smell turned out to be a bag of moldy *shunkleesh*, innocently packed in a passenger's bag. In this post 9/11 world, I strongly advise against transporting *shunkleesh*, especially from a country designated by the Bush Administration as a terrorist nation. Just don't do it, okay? We have enough bad press as it is, *thank you very much!*

For those of you who don't know, *shunkleesh* is one of those food items that you need to have fully stocked in your home at all times. Not just because it's critical to your identity as an Arab-American. And not just because it tastes delicious with fresh homemade bread and hot melted butter, or when it is sliced up and mixed with some extra virgin olive oil, onions, and tomatoes. But also because it could, very well, save your life.

It's true. Ask any pharmacist.

Shunkleesh is a cheese, right? Cheese is basically mold. Mold is basically penicillin. *Shunkleesh* can be used as an antibiotic—and its serum, as a possible vaccine for the Avian Flu. I swear I read something about *shunkleesh* curing some rare disease in lab mice. It's potent enough. Just keep a little vial locked up in your medicine cabinet, and you should be all right.

See how cool us *Araaabics* are? Once again offering our contribution to the world of science! First we invented Algebra, then the alphabet, and now look, we're curing diseases left and right! We are *sooo* cool!

※ ※ ※ ※ ※

Pssst ...!

Hey ...! Come here ...!

We gotta talk.

It's serious.

Shut the door.

Sit down.

Look, I was just down playing everything for a minute because I didn't want to set off a massive panic alarm, but I'm serious, we've got a big problem on our hands. I'm talking HUGE. And if anyone finds out about this one, we're screwed, big time. For real. It's so big that it's gonna go down as one of those Top 10 Bloopers in the History of the World. And it won't be a funny one, either. It will be right under that whole Trojan Horse slip-up.

Yup, it's one of those fatal blunders where you just want to find a remote corner of the world, go under the blankees, and hide until everyone's completely forgotten about the whole ordeal. It just makes you feel like a big buffoon. I'm kinda feeling like that right now because, on some small level, I contributed to this big mess. And what used to be a relatively minor problem has now blown way out of proportion.

You see, people who are culinarily impaired (like me), get all excited about making *shunkleesh*, especially when it's their first time. It's like this big *to-do*. They do all the preparation work of draining the water from the cottage cheese, spicing it up, and rolling them into round balls. Then they prepare them to be stored away. What they do is cover them up in tons of newspapers and rags, find a remote spot, and hide them there until they dry up. This may take weeks, months, even years, who knows? The problem occurs when sometimes they hide the *shunkleesh* balls in these secret dark corners and inadvertently forget about them.

It's completely unintentional. You just get wrapped up in the excitement of it all and totally lose focus. See, you spend like three days preparing, nonstop. And, of course, you're in the moment: you got a scarf on your head, you're barefoot in the kitchen, you're singing old folk songs, the sun is shining, the music's playing, and you're feeling great! You're feeling all domestic and stuff.

You're happy because you're draining the cottage cheese. You're happy because you're rolling up cute, little, adorable balls. You're happy because you're barefoot, dancing around the kitchen. You, *Ms. 'Metropolitan-fast-track-career-woman,'* are doing something noble. You are carrying on the tradition of your great ancestors—those fierce warrior women who made cheese for their hungry, lion-hunting husbands.

You're excited. This is gonna be great! You round up all the balls and secretly contemplate where you're going to store your special stash. Then, finally, you store them. But, like everything else in life, time goes on. And life goes on. *Your life goes on.* You check on them in about a week, drain the water-soaked cloths, change the newspapers underneath, then get back to work. You go on and get distracted again. Three weeks later you check them again. Change the dressings and get back to your life. You take a spinning class at the gym, start a new diet—two months later, check them again—enroll in college, get a new job, apply for a Ph. D. Check them again. Get married, have kids, finish your Ph. D., apply for an overseas fellowship. And, by that time you, completely forgot about the *shunkleesh* all together, let alone where on earth you stored them!

I made my first batch when I was 23 years old.

For the life of me, I couldn't tell you where they are now.

I have not a clue.

The problem is that I'm not the only one. If you take into consideration all the batches that probably didn't work out and were discarded, plus if you factor in all the subsequent good batches that were mislaid, and then multiply those numbers by the amount of balls prepared in any given year …

And, I think … I think something just went terribly wrong!

Let me explain.

We all know that when George W. sent Collin Powell to the U. N. to testify that Iraq had Weapons of Mass Destruction, Bush believed his information was solid. It was a slam dunk, remember? Powell *(M*'%^**#*'s had to play a brother!)* sat in front of the entire world and displayed satellite photos of material storage facilities and on-site decontamination vehicles. Photographs of hidden chemical bunkers, along with phone conversations, were also used to support the case for going to war with Iraq. We all watched and waited as the weapons' inspectors fruitlessly searched for the WMDs.

We know now that it was all a big mistake.

Talk about a blunder!

The Bush Administration kinda mumbled something about there not being any weapons in Iraq after all. But, the truth is, we really haven't even heard as much as a *"Ooops! My bad. Sorry 'bout that."*

But, mistakes aside, it leaves the rest of us to question what made them suspect that WMDs existed in the first place? If it wasn't weapons, then what substance were their radars detecting? What exactly was it that they picked up?

Perhaps, just perhaps, the *shunkleesh* was giving off some sort of unidentifiable radiation, and all your sophisticated, multi-kazillion dollar, high-tech equipment mistakenly delivers information of hidden WMDs. Like, what happens if, all of a sudden, the toxic radiation given off by a million missing-in-action *shunkleesh* balls—*all throughout history*—have finally amassed enough wave energy strength to generate a false positive, thereby shaking the whole world order and thrusting us into a massive war with Iraq—the cradle of civilization where the first cheese balls were probably lost thousands of years ago?

Huh?

Answer me!

Seriously!

Maybe it was just the *shunkleesh—and nothing else!*

We don't know!

Look, in order to understand the scope and magnitude of this whole thing, you have to realize that *shunkleesh* is no ordinary cheese. Let me explain. British researchers recently discovered the smelliest cheese in the world. It's called *Vieux Boulogne*. *Vieux Boulogne* is a soft cheese that hails from *Boulogne-Sur-Mer* in Northern France. It is aged between seven to nine weeks and has a rind brushed with beer. Researchers say that the horrific, pungent smell is created by the beer as it reacts with enzymes in the cheese. The smell is unspeakable.

They obviously never heard of *shunkleesh*.

It's estimated that one really good ball of *shunkleesh* has the power equivalent of a thousand atomic bombs.

Given all that we know now, is it not conceivable that *shunkleesh* could be the real reason we went to war with Iraq in the first place?

Why not? It could happen!

Listen, it makes perfect sense. Iraq is a Middle Eastern country, right? Women all over the Arab world have been making *shunkleesh, macdouse,* and who knows what else for thousands of years. Plus, think about it, Baghdad, Babylon, they were ancient cities. Who knows what's buried under all that rubble?

I don't care what you say: it's all a big conspiracy as far as I'm concerned. The government knows the truth; they're just keeping hush-hush about it. Oh sure, they'll acknowledge that they acted on faulty information—but they'll never say *what* that faulty information was. Just like Cheney pulling the trigger on his hunting buddy—faulty info! *Uhh ... they told me it was a quail so I shot at it.* It's just way too embarrassing for everyone. Imagine the crisis in the Pentagon after this pretty little fiasco!

War over cheese? Oh man! We'd never be able to show our faces in public again. In one fell swoop, "America the Great" would lose every cool point it's ever earned. It would be like Superman turning into Elmer Fudd right before your very eyes.

You think the world is laughing at us now? Oh no. Wait till the press gets a hold of this one.

We're done.

At least Bush is being honest about this Gulf War. It's certainly not a war over oil, that's for sure.

And now Iran?

And North Korea?

Oh, man! We're screwed! My dad was right; the end *is* near.

Because you just know they have their own little funky, freakish, ancient foods, too.

No wonder France was so staunchly opposed to the war. They've got *Vieux Boulogne* to worry about.

And people know about *that* cheese.

It's over.

We're done.

Chapter 22

The Art of Grapeleave Picking and Baking Bread: Your Key to Legitimacy

Grapeleaves
Dude. Listen. … This doesn't make you legitimate. At all. It's really naïve to actually believe that, okay? Come on, guys? *The Art of Grapeleave Picking?* Get real! There is no freakin' art! Just pick up a Tahini bucket, go to the park, and start picking! Look, I just tricked you with the title because I needed a place to talk about grapeleaves somewhere in the book, so I just put it here, okay? Don't be mad. Just go out there and pick some grapeleaves.

All right! All right! *(Jeez!)*

"Ding!" (waving a plastic magic wand.)

There! I just validated you. Are you happy, now?

All right, look, you actually should go grapeleave picking. In fact, you should go with your grandmother. Then you'll be validated for real. I've done it a million times with my *sito*, and it was great. I don't know how to explain it, but, every so often, something just comes over me, and I have this sudden urge to go grapeleave picking. On days when I feel like a real *sit-el-beit*, I'll put on my four-inch heels, wrap a scarf around my head, put on silver hoop earrings, tie my shirt in a cross-halter, fold up the jean cuffs, put on some red lipstick, grab my mango-banana drink, head to the park, and start picking grapeleaves. I might even sing an old song or two. On rare occasions, I might bust out the old Harry Bellefonte classic Banana Boat *"Day-O"* song.

I'm just weird like that.

You don't have to go through all that, though. As a matter of fact, skip the whole thing. Just go to the supermarket and pick up a jar of grapeleaves.

Now, *making* grapeleaves? That's a whole different ballgame all together. That actually does count as real legitimacy. Cooking, in general, is a very serious thing for the Arabic woman. Her whole reputation depends on how well she can cook. But grapeleaves? Grapeleaves are the litmus test. They're often the deciding factor in whether or not a man decides to go through with a marriage deal or not.

How *well* you make grapeleaves determines your place in the Arabic community. Granted, it's not the ultimate status symbol but it's damn close. If I asked you right now, "who makes the best grapeleaves in the world?" in an instant, you'll know, but you'll never tell. Because you know how vicious these women can be. They're monsters. They're constantly scrutinizing and inspecting other women's grapeleaves. Haters! Always trying to keep a *sito* down, you know? My advice: just keep your mouth shut and remain diplomatic, no matter what manipulative tactics they use.

The next time you're at a bridal shower take a close look at the women. Carefully watch their eyes as the approach the tray of grapeleaves in the food line. Don't say a word. Just watch. You'll see. Never noticed before, did you? Well, you've got a lot to think about now, don't you? Those ladies had you believing that everything was cool between them, pretending like they're best friends. They kiss each other and compliment each other, just like they all did in the bathroom, back in Chapter 17! It's sick! But it's true.

Greeks have the same problem, I'm sure.

Look, grapeleaves are a big deal, and there are so many more things to learn, but that would take an entire other book. So, suffice it to say that the single most important thing for you to know is this one rule: the smaller the grapeleave, the higher the status. It's as simple as that. The women who make the real teeny, tiny grapeleaves, carry the greatest prestige and are the most envied. No matter what they put into it, no matter how it tastes, no matter how long it simmered in the pot, it all boils down to just one thing …

Size.

Baking Bread

"If you bake bread with indifference, you bake a bread that feeds but half a man's hunger."

—*Khalil Gibran*

Bread is the staple of life. And when it's made with love, it nourishes the soul. Baking bread is one of the most beautiful, spiritual gifts that I can think of. It's a very hard thing to do. It's time consuming, labor intensive and requires a lot of patience. And it's how our mothers and grandmothers expressed their love for us. They baked bread from their hearts to feed their children.

They nurtured their bread just like they nurtured their children. They took raw ingredients: flour, water, salt, and yeast, and, out of it, created *ageen*.[151] When the *ageen* was born, they kneaded it over and over again, with their bare hands, instinctively knowing when to press down tough and when to soften up a bit, depending on the individual nature and texture, of course. Working with the *ageen* was rough at times, but definitely worth it. Then, when it became a healthy enough size, they let it rest. Because *ageen*, especially baby *ageen*, needs to rest.

Ahhh ... sleepytime (yawn)

Later, when it "grew up" a bit, she took the *ageen* out again and divided it into little balls. And from the main *ageen*, many little ones were born. She laid all the little ones out on the kitchen table. Each one—side by side—and then put them to rest once again. Nap time. Growing up requires a lot energy. She covered them all up with big blankees and stacks of heavy, black winter coats to keep them nice, warm and cozy, and all bundled up just right. Then she would shut off the kitchen lights, grab a fresh cup of hot coffee, and put her legs up on the sofa. She, too, needed to rest.

All the *ageen* would sit quietly on the kitchen table—all snuggled up—nice and comfy. Sleeping very softly and quietly.

---

151. Dough.

"Go to sleep ... go to sleep ... go to sleep, little ageeeeny ... La la la, la la." (yawn, eyes fluttering, trying to stay open but losing the fight).
(Shhh! Be quiet! The ageen is resting!)

Then, a few hours later, she got up and started baking the bread.

Carry on that tradition. It bonds mothers and daughters. What more beautiful gift is there than to bake bread with your bare hands and offer it to the people that you love the most?

My mother loved it when people ate her homemade bread. On a bitter cold, dark, snowy winter day, when you were tired, after an exhausting day at school, you'd open the kitchen door and be overwhelmed with the aroma of fresh baked bread. She would tell you—as the steam rose from the hot loaf that she held in her kind, gentle hands—to take off your coat, grab a cup of coffee, and get piece of hot bread. Melted butter dripped off the edges as you took your first bite. And you knew then, that you were home.

Then we'd sit and talk for hours, drink coffee, and eat her delicious bread.

That was her gift to us.

Thank you for the memories, mommy.

And for everything, else.

Chapter 23

In Conclusion

So, there you have it.

You are an Arab-American female.

It's a beautiful thing. And sometimes it's a painful thing. You are wrestling with two of the most diametrically opposed cultures on the face of the planet—and you are surviving.

In my heart, I know that it would have been better to have lived in Syria and never to have come here in the first place. If I had been born and raised over there, I would never have been confronted with, and been forced to make, the specific choices that I have had to make here. Life would have been simple, and I wouldn't have known a different way.

I also believe that life would have been much easier if I weren't Arabic, at all. As a straight-up American, things would have been totally different. Life would have just been a lighter ride. Black would be black. And white would be white. No gray. No uncertainty. No confusion. Less drama. Less passion. No torture.

If I had been strictly one or the other, everything would have been easier.

But who would I be if I weren't American?

And who would I be if I weren't Arabic?

In my work, I have done some amazing things. And in my personal life, I am proud to say that I have traveled all over the world, walked on the edge a bit, and have done many adventurous things. I even took a flying lesson when I was fifteen-years-old. As an American, I've been able to take advantage of the countless opportunities that this great country has offered me.

But I've also been tormented by the confusion of being an Arab-American female because I am, by nature, a black and white thinking person. I need clarity. I can't function without it. I tend to go to extremes when I feel confused inside—anything to stop the ground beneath me from shaking. To be a traditional girl raised in America. To be at my very core, a Syrian village girl and yet to possess the fiery, independent free-spirit of an American girl is not an easy thing to do.

But again, if I were either/or, I wouldn't have the depth, complexity and insight that I do. And I wouldn't be the person that I am today. And, to be honest, I kinda like me.

Being both means that I can holla' with the boys and I can wail with the girls.

I like that.

So, Cheers! Cheers to you, my friend! Here's to the girl who can proudly cherish her ethnicity and traditions, while simultaneously embracing the great American spirit of independence and strength. Here's to you, the girl who can navigate through sheer madness, and in the end appreciate her blessings. And here's to you, the girl who can dance in that ancient land with as much grace as she can glide on that thin piece of ice called America. You are truly amazing!

Look, it took a very long time for me to get here. And, I am so happy I finally arrived. Despite so much torment trying to sort things out, I wouldn't trade my experience for the world. I see the journey as a beautiful thing. Like a piece of coal that withstands the enormous pressures of the earth's dynamic forces, enduring unimaginable temperatures in an unpredictable environment; in due time, it emerges as a most perfect creation. It emerges as a stunning diamond.

I truly believe each and every one of us are all diamonds created to shine brilliantly. Some are still in the process, some are done, and some haven't even started yet. No matter how badly you want it, though, it's simply not something you can rush through. The process takes time. But, as sure as night turns into day, each woman, in her own time, will shine, in her very own unique way.

Its so true—Arab women deal with very serious issues that they often feel powerless to change. The key word, though, is feel—*feel* powerless to change—not are powerless to change. And that's critical to understand.

I honestly did my best to break it all down for you so that hopefully you could understand yourself better and not feel so alone, or so crazy. But the bottom line is that nobody can figure it out for you. Nobody. That's why this is just a guide. You gotta navigate your own path, make your own mistakes, and of course get heat for it. Just make up your own rules along the way. Trust yourself. And be free. Whatever being "free" means to you.

Jump and play in each different, fascinating world.

Hop the fence once in a while.

Holla' at the boys. Make *shunkleesh* with the girls.

Be adventurous. Explore. Enjoy.

You'll find your way. I know you will. God will guide you.

That, my friend…

I promise.

GLOSSARY

Alla Khaleekay—A blessing that means God keep you alive.

Arabic coffee (n.)—Arabic coffee (makes espresso look totally wimpy).

Arak (n.)—100 proof alcohol. Unless it's homemade, then I think it jumps to 1,000 proof. The important thing to know is that it's a really strong drink. In fact, it's so strong that you have to cut it with water to drink it.

Arees (n.)—The groom.

Argeelee (n.)—A shisha, or hooka.

Aroos (n.)—The bride.

B'tehkay Arabay?—Literally translated, Do you speak Arabic?

Bizzer (n.)—Seeds we snack on. That's all they are but, they are very important in Arabic culture. There are three basic types (see Chapter 14).

Corona (n.)—A beer I really like to drink. And one that I am going to have when this book is completed.

Dupkee (n. and v.)—The *dupkee* is our cultural line dance. When we *dupkee*, we basically dance around in circles for hours. We hold hands. We sing. It's *waaay* fun, and we never get bored! It's just like a serveece ride but without the car!

Foo-Foo (n.)—A bubble-gum brained female with a very small I. Q. She smiles constantly, has fatal fashion sense and wants to get married in the worst way. Her signature style is ruffled, frilly, outdated '70's blouses, but her special trademark is long, curly, over-sprayed '80's hair. She is to Carson Kressley what Kryptonite is to Superman. In fact, reports have recently surfaced of gay men suffering massive heart attacks upon random sightings. A code red alert has been issued by the Global Fashion Police, and she is suspect number one on the *Extreme Makeover Most Wanted List*. Radical environmentalists want her dead or alive as she is the single most potent threat to the ozone layer.

Green Card (n.)—The green light to stay in the USA permanently. Most often obtained by marrying a U.S. citizen.

Hafli (n.)—Arabic party.

I Love Your Green Card … ahhh … I mean Your Green Eyes—A gift for you—if you're smart. And a mistake for him because he's not. It's a careless Freudian slip by a man who is trying to sweep you off your feet so that he can get you to marry him—not for love—but for the green card.

LAP (n.)—Lebanese-American Princess.

Macdouse (n.)—A horrific looking delicacy, often resembling a really gross … *um … forget it. Macdouse* is pickled baby eggplant stuffed with garlic, walnuts, and red peppers. It is robust and full of flavor. The garlic is so potent that it should only be eaten with the closest of friends. The longer this delicious delicacy is aged, the more fabulous the taste. Served with bread and hot tea, it is truly to die for (just don't look at it while you are eating it).

Maté (?)—We really don't know what *maté* is, but it's a very special hot drink that is served when people really like having you around. (All right, since we're at the end of the book, I'll tell you what it is: it's *Yerba Maté,* the very popular South American drink which is packed with antioxidants and nutrients.)

Muktabee (n.)—The library. And one of the best places to meet lots of guys. No, really, it is!

SAP (n.)—Syrian-American Princess.

Shunkleesh (n.)—So dangerous, that you might be arrested for possession. A pungent, horrific-smelling, aged cheese that can also be used as a very powerful lethal weapon and is frequently swapped on the black market. It is slightly less deadly than ricin and more abundant than uranium. The latest figures point to some one million lost and forgotten *shunkleesh* balls in remote locations all over the world. A government-issued warning suggests they are likely giving off toxic levels of radiation at this moment. This ghastly smelling cheese, however, is absolutely delicious to eat.

Sit-el-Beit (n.)—The lady of the house. It is the common name used for the female (usually married, but not always) who takes care of the household. She does it all: cooks, cleans, serves coffee and entertains with grace and ease. She might be described as the Arabic version of a slick marketed, pre-prison Martha Stewart. She is the perfect hostess and ultimate homemaker.

SLAP (n.)—Syrian-Lebanese American Princess.

Tabal (n. and v.)—When used a noun, it's a loud drum. When used as a verb, it's a fun Arabic party, usually the day before a wedding takes place.

Tfadlaay—A warm expression of hospitality. Literally translated means a bunch of stuff: "have a seat," "stay for a while," "come on over," "join in the fun," "help yourself," etc.).

The Patriot Act (n. or v. ?)—Shhh! ... I can't tell you.

Um Kalthoum (n.)—The greatest Middle Eastern artist of all time. This classical Egyptian vocalist was adored by the Arab world. One of her greatest pieces of work, *Inta Omri* ("You Are My Life") remains a masterpiece today.

Waaay-laaay!—Overdramatic wailing sounds that women make during a crisis—or during an event that they would like to *manipulate* into being a crisis.

Zalghouta (n. or v. —still debating that one.)—A *zalghouta* is a very loud Arabian expression of excitement and joy. And in other contexts, an expression of strength, unity and fervor. It's also a really cool battle cry. [152] In fact, it sounds very much like Hollywood's portrayal of an American Indian battle cry. It's a high-pitched, rapid, tongue-firing sequence that goes something like this: *La-la-la-la-la-la-la-la-la-la-leeeesh!*

---

152. At least it was back in the day.

Welcome to the First-Ever *Zalghouta* Challenge Sponsored by Dalel B. Khalil

As you all know, I have sat on this coveted throne for over two glorious and memorable decades. For twenty plus years, I was there when many of you exchanged your wedding vows, baptized your children, and celebrated countless occasions across the land. It was I who was summoned to make the traditional ceremonial call, to bring life to your events. I gave freely of myself, and when they chanted my name, without hesitation, I obliged.

I feel as if I have served my duty well, providing the Best Damn *Zalghoutas* Period! In every instance, and regardless of any throat or vocal cord discomfort and/or injury, I gave with passion. The *zalghouta* is a primal call, one that embodies the spirit of our rich, strong ancestry. It is a role that I have fulfilled with conviction and honor. I want to make it clear that my genuine love and loyalty for this position is out of the pureness of my heart—not blind ambition, glory, or fame. It is with great pride that I had been chosen to serve in this capacity and that I have sustained this position for so long a duration.

Suddenly, however, and out of nowhere, there are those who are questioning my ability. It has come to my knowledge that certain individuals are arrogantly coming forward to challenge my legitimacy as the rightful *Zalghouta Queen* of my particular village. They are unabashedly proclaiming that they—not I—are the Best Damn *Zalghouta Queen* Period!

These wretched individuals (and you know who you are!) believe that they, not I, have what it takes to carry on this tremendous responsibility. I take this as a direct threat and I'm ready to take it outside! But, I am a woman of peace and it is not my desire to wage war against my fellow countrywomen. After all, it is the collective will of the tribe to determine who will represent them. However, I will not surrender without a damn good fight! I will gracefully concede *only* to the woman who is worthy to take my place. And my successor had better prove that she is worthy to knock my a** off (or she better run like hell)!

Therefore, I am sponsoring the *First-Ever Zalghouta Challenge*. This competition is open to everyone, but I especially call upon those who have had the audacity to challenge me directly.

In the future, I strongly advise each village to hold its very own *Zalghouta Challenge,* ordain their own *Zalghouta Queen,* and settle all frivolous, jealous, immature disputes once and for all. Oh, and take my advice—have a lawyer present.

The challenge will take place atop the highest mountain at a date and time of my choosing.

Be ready because, girl, I am so ready for you!

Respectfully yours,

Dalel Khalil
Official Zalghouta Queen